THE LIVES THEY SAVED

"It wasn't until I got to the waterfront, loading people onto a boat, that I started to feel yes, this is why I'm here. If I do anything today, I'm going to keep this child from dying in the World Trade Center. And I did," said paramedic James Creedon, Battalion 14, EMS, FDNY. "If I ever doubt I did my job that day, I can point to that and say there's one three-year-old girl who got away safely and reunited with her mother and that was because of me."[1]

THE LIVES THEY SAVED

The Untold Story of Medics, Mariners,
and the Incredible Boat Lift that Evacuated
Nearly 300,000 People From New York City on 9/11

L. DOUGLAS KEENEY

Essex, Connecticut

An imprint of Globe Pequot, the trade division of
The Rowman & Littlefield Publishing Group, Inc.
4501 Forbes Blvd., Ste. 200
Lanham, MD 20706
www.rowman.com

Distributed by NATIONAL BOOK NETWORK

British Library Cataloguing in Publication Information Available

Library of Congress Cataloging-in-Publication Data Available

ISBN 978-1-4930-7300-9 (paperback)
ISBN 978-1-4930-4811-3 (e-book)

♾™ The paper used in this publication meets the minimum requirements of American
National Standard for Information Sciences—Permanence of Paper for Printed Library
Materials, ANSI/NISO Z39.48-1992.

Contents

Foreword

THE GENERALLY RECTILINEAR-SHAPED ISLAND OF MANHATTAN LIES ON a north-south axis with its southern tip protruding into New York Harbor. On September 11, 2001, as many as 500,000 people were suddenly cut off from the rest of Manhattan by the collapse of the World Trade Center, with more than one-quarter of a million of them on that southern tip of the island. That area is called Lower Manhattan.

On October 1, 2001—20 days after the attacks on the World Trade Center—the Fire Department of New York City began a series of interviews with 503 of the rank-and-file firefighters and EMS first responders who had been at ground zero. The interviews lasted for five months and concluded on February 1, 2002. All told, 7,050 pages of oral histories were generated that covered virtually every aspect of that day, starting with the quiet of the morning, then to the attack, to the collapsing buildings, and finally to the rescues and evacuations. The depth of the accounts given by each person vary, but, on the whole, they detailed each person's response, where they were, the events that unfolded around them, what they saw when they arrived, what they did, who they rescued, how they survived, and so on. Taken together, these interviews give us an engaging and powerful history of that day, in the raw language of oral histories the likes of which rival any Stephen Ambrose-styled book on World War II.

As an author with extensive experience using oral histories, what jumped out at me from these accounts was not what was known about 9/11, but rather the unexpected tellings of the unknown. For example, the towers were mentioned 3,794 times and the leaders on the ground, the department chiefs, were mentioned an average of 300 times per person—Chief Nigro, Chief Ganci, EMS Chief Kowalczyk, and the others. For sure, that was as it should be—the chiefs were the leaders and interacted with dozens of responders. The towers were their mission that day so it would be expected that hundreds of respondents would mention one or both. But other things came up that were not expected. Mentioned more frequently than any department chief were no fewer than 505 mentions of a boat, 304 mentions of a ferry, and 245 instances when someone talked about evacuating people to the river or to the water.

Several sources were essential in the writing of this book, foremost among them the 503 oral histories known as the World Trade Center Task Force Interviews, as collected by the New York City Fire Department. Although these interviews took place within months of 9/11, a time when memories were surely fresh and recall would be acute, around the base of the towers there was so much confusion, so much dust and debris and the shock of death and injuries that timelines, sequences, and even people identified at one location or the other were often guesses or flat out inadvertent mistakes. However, by cross-checking one respondent's recall with another, and conducting my own interviews, things started to fall into place. Because of the detail and depth of information in the Task Force Interviews, I have chosen to use them as the clothesline on which I hang the rest of the story—the rescues, the response of the boat captains, the bravery shown by those who kept going back in to dig out more survivors, and, ultimately, the impetus to evacuate Lower Manhattan by boat. I identify these interviews by concluding a quote with something along the lines of "as told to an interviewer." From their second quote onward, I simply say "they said," or something to that effect

An equally important resource were the boat captains. While no central collection exists for their stories, some diligent maritime reporters were in tune with the events unfolding along the waterfront and they wrote numerous contemporary accounts for which I am grateful and acknowledge as and when used.

A second collection of oral histories came from an ambitious project called the September 11 Digital Archive run by the Roy Rosenzweig

Center for History and New Media and the American Social History Project/Center for Media and Learning at George Mason University. Designed to be a permanent record of firsthand experiences, survivors were encouraged to leave their experiences, and hundreds, if not thousands, did just that. However, many of the best accounts were contributed anonymously, so when I use one for a quote, I identify them as contributors to the "digital archives." See https://911digitalarchive.org/about for more oral histories.

There are several ways to indicate the Twin Towers of the World Trade Center. To some they were 1 WTC and 2 WTC or WTC 1 and WTC 2. To others they were the North Tower and the South Tower. However, because "north" and "south" are important references in the telling of this story, throughout the book I have chosen to call them the North Tower (WTC 1) and the South Tower (WTC 2). The other buildings in the complex are identified by using the protocol then in use, for instance, WTC 3, WTC 7, etc.

Similarly, there are two ways to reference the West Side Highway. The original West Side Highway was a long, wide six-lane thoroughfare that ran alongside the Hudson River as far up as 72nd Street. Years ago, however, during its reconstruction, the name was changed to West Street. Still, a majority of the interviewees used the old name (West Side Highway), and not the new name (West Street). Because the old name has a useful geographic reference (West *Side* Highway versus West Street), I have chosen to use the old name, West Side Highway.

And then there are the two walking bridges that cross the West Side Highway. One was near the North Tower and one was near the South Tower. As best as I could tell, there was no formal name for either of these bridges so, again, because geography is important to this story, I identify them as the North Pedestrian Bridge and the South Pedestrian Bridge.

So, how many people were evacuated by boat? It's hard to say precisely. In early reports, fantastic numbers were tossed about—500,000 to 1,000,00—and for some reason those numbers stuck. But the math never really added up. Most accounts agree that there were roughly 130 to 150 vessels involved in the evacuation of Lower Manhattan. The largest boats were the 6,000-passenger Staten Island ferries, the smallest were some rubber dinghies that carried two or three passengers. In between were tugboats, dinner cruise boats, working boats, and police/rescue boats, the latter generally carrying 20 or so passengers, but doing many, many trips. However, the most frequently used boats during the evacuation of Lower Manhattan were ferries and among them were 20 plus ferries of NY Waterway each capable of carrying 149 or so passengers per trip.

Then there is the count itself. As some of the boat captains later admitted, so fast were things happening and so traumatic were they that in those first few minutes of the attack, counting passengers was at best spotty. When things finally settled down, however, the mariners were exceedingly mindful of their licensed, legal passenger limits and, while some overloaded their vessels, nearly everyone was counted, and loads were adhered to.

That said, when combing through official records, some boats are listed and some are not, and many of those listed have no numbers associated with their participation—that is, we know they were there and evacuated people, but nothing clearly indicates how many people they took on. In such cases, other data were used to generate reasonable estimates starting with the capacity of the vessel, the time they began evacuating people, how long it took the vessel to reach their destinations, and therefore how many loads were theoretically possible. The long and short of it is this: Nearly 270,000 people were evacuated from Manhattan by boat on September 11. This includes a small margin for the early confusion and a margin for the few vessels that had no passenger records. That said, anything above and beyond that would scarcely move the needle, and certainly not change the total in any significant way. To sum it up, September 11, 2001, represents the largest single-day boat lift in history and one of the greatest rescues in modern history.

Twenty years have passed as of the writing of this book, an impossible length of time, it seems, considering how fresh it feels to those who lived through that day. At 8:46 a.m., the attack began when American Airlines Flight 11 crashed into the North Tower. At 9:02 a.m. United Airlines Flight 175 was flown into the South Tower. Hundreds died instantly. The horrors continued until both towers collapsed. At 10:28 a.m. the World Trade Center towers were no more. That day thousands died including 343 first responders.[1]

That people were evacuated by boat is well-known to some but no one has chronicled the battle with death that took place around the base of the towers and how some 2,000 victims with injuries were carried to the waterfront by first responders and whisked away to hospitals by boat. In fact, it was in this little known and absolutely critical partnership between land and sea that so many lives were saved and out of which emerges a powerful history of courageous medics and mariners who united against an attack on the United States.

What the EMTs did to pull people out of the debris and get them down to the water, how the boat captains braved the dark-as-night cloud that hid Manhattan; all of this has been a missing piece of the September 11 story for two decades. No longer. There will be some errors—oral histories can be imprecise, memories change, facts may have been clouded by the fog of the collapse—but nothing diminishes the courage, determination, and sense of hope that powered tired muscles and delivered some 270,000 survivors back to their loved ones.

CHAPTER 1

September 12, 2001

The Day After

NEW YORK CITY FIRE DEPARTMENT DEPUTY CHIEF MEDICAL OFFICER David Prezant thought about the attacks of 9/11 and the evacuation of Lower Manhattan by boat. He could understand those who evacuated Manhattan by walking up Broadway or crossing over the Brooklyn Bridge. He could understand the unique nature of the attacks themselves. But there was one thing he didn't understand. "There was an interesting triage concept when the first building collapsed, which was unknown to us," he later said. "That is, that a lot of people were evacuated to Staten Island and to Jersey City . . . ferries were just picking up the wounded and taking them, and some fire boats and some police boats as well. Why not take them around the bend in Manhattan up to Bellevue Hospital or up the East River to Cornell?" he asked.

The answer, he realized, was found in the smoke, debris, and carnage around him. Manhattan had been attacked. "Manhattan," he said, "may not exist for long."[1]

CHAPTER 2

September 10, 2001

The Night Before

ON SEPTEMBER 10, 2001, A MAN BY THE NAME OF JOHN MCFARLANE boarded the P&O ship *Royal Princess* looking forward to a leisurely cruise along the Eastern Seaboard of the United States. The ship was embarking passengers from the Manhattan Cruise Terminal on the Hudson River, a cluster of piers and passenger terminals north of the *Intrepid* aircraft carrier, a popular museum on the west side of Manhattan. The *Royal Princess* looked oddly out of place. It was an ocean-going passenger liner docked against a backdrop of towering high-rises, skyscrapers, and deep canyons of streets crowded with busy office workers. But it was precisely that contrast, that visual incongruity, that charged the air with a sense of excitement.

At roughly six o'clock that evening, the tide peaked at 4.6 feet above sea level, flooding the vast network of rivers, streams, mudflats, coves, and deep-water channels of New York Harbor with waters sufficient to give deep draft vessels like the *Royal Princess* safe passage out to sea. Two hours later, the captain slipped the lines and eased his ship away from the docks and into the harbor. He turned the bow downstream parallel to the city, giving his passengers a breathtaking view of Manhattan. They steamed past the *Intrepid*, then Chelsea Piers, a vast embarkation point for numerous cruise boats and harbor tours, then past the New York City Fire Department's iconic 129-foot fireboat the *John D. McKean*, and finally past the tucked-in boat harbor at the North Cove Marina. The *Royal Princess* turned into the Upper Bay and past the Statue of Liberty as she picked up the ebb tide flowing out to sea. To her left, the two towers of the World Trade Center stood boldly against the night sky, impervious to the gathering storm swirling around them, casting a silent but watchful eye over the harbor. A passenger by the name of Shirley Pantaleo was standing on the promenade deck. She had a camera and took a photo of the towers at 9:45 p.m.[1] Then, as if on cue, the towers slipped from view into the darkness. The night came to an end with a flurry of lightning bolts electrifying the sky as a thunderstorm passed over the city.

Those bolts of lightning were caught by a video camera placed in a window looking out from the 92nd floor of 1 World Trade Center, the North Tower, by an artist in residence from Australia named Monika Bravo. She was exceedingly uncomfortable on the 92nd floor. She had gone so far as to paint her studio black and shutter the windows, but nonetheless she braved this spot high in the sky because she wanted to film the images of clouds, and what better place than in the clouds themselves? For seven hours her cameras rolled, capturing the dark cumulus clouds and lightning. At midnight she shut things down, popped out the cassette, and went home. When she awoke the next morning at 7:30 a.m., she was shocked by what she had done. Never before, she later said, had she ever taken the film home.[2]

Carmen Taylor was up early the morning on September 11. As a tourist on vacation from her home state of Arkansas, Carmen wanted to take the morning ferry to see the Statue of Liberty. As a photographer herself, she was hoping to get some spectacular images to add to her collection, and she couldn't have picked a better day. The overnight storm had cleared the air and the morning sun welcomed her with open arms. It was a bright and clear morning, the sky flecked only by occasional clouds and gently tempered by a soft, easterly breeze blowing out to sea.

Carmen was able to get plenty of beautiful shots before heading back to Lower Manhattan. As her ferry returned, Carmen positioned herself toward the bow so she could have an unobstructed view of the colossal towers. Halfway across the harbor, she heard something from overhead and automatically raised her camera.

Little did she know that she would take the picture of a lifetime.

CHAPTER 3

"There should be a law against working on such a beautiful day."

New York Harbor, September 11, 2001
7:45 a.m.

IT WAS TUESDAY MORNING, SEPTEMBER 11, 2001. A RED FIREBALL OF A
sun came up silhouetting Lower Manhattan with a glorious sunrise. From
the docks at Caven Point, New Jersey, a marine terminal directly across
the harbor, the view was postcard perfect. The whole of Manhattan spar-
kled in a surreal, Disney-esque image of some City-of-the-Future what
with its tightly clustered buildings and the two giant towers split by shafts
of brilliant sunlight streaking down the canyons of the city and bouncing
from steel to glass to steel and out to the sea. The sky was a brilliant blue.
Wisps of white clouds drifted on a gentle easterly breeze.

Assistant Vessel Master Liz Finn of the US Army Corp of Engineers
stood on the docks with a group of boat captains who commanded a fleet
of seven ships specifically designed to remove hazardous debris found
floating in New York Harbor, the East River, and the Hudson River.
Finn's ship, the *Gelberman*, was an 85-foot-long vessel with a seven-ton
crane amidships that could pull a tree out of the water with ease. A sister
ship, the *Driftmaster*, was built with the hull of a catamaran so it could
skim the surface and scoop up almost anything else that floated.[1] "Most
people go around stuff in the water," said Station Chief Rich Bulvid. "We
go after it."[2] Before Finn walked off the docks and back to the buildings
to attend a series of maritime safety meetings, she paused long enough
to look at the sunrise, no doubt marveling at the magnificent view of the

city. The morning temperatures were pleasingly mild, and the breeze was fresh with a hint of saltwater in the air.

Petty Officer Carlos Perez of the US Coast Guard didn't stop to admire the sunrise or the view as he walked near the waterfront on Staten Island, and it wasn't because he hadn't noticed or didn't care. Quite to the contrary. Perez knew New York Harbor as well as anyone, all 146 square miles of it, complete with its deep-water channels that run under its bays 40 to 50 feet deep, the East River and Hudson River meeting at the Battery, the tidal inflows and outflows, and the 600-plus miles of coastline that he patrolled.[3]

Tall with close cropped hair and dark piercing eyes, Petty Officer Perez went to a community college and then held several jobs before a Coast Guard recruiting commercial caught his eye. He enlisted, moved up the ladder, and did a tour on a cutter in Puerto Rico before being sent to Coast Guard Station New York on Staten Island. On 9/11, he was to be the coxswain on one of the station's emergency-response boats called "ready boats." Perez walked toward the station no doubt casting a watchful eye toward the docks where a half-dozen Coast Guard boats rocked against their cleated lines. Not far from where he walked, out toward the Atlantic Ocean, the Verrazano-Narrows bridge soared 228 feet above the entrance to the Upper Bay connecting Staten Island to Long Island. Above him, seagulls *awk-awked* in the sky, circling on the gentle breeze. The harbor's water gently lapped against the hulls of the boats with those distinctive orange stripes on their bows.

Perez went inside the station, got a cup of coffee, and shuffled into the briefing room for the morning updates. No doubt there was the glazed-look of repetition among the blue-shirted coasties as the briefer covered the graphs and charts with the hieroglyphics marking atmospheric inversions, low pressure systems, winds aloft, dewpoints, temperatures, and cloud formations, plus important nautical data like currents and tides—low tide would occur at 8:44 a.m. that morning—plus any navigational hazards caused by the weather the night before. Basic emergency procedures and frequencies were covered, they reviewed updates to the notices to mariners, then talked about a diving outfit that was working the harbor around the Verrazzano-Narrows Bridge. "Give them wide berth," the briefer said, or something to that effect. The meeting broke up with an informal summary of the weather that brought smiles to the boat crews. The skies over New York City would be "beautiful all day," said the briefing officer, and the harbor waters would be "smooth as glass."

Perez pushed back his chair, got up, and headed to the chart room. Today was his maiden voyage as commander of one of the station's fast-moving, twin-engine, 300-hp search-and-rescue vessels. His boat had the rather unromantic name of *41497*.[4] It was a modified cabin cruiser with an enclosed pilot house and open deck. If there was an emergency in the harbor, if a boat took on water or a passenger went overboard or a container ship ran aground on the tricky mud flats inside the lower bay, he'd be the first Coast Guard boat on the scene, rain or shine, snow or sleet. "We're so familiar with [New York Harbor]. Almost every day we're going out. We know the area, we know landmarks, we've worked with many of the pilots and boats and tugs and run into them everyday. We do a hard day's physical labor," said one of his fellow coastguardsmen. "We're constantly adapting to whatever the situation is."[5] With dozens of ferries, tugboats, and container ships, plus fuel barges, lighters, pleasure boats, and even Corps of Engineers drift vessels all using the harbor, there was always a "situation."

On the other side of Staten Island, up the Kill Van Kull channel, New Jersey state trooper Joseph G. DeMarino was about to start his shift at the helm of a 45-foot harbor patrol boat. DeMarino was part of a section of the New Jersey State Police who had the unique job of patrolling not the interstate highways but rather the waterways around the marine terminals, oil refineries, and container ships on the New Jersey side of the massive complex of the Port of New York–New Jersey. "We lived on the water," said DeMarino of his three-man boat crew. The area they patrolled included the sort of waters that a weekend sailor would try hard to avoid, including the industrialized waterways in and around Port Elizabeth, Port Newark, and the Bayonne terminal. These were waterways edged by industrial docks on one side and a combination of tricky saltwater marshes and a sailor's nightmare of abandoned piers and invisible underwater obstacles on the other. DeMarino's crew would watch for stowaways, for things that had fallen into the water and were now a hazard to other ships, and for just about any sort of criminal activity one could find on land or sea. To that end, they carried shotguns and automatic rifles.[6]

On this day instead of weapons, they would need every knot of speed their engines could give them.

— —

Across the harbor from Staten Island, a mile or two up the Hudson River on the west side of Manhattan, was New York City Fire Department's fire station Marine 1. Berthed there was the fireboat *John D. McKean*, one of the services largest fireboats, a handsome ship built in 1954 and painted fire-engine red with a rising bow, low gunwales, and a raised pilot house done in a soft white with black trim. Using water drawn from the river, the *John McKean* could draft the equivalent of three standard-size swimming pools in 60 seconds and, through her deck guns called monitors, throw 19,000 gallons of water on a fire a minute, ten times what the average land-based fire engine could pump. In years past, fireboats in the Marine Division had been called upon to put out fires on ships, piers, and old warehouses on the waterfront, and even car fires on the bridges over the harbor using their water cannons. When the US Navy paraded their ships during Fleet Week or when New York City was the maiden port of call for a new passenger ship, the *McKean* would position herself in the middle of the harbor and shoot an impressive 40-foot arc of water under which the important new arrival would sail triumphantly into the harbor. Some went so far as to say the fireboats of New York were as famous as any other attraction in the city, although nothing could match the Twin Towers.

As the *McKean* rocked against her lines, the station's interim chief, Covering Officer Captain Edward Metcalf, FDNY, came into the kitchen for the morning crew change. Metcalf was mechanically inclined and spent many of his weekends as a maintainer for the combat helicopters of the New York National Guard. On the morning of 9/11, he was standing in as a substitute for the station's chief who was away on leave. "It was my first tour on a boat," said Metcalf. "I didn't know the guys.

I didn't know the boat. I was a captain of fire operations."[7] "Calf," as he was known, said hello to the new crew, presumably including firefighter Tom Sullivan, a bulldozer of a man who was a natural leader, and to Greg Woods, who doubled as a lifeguard when he was off-duty and to James Filomeno, who was digging into a heaping plate of food in front of him.[8] "There should be a law against working on such a beautiful day," said engineer Billy O'Brien. O'Brien got his share of slack because engineers knew their boats like a conductor knows an orchestra. Metcalf laughed and the noise level swelled as the men shot barbs back and forth, a fire-boat station being more than a second home for most of them. Metcalf looked around the room. *It would be a good day*, he thought approvingly, such being the influence of a warm, sunny day on those who worked the waterways of New York City.[9]

Peter Johannsson was on a New York Waterway ferry that was running between the bedroom community of Weehawken, New Jersey, and the Wall Street terminal at Pier 11 on the East River. At 8:32 a.m. his ferry passed between Governors Island and the tip of Manhattan about to make the turn up the East River. His boss, Arthur E. Imperatore Jr., a trucking magnate and the founder of the company, would no doubt be pleased by the day's take. Years ago, Imperatore realized the need for a fast-boat ferry service between the bedroom communities of New Jersey and the forest of office towers in Lower Manhattan. He painted his ferries blue and white, so they'd stand apart from the slower orange Staten Island ferry boats, then he equipped them with powerful engines so they could do a run in under 15 minutes, or nearly half the time of his competitors. As the financial district grew, so too, did his business; and Imperatore now had a fleet of 24 ferries, 22 of which were in the water the morning of 9/11, ready to reap the bounty of the day's good weather. Peter Johansson watched as they banked left and navigated up the East River toward Pier 11. They would dock precisely on time.

And so it began on a morning as beautiful as any on the waterfront of one of the busiest ports in the United States, a new day as yet untouched by humans; a day waiting to unfold in all its glory. The brackish smell of seawater suffused the air as small waves curled up and expired against the countless pilings, wharves, and seawalls that lined the harbor. Deckhands, captains, mariners, and stevedores coiled their lines, pulled their hawsers, and shouted out commands as engines came to life and propellers churned the waters into a frothy white as boats began to back out from their docks. Ticket-takers began opening their booths around the Battery; tourists would soon come out in droves on a day as perfect as this.

Countless workers began manning the cranes that would lift containers off the ships and swing them onto the backs of semitrucks waiting to haul loads across the United States. Ferries were speeding across the upper and lower bays and up and down the rivers to and from the bedroom communities of Long Island or New Jersey. It was commerce at its best; energetic, exciting, finely tuned, and refined by years of repetition, an interplay of people and machines connected, more than they knew, by the harbor itself.

Ken Peterson, the port safety officer for Reinauer Transportation Company, a major tugboat operator in New York Harbor, and captain of the tugboat *Franklin Reinauer*, an orange and red 81-foot workhorse with a 2,100-horsepower engine, started his morning at the company's docks on Staten Island, where a half dozen of his tugs were berthed. He checked in early.[10] Park rangers working the national parks around the harbor began preparing their utility boats to shuttle their staff out to man the ticket counters and snack bars on Liberty Island and Ellis Island for the hordes of visitors who would walk through the immigration buildings or marvel at the beauty of the Statue of Liberty.[11] The orange giant of a ship, the 6,000-passenger ferry called the *Samuel I. Newhouse*, was at the midpoint of her five-mile run between the Whitehall Terminal in Lower Manhattan and the St. George Terminal on Staten Island. Captain James Parese manned the helm, a respected mariner on the harbor. Parese could make the trip in 25 minutes, give or take, then turn around and run the course in reverse. His schedule called for him to head back to Manhattan at 8:47 a.m.

Tourism is a big part of the daily shot in the economic arm of Lower Manhattan, and good weather meant good business for the operators of the harbor cruises and dinner boats that plied the waters of New York Harbor. There were the established outfits with big ships that were well- known to almost anyone who'd ever gone on a harbor cruise—Circle Line, Spirit Cruises, VIP Yacht Cruises—while others offered a more personalized touch. Patrick Harris, for one, looked forward to a fatter wallet by day's end. A nautical-looking captain with the peppiness of an east coaster, Harris ran a charter operation out of Manhattan's North Cove Marina on his 70-foot sailboat the *Ventura*. His stock-in-trade was a three-hour dinner cruise on the harbor, complete with a bucket of champagne and the incredible sights and lights of New York's skyscrapers as seen from the dark, silent waters of the harbor.

Sometime before 8:30 a.m., Harris, with cup of coffee in hand, sat down in the helm of his boat and leaned back, glancing approvingly at the city that lay just beyond the edge of his marina, a familiar forest of high-rises punctuated by the two colossal steel-and-glass towers that soared almost 1,400 feet into the sky. Just two blocks away, beyond the Winter Garden and the World Financial Center, thousands of New Yorkers tied to the ebb and flow of business and commerce were now emptying out of the subway, PATH, and ferry terminals in Lower Manhattan, briefcases in hand, pocketbooks over their shoulders, Blackberries pressed against their ears. Shoulder-to-shoulder they hustled up the stairs to street level, filtering out into the rabbit warren of sidewalks hemmed in by buildings punctuated by the silver colossal. Here, 14,154 of them would split off from the pack and pass through the enormous glass-and-marble lobbies and ascend the elevators to take up battle stations in the pods, cubicles, or well-appointed private offices where they would go about the combat of world commerce. But not Captain Pat, as Harris was known. Soon enough he'd be polishing brass and washing the decks for tonight's charter, but for now, on this glorious September morning, the most pressing need in his world came down to a cup of coffee on this magnificent yacht with the ever-so-familiar lapping of the Hudson River against its hull. He had his boat and the unbridled optimism of a man on the edge of the open seas. Harris sipped his coffee, content in the knowledge that 25 years ago he had abandoned that rat race for, well, for *this*.[12]

To the south of Battery Park City, standing in the water just beyond the seawall near the tip of Manhattan, was a wood piling driven into the seabed on top of which was a weather-beaten box. Inside that box, an electronically generated audio signal chirped every six minutes. This chirp, or soundwave, raced down a six-inch-wide tube some ten feet until it hit the surface of the water and bounced back up. Every six minutes this signal chirped and every six minutes the time it took to travel back and forth was measured. X number of seconds meant the water level was this many feet above sea level; Y number of seconds meant the water level was that many feet below sea level. Up and down the water levels would rise and fall, a 12-hour and 15-minute cycle regulated by the moon and recorded by this box. From boxes stationed around the harbor, these chirps were merged, and a tide table was produced on which the captains of deep draft vessels depended. A ship such as the *Queen Mary* would leave her pier and risk the shoals of Buttermilk Channel only when the chirps forecast water levels high enough to clear the bottom of the bay. Equally, on this chirp would captains decide when to go upstream or downstream, to work with the currents, or foolishly—perhaps ignorantly —to labor against them. In short, this chirp was the metronome of life on the waterways of New York, it influenced everything that moved.

On September 11, 2001, the sum of those chirps was processed and merged with the chirps from all the boxes around New York Harbor, generating a tide table that said low tide would occur at 8:44 a.m. To a mother pushing a baby stroller around Battery Park, at 8:44 a.m. the water levels would appear to be so low that looking over the railing might seem like looking over the side of a small ocean liner, so precarious was the drop to the waters below.

Moreover, in the minutes that followed, the tide would reverse itself and start to come in, and the currents around Manhattan's seawall would start running fast and strong—strong enough to pose a danger to even the most physically fit of all swimmers.[13]

And then, with each chirp after that, the currents would strengthen yet again.

CHAPTER 4

"Lower Manhattan is really MCI (Mass Casualty Incident) City."

8:30 a.m.

TO THE AVERAGE NEW YORKER, THE FIREBOATS, FERRIES, AND SMOOTH-as-glass waterways of New York Harbor were a mere backdrop to their daily lives—their city was no more an island than a yellow cab was a boat. Subways, streets, buses, and crowded sidewalks edged with honking cars, messengers on bikes weaving through the traffic, and Starbucks crowded with secretaries and assistants waiting for a cappuccino—that was the real world. The tugboats, ferries, and container ships were mere footnotes to life. Beautiful, yes, but little more. New York was a *city* and a vibrant one at that.

A businessman by the name of Jonathan Segal worked in Lower Manhattan but commuted nearly two hours from his home in New Jersey. As he usually did on such a spectacular day, he took the ferry across the Hudson River into Manhattan rather than the somewhat dark and closed-in commuter train. The deciding point in his daily routine—train or boat—came when he reached Hoboken, New Jersey, a bedroom community nestled up against the river directly across from the city. "Occasionally, I will take the PATH train into the World Trade Center basement," he said in his digital archive. "But unless I have early meetings or if it's raining, I stick to the ferry. It's the most beautiful way to come into the city. The Twin Towers ahead, the Statue of Liberty and Ellis Island to the right, midtown skyscrapers on the left."

Segal got on the ferry and ran into a colleague and together they talked, the boat skimming the river as they headed toward the terminal at the base of the World Financial Center. He got off and crossed the West Side Highway to Liberty Street and walked toward his office on Broadway. That the entire World Trade Center complex would be reduced to smoking ruins before lunch was, judging by the tone of his comments, the furthest thing from his mind.[1]

At 8:30 a.m., the chatter of morning arrivals filled the air as businessmen and women rolled into work filling up the maze of cubicles and offices inside the World Trade Center. Some of the morning arrivals got down to business right away and gave themselves over to a computer screen or a conference call; others had their first mindless conversation around a water cooler or a coffee pot. Last night's *Monday Night Football* game between the New York Giants and the Denver Broncos had been a close game won by the Broncos 31–20 against a Giants offense that had put up an admirable 300 yards. The sudden thunderstorm that roiled the city caused annoying flight delays and cancelations but had cleaned the air. Everyday problems were talked about. A babysitter forgot to walk a dog, there were late dinners—and now some hangovers—but today was Tuesday, the back-to-work reality of another day and another dollar well underway. Before it was over, tens of thousands of workers would enter and exit the Twin Towers, and tens of thousands more would come down to gawk at their height.[2]

On Long Island, Deputy Chief Zachary Goldfarb, Division 3, Emergency Medical Services, New York City Fire Department, had just completed an overnight tour as the service's citywide chief. The department's roughly 2,900 EMTs attended to the biological needs of this city of eight million residents. They splinted broken legs, treated heart attacks, and raced to the scene of 9-1-1 calls with stethoscopes around their necks in ambulances that were emergency rooms on wheels. The day before, Goldfarb had visited several of his stations to make sure their mass-casualty assets were well stocked. While there was always room for improvement, he was pleased by what he saw, and, in these morning hours at the end of a long shift, he was at his desk finishing a stack of reports. Goldfarb went through his paperwork as fast as he could. No doubt at some point he saw the two silvery towers that seemed to reach up into the sky and touch the clouds.[3] Few places had become such visible symbols of America's financial prowess as the towers of the World Trade Center, but ever since they opened in 1973, fewer places had given Goldfarb and first responders more sleepless nights.

The World Trade Center was a city in its own right with seven skyscrapers squeezed into 16 acres of Lower Manhattan, the tallest of which were the two 1,368-foot steel towers: WTC 1, the North Tower, and WTC 2, the South Tower. Save for a few feet here and there, and antennas that crowned the North Tower, they were identical twins—110 vertical floors each stacked one on top of the other, each floor an acre in size, with a total of ten million square feet of real estate.[4] The towers were grouped together with five additional buildings—WTC 3, a 22-story Marriott hotel between WTC 1 and WTC 2, the 9-story buildings of WTC 4 and WTC 5, the 8-story WTC 6, and the 47-story WTC 7— plus a handsome five-acre area called Tobin Plaza, with fountains, sculptures, and plenty of room for open-air concerts at lunch time. Not to be overlooked, there was an interconnected underground shopping mall with restaurants, retail stores, and fast-food outlets, multiple levels of underground parking, and the adjacent World Financial Center complex of buildings. You could eat at the World Trade Center, pick out a new wardrobe, buy a new book, plan trips, spend the night in a luxury hotel, and catch a train home, all without leaving the site. Said a newly transplanted nurse from Hawaii in her digital archive: "The WTC is a big part of [my] daily life, whether for shopping, eating at the falafel stand across Liberty, catching the subway or buying something special to cook for dinner nearby at the Amish Market."[5] And that was precisely what caused those sleepless nights for the first responders—twin towers each standing 110 stories with as many as 15,000 people tightly packed into that real estate, most of it vertical, for a total of as many as 50,000 people located somewhere in the complex. "You have to realize that we are talking about a small imprint [of] New York City that was larger in population than many small cities in America," said Goldfarb.[6]

First responder and medic Lieutenant Amy Monroe, Battalion 4, EMS, FDNY, lived in Lower Manhattan and worked out of a station near the East River. "I know the area and the World Trade very well," she said in her interview after the collapse. "Lower Manhattan is really MCI [Mass Casualty Incident] City. We do MCIs all the time [there]."[7] To cut the response time, ambulances were stationed around the perimeter of the complex, each with a two-person EMS crew trained in basic and advanced life-support skills. They could quickly respond to a life-threatening emergency, bringing with them an impressive array of tools. In their ambulance they carried some combination of Stokes baskets, long boards, scoop shovels, slings, respirators, portable suction, defibrillators, plenty of pads, stair chairs, splints, oxygen tanks, nebulizers, saline, needles, meds like albuterol, chemical antidote kits, and, for their own safety, protective gear like a safety coat, a vest, and a helmet. Plus, there was a plan. If a major accident were to occur anywhere within the complex of the World Trade Center, there was a tested, practiced, and drilled preplan that included critical information such as engineering and architectural diagrams of the towers, inventories of the EMS assets on-site, and the best evacuation routes to Uptown hospitals. Said Goldfarb of this preplan, "It included the best approaches, any unique aspects of the buildings like underground access, staging locations [for the arriving ambulances], what resources were on-site that could help us—like a first-aid room, medical team, or response capabilities—what the nearest hospitals were, and what the best road accesses were."[8]

The linchpin to the preplan, or, for that matter the linchpin to any preplan for a mass casualty incident, was the transport plan to evacuate patients from an incident as quickly as possible; that is, to triage the injured and send them off to the hospitals most appropriate to the severity of their wounds while funneling the walking wounded offsite to a safe place well away from the incident. Time was of the essence. Bottlenecks were to be avoided at all costs. Transport was key, and to that end the World Trade Center was well served. Four major roads form a perimeter around the complex. On the west side of the buildings, running parallel to the Hudson River, is a thoroughfare called the West Side Highway. This enormously wide road has multiple lanes going both ways divided by a median. It's the primary route along the west side of Manhattan.

On the opposite side of the complex, to the east of the buildings and parallel to the West Side Highway, is Church Street, a four-lane thoroughfare with another straight shot uptown. It, too, provided excellent ingress and egress, although it was more complicated and narrower.

Two cross streets completed the perimeter, one to the north and one to the south. To the north, running just 100 feet or so from the base of the North Tower, was Vesey Street, a cross street that connected the West Side Highway and Church Street. To the south side of the complex was Liberty Street. Liberty connected the southern end of the West Side Highway and Church Street and was close to the base of the South Tower. Both cross streets were essential to any successful evacuation of the complex, but it was the seven lanes of the West Side Highway and the four lanes of Church Street that were burned into the hard drives of every first responder. If there was an MCI at the World Trade Center, the West Side Highway and Church Street were the fastest routes to the hospitals Uptown. In a word, the West Side Highway and Church Street were the way out.

EMT Mary Merced, Division 3, EMS, FDNY, Chief Goldfarb's assistant and driver that morning, waited outside his door as he finished his paperwork. At 8:30 a.m. Goldfarb officially signed out, got in his car, and started his drive home. Goldfarb asked Merced to tune the shortwave radio to the channel used by the special operations forces of the New York City Police Department. They listened to the chatter as they drove, Goldfarb getting a feel for the rhythm of the day before he went off the grid, New York City being a busy place even in the early morning hours. The chatter seemed normal, everything sounded okay.

In hindsight, it might have been better if the radio had been turned off.

Sixteen minutes earlier, at approximately 8:14 a.m. on September 11, somewhere in the skies over Pennsylvania, American Airlines Flight 11 bound for Los Angeles was hijacked by terrorists and began a turn to the south, a turn that continued until the Boeing 767 was headed toward New York City. By 8:40 a.m. Manhattan would have clearly been visible from the cockpit as it entered the city's airspace. The terrorists began a rapid descent to just a few hundred feet above the ground as the plane reached the Hudson River. Later it would be determined that Flight 11 raced the entire 13-mile length of Manhattan at the breakneck speed of 466 miles per hour. Looking out a passenger window, the forest of buildings that comprised one of the largest cities in the world must have seemed like a terrifying blur.[9]

CHAPTER 5

"We had a view of the World Trade Center."

8:45 a.m.

ACROSS NEW YORK CITY, FIREHOUSES AND EMS CREWS WERE CHANGING shifts. Fresh crews arrived to take over for those that covered the night before. As Deputy Chief Zachary Goldfarb made his way home, EMS day crews were rolling out to their staging area, prepping their ambulances that guaranteed a response time of less than ten minutes. The 9-1-1 dispatch computer systems could sweep the field to find the ambulance nearest to the location of a caller and send it out to attend to the emergency. "It's called our CSL—our Cross Street Location," said EMT Jennifer Beckham, EMS, Flushing Hospital Medical Center, Unit 52 Frank. "We had to remain plus or minus 3 blocks of our CSL."[1]

EMT Orlando Martinez, Battalion 4, FDNY, and his partner, EMT Frank Puma, also of Battalion 4, picked up their ambulance from Fire Station 4 on South Street down by the East River, and drove to their designated staging location, Church Street and Barclay Street. They parked one block from WTC 5 on the east side of the World Trade Center complex, just up from the Millennium Hotel. Not feeling particularly pressed for time on this beautiful September morning, Martinez and Puma walked to their favorite deli for some food. They sat down at the counter and gave Debbie, their waitress, their order. With the enormous Twin Towers not more than a few hundred feet behind them they tuned their portable radios to the citywide frequency and got ready to eat.[2] Their call sign was 01 Adam.

EMTs Alexander Loutsky, Battalion 4, FDNY, and Ralph "Eric" Ramos, also of Battalion 4, were in vehicle 219 headed to the other side of the World Trade Center not more than four blocks from Martinez and Puma, although they may as well have been on the other side of the moon so vast was the complex. Ramos and Loutsky were navigating the streets toward Liberty Street and the West Side Highway aiming for the corner to the west between the Marriott Hotel, called WTC 3, and the South Tower. They, too, were in no particular hurry, such being the tempo of things when the skies are blue and the winds calm. "We had just exchanged vehicles at battalion around a little after 8:30," said Loutsky. "We were around Pearl Street and we had a view of the World Trade Center, which was only a few blocks away." As they neared the Brooklyn Bridge, the Twin Towers grew larger, two buildings so tall that to one standing at their base it was nearly impossible to see the tops. Loutsky and Ramos were shooting the bull. "We were talking small talk," Loutsky said, "football, politics, people talk."[3] Their call sign was 01 Charlie.[4]

Across the East River, over in Brooklyn, EMT Sean Cunniffe, Battalion 31, EMS FDNY, and his partner Jarjean Felton loaded their ambulance and headed down Flatbush Avenue to their cross-street staging location, where they would sit and wait for a call. As was their morning habit, their first stop was for the 99-cent bacon, egg, and cheese special at their favorite diner. "Can't pass that up," said Cunniffe.[5] With penlights and trauma sheers stuffed into their cargo pockets, they grabbed their handheld radios and went inside and sat down at the counter, one ear tuned to the chatter for their call sign, 48 David.

With Loutsky and Ramos on one side of Lower Manhattan, Martinez and Puma on the other, and Cunniffe and Felton across the bridge, EMTs more or less surrounded the World Trade Center. Completing the picture was Firehouse 10 on Liberty Street, the cross street just below the South Tower. Firehouse 10, or 10-and-10, as it was called, was home to Ladder 10 and Engine 10. The firefighters of 10-and-10 had a patch that depicted a mustached fireman standing atop the World Trade Center, one foot planted on each of the towers, an ax in one hand, a hose in the other. They were the protectors of the Twin Towers. They dared any fire to touch them. But in less than two hours, 10-and-10 would be reeling from the collapse of the towers, and the streets around them would be blocked, or nearly so. Indeed, in less than two hours the well-constructed and rehearsed, totally detailed mass casualty incident preplan for the Twin Towers would be activated and would function, save for one key element. In the attacks that would occur, a sky full of steel and concrete would rain down on Lower Manhattan leaving a deadly pile of I-beams and shredded construction debris blocking off the West Side Highway, Vesey Street, and almost all of Liberty Street.

For all practical purposes, anyone below the North Tower would be cut off from Uptown Manhattan as certainly as if they were stranded on a deserted island in the Pacific. And, and for that, there was no preplan.

Except the harbor.

And at 8:44 a.m., the boxes measuring the water levels chirped low tide.

CHAPTER 6

"Eric, look at that!
Look how low that plane is."

8:46 a.m.

ALTHOUGH AROUND HIM HISTORY WAS TURNING, ROBERT LAROCCO had no idea about any hijacking over Pennsylvania. For now, his world revolved around a single cup of coffee. Larocco was early for an appointment in Lower Manhattan, so to kill some time he headed over to the Village to grab a cup of joe at a local diner he knew. A splash of sunshine warmed his face as he breathed in the crisp morning air, a beautiful day unfolding if ever there was one. He walked past a small pocket park where some early risers were setting up a farmers' market, but then he heard something that was out of place, and he wasn't the only one. It sounded like an airplane, but one in trouble, like the engines were straining, he would later say, and others thought so too.

"Everyone stopped what they were doing," said Larocco. He looked south toward the tip of Manhattan but didn't see anything, not immediately, not until he caught sight of a jet through a gap in the buildings. "Normally, over Manhattan, a plane flies very high. But then, for six or seven seconds, flying out of the northeast, headed southwest, was this jetliner, like the kind of thing you would go on to go to Miami Beach or Vegas or something like that. It was flying very low, probably about 350 feet. As it passed over us, it wobbled just a little bit."

Larocco followed the plane with his eyes but no sooner had it appeared, than it disappeared from view. He came to the reasonable conclusion that the airliner was headed to Newark Airport in New Jersey, so he put it out of his mind until he heard another noise. "I started walking to go where I was going to have breakfast, and then I heard a dull thud; not an explosion but an actual dull thud with a little bit of metal to it."[1] The sound came from the direction that the mysterious jet had been flying, so Larocco concluded that it had dropped an engine or had some other problem, but in the next instant he knew that he was wrong. "You normally can't see the [World Trade Center towers] from where I was. But going from west to east was a cloud of white smoke with dust."[2]

EMT Frank Pastor, Battalion 31, EMS FDNY, and his partner EMT Mala Harrilal were parked at their cross-street location in Brooklyn's Red Hook section on Long Island near the East River. They had a perfect view of Lower Manhattan and the towers. "We were sitting there, and we were looking at the city," said Pastor. "All of a sudden my partner says to me, 'Frankie, that plane seems to be low.'"[3]

Orlando Martinez and Frank Puma, the EMTs that were waiting for their breakfast, felt the building they were in shake, a "rumble" as they later described it. Debbie, their waitress, asked what was going on. Puma thought a manhole cover had blown off, as if such a thing could make a building shake.

"Shouldn't you guys go outside and check what's going on?" the waitress asked, looking at Puma.

They waved her off and told her if they were needed they'd get a call, but then Martinez had second thoughts and told Puma to go outside and check things out. "So, Pu goes outside and doesn't come back for a minute. The food wasn't ready yet. So, I said, 'You know what? Let me go out and see what's up with Puma.' I went outside and looked around the block. I saw Puma. His mouth was just dropped. He was looking up. I look up, too, and say, 'Oh shit. That's gotta be bad.'"[4, 5]

Loutsky and Ramos, the other EMTs near the Towers, saw the airliner as well and also thought it was too low, but not in their wildest dreams did they think it would ram into a building. They were talking when the airliner caught Loutsky's eye. "Eric, look at that! Look how low that plane is!" yelled Loutsky. "It's gonna hit. It's gonna hit!"[6]

Ramos looked up and they both saw it, although they could scarcely believe their eyes. "A few seconds later, it exploded, just went in, and exploded," said Loutsky. "We just shook. We shook."[7] Loutsky quickly picked up his radio and started to call dispatch, but first he composed himself because he wanted to get this right. He guessed the airwaves would soon be a blur of transmission with voices piling on top of voices; he had to get this call right.

"01 Charlie for the priority," Loutsky called in.

"01 Charlie, go," answered dispatch, acknowledging the priority.

"01 Charlie. We have just witnessed a plane hit the World Trade Center," said Loutsky, his words measured and even.

There was a slight hesitation. Dispatch asked for a repeat.[8]

Before Loutsky could answer, Martinez and Puma in 01 Adam hit the airwaves. "I grabbed for my radio and yelled over the air, '1 Adam. A bomb just went off in the Trade Center,'" said Puma.[9] "We were running [to our vehicle]" said Martinez. "We were a block away [from the North Tower]."[10]

───

At 8:46:40 a.m. American Flight 11, a wide-bodied Boeing 767 jet-liner with 92 passengers and crew members on board, slammed head-on into the north side of the North Tower, impacting the building between the 93rd and 99th floors at some 450 miles per hour, killing scores of people instantly. Because Flight 11 was on a transcontinental route it carried 9,717 gallons of highly flammable jet fuel. The fuel ignited whooshed through every possible opening in the building, gulping fresh oxygen wherever it could, racing down elevator shafts and exploding out into connecting lobbies burning and killing as it went until hit the B4 level, four stories below ground, and flamed out.[11]

Above, at the impact site, a geyser of fire and debris shot out of the side of the building sending rivers of flaming jet fuel down onto Tobin Plaza below. A portion of the plane's flap, engine parts, and at least one passenger landed on the ground dead.[12] Elevators and stairwells were severed or crushed leaving them inaccessible. Fire, smoke, and heat rose toward those who were trapped in the top floors. The restaurant, Windows on the World, on the 106th and 107th floors, was filled with some 170 people for a morning conference, all now cut off from escape 1,300 feet above the harbor.[13]

Time suddenly froze as a blizzard of transmissions rendered the airwaves useless. "There was so much noise when the first call came over, everybody just went like ballistic over the radio," said EMT Faisel Abed, Battalion 8, EMS FDNY. "There was 01 Adam, [who were] like under the building at that time, and then there were a couple of other units that said, 'we will go, we will go.' It sounded legit. It did sound legit, but in the back of our minds, we thought maybe it's one of the generators that blew up, something electrical, something mechanical. It's just such a tall building, things happen, you know?"[14]

To eliminate any doubt about the severity of the situation—that it wasn't as simple as a generator—Lieutenant Rene Davila, Battalion 4, EMS FDNY, got through to dispatch and confirmed that an airplane had hit the tower, thus becoming one of the first senior EMS officers to do so. Davila told dispatch to notify the command's senior staff and to roll their mass casualty assets. This was going to generate a lot of patients, Davila said to himself; this was going to be the mother of all MCIs.[15]

A plume of black smoke began to stream downwind from the North Tower etching a line 900 feet in the sky toward the Atlantic Ocean. EMT John Ruthmund, Battalion 22, EMS FDNY and his partner were driving across the Verrazano-Narrows Bridge when they saw the line of smoke. It didn't make sense to them, not on this postcard-perfect day. "We had no idea what was going on. The only thing we knew, there was a fire, and we knew that from looking over off the bridge that a plane had hit it, but we thought it was a Cessna, like a little tiny private airplane. Nobody had a clue it was a commercial liner." Ruthmund and his partner made their way to Lower Manhattan and parked their ambulance at Liberty and West Side, but when they saw the burning tower, they thought better of it and moved their truck further away.

Captain Paul Mallery, Ladder 10, FDNY, was coming off a 24-hour shift at 10-and-10. He wasn't going home, not yet. He was scheduled to work at a polling station for a candidate up for election that day, so he stayed in the firehouse and took a shower. While washing, Mallory heard the explosion and probably felt it too, so he quickly got out and dried off and joined the others by the window. "You can't see Tower 1 because it's blocked by Tower 2," he said, speaking of how close they were. "But we did see papers start fluttering down from the sky. We said, 'Uh, this can't be good.'" Someone flipped on the TV. "You could see the building on fire. We were saying, 'What was it? Some guy being a wise guy? [A] little Cessna being cutey-cutey trying to thread the needle between the two buildings and he missed?"[16]

But deep inside, they knew cutey-cutey wasn't it. No matter how you cut it, a Cessna is too small for anything like what they were seeing. At best, a Cessna can hold 40 gallons of gas, a mere matchstick compared to the thousands of gallons of highly volatile jet fuel that is carried by a Boeing 767. No, the 9,717 gallons of highly volatile jet fuel that was carried by this Boeing 767 could burn through anything. The massive fireball alone was proof of that: It had been large enough to swallow a small house.[17]

Jonathan Segal, the commuter who took the ferry in from Hoboken, New Jersey, was still on his way to work when the jet hit the North Tower. "I was on the south side of Liberty Street walking up the sidewalk that sits across the road from the Twin Towers," he later wrote. "I have a clear picture of a large piece of metal flying down toward me and the street. I sprinted up the street zigzagging around falling fire, metal and concrete." Segal made it to Washington Street where he crossed over to the 10-and-10 firehouse and ducked under the overhang. "It is a beautiful, old fire station with an arched brick doorway, and I ran under that trying to get out from under the raining debris. A firemen ran outside and looked up at the towers." Another one grabbed Segal and pulled him inside and pushed him back to a corner where two other civilians were sheltering. "The second imprinted memory of that day was hearing one of them scream out 'Let's go boys! Suit up! We've got work to do!'" said Segal. "The firemen were in their trucks and on their way within a minute because when I looked up, all their vehicles were gone, and they had closed the garage doors to the station. Those men were in the [North Tower] within two minutes of the crash and I later realized that most, if not all of them, might not have made it out."[18]

Across the five boroughs, radios and data terminals chattered to life, sending shock waves of urgency through the EMS community. Battalion 22 on Staten Island activated their preplan. Units were directed to Liberty and the West Side Highway not far from Orlando Martinez. Battalion 4 was directed to the tower. Some EMS units were sent to the West Side Highway and Vesey, some to Church and Vesey, some to Liberty Street. *Turn out coat? Check. Helmets? Check. Staging area? Check.*

Still, the news was unclear. The radios were jammed with transmissions that contained a laundry list of possible reasons for the sudden smoke coming out of the tower. EMS Citywide Dispatch cleared things up when they broadcast an urgent "10-40," a code that meant a mass casualty incident on the order of a plane crash or a train derailment had occurred.[19] Next came word that the 10-40 was assigned to Box 8087.[20] To all who heard it, Box 8087—an old but useful fire department code system for the thousands of manual fireboxes on the streets around the city—signified that the MCI was at the corner of Vesey and Church Streets, which confirmed the worst—that there was an MCI at the largest and most iconic structure in America, the World Trade Center.[21]

⸻

"Did you hear that?" Merced asked over the noise of the radios, as if her passenger, Chief Goldfarb, could have missed it. Goldfarb asked her to repeat it, which she did. "It was unbelievable," said Merced. "An airplane crashed into the World Trade Center."[22] Goldfarb picked up the radio and told dispatch to assign him the job then called the incoming citywide chief and told him he was going to Lower Manhattan. "From what I could see from a distance, it was not a Cessna that hit that building," said Goldfarb in his interview. "It was obviously something big that hit that big building." Then he added the terrible but unspoken truth that was no doubt going through the minds of the responders in the countless ambulances, fire stations, and police units. "I knew that building was going to be full of people," he said. "Experience told me that we were going to have a lot of patients."[23]

"We should be able to get to the tunnel," said Goldfarb to Merced. "Let's take the Battery Tunnel."[24]

Merced hit the emergency lights and floored it.

"We noticed smoke coming off the first building."

8:47 a.m.

AROUND NEW YORK HARBOR, WORRIED EYES TURNED IN THE DIRECTION of the smoke, although what it meant was entirely unclear. Captain James Parese was in the pilothouse of the ferry *Newhouse*, ready to depart Staten Island, when he saw the smoke. "We were leaving St. George dock at approximately 8:48 a.m., heading north for Manhattan," said Parese. "When we entered the pilothouse, we noticed the smoke coming off the first building." Parese, a well-known figure on the harbor, was experienced and well liked with a confident gaze that spoke to his comfort on the water. His usual uniform was a white shirt with dark slacks and a clip of keys on his hip. With a passenger capacity of 6,000, the 310-foot long, 3,335-ton burnt-orange ferry connected Lower Manhattan to Staten Island using the Whitehall Terminal on Manhattan and the St. George Terminal on Staten Island. The double-sided bow of the large boat allowed the *Newhouse* to enter a slip without backing out, which meant not only a fast turnaround but a design that allowed the entire system to operate like clockwork, back and forth to Staten Island, one ferry arriving, one departing, rarely if ever off schedule.

Parese knew the tower was burning but he also knew that New York's fire department was one of the finest in the nation. Surely they knew what to do. Parese got underway, departing the terminal as scheduled and headed across the harbor, one eye on the water, one on the tower.[1]

Jersey City, New Jersey, lies directly across the Hudson River from the Twin Towers. A city of sparkling steel high rises, Jersey City boasts a vibrant waterfront with a magnificent park, excellent docks for ferries and tour boats plus a footbridge that connects it directly to Ellis Island. But for all of that, it was the view of Manhattan that everyone remembers. Paramedic Mickie Slattery was having breakfast at a coffee shop along the waterfront. She wore a white shirt and blue cargo pants, the uniform of a critical care paramedic with the Jersey City Medical Center and the perfect outfit for the delightfully warm day. From her table, she was enjoying her postcard-perfect view of the distant towers when she suddenly saw a fireball blossom out of the North Tower and a stream of black smoke tailing off to the right. That can't be good she thought, and it triggered memories that lay just beneath the surface: In 1993, terrorists had set off a bomb in the underground parking garage of the towers and Jersey City had been inundated with survivors. It happened without any warning and without any coordination with the city and they had been ill-prepared to help. If the line of smoke coming off the distant tower meant what she thought it meant, Jersey City would again be receiving casualties. Slattery was going to be prepared this time. She immediately got up and drove back to her hospital and began to stock her ambulance with extra bandages, nebulizers, splints, water, and more.[2]

—◆—

Perez's Coast Guard Station New York was situated on a handsome campus of buildings that ran down to the Staten Island waterfront with an unobstructed view of Manhattan five miles across the harbor. A flagpole stands between the docks and the buildings that house the Coast Guard station's operations center including the chart room where Perez was getting updates. Next door, in Fort Wadsworth, a second Coast Guard operations center, called the Vessel Traffic System, was monitoring every ship that was entering, transiting, or leaving New York Harbor. Inside the Vessel Traffic System center, Coast Guard personnel watched a bank of radar scopes and video monitors that included a bank of closed-circuit television feeds from cameras that had a perfect view of Lower Manhattan.

At 8:47 a.m., on Tuesday, September 11, 2001, all those cameras showed a line of smoke coming off the top of the North Tower of the World Trade Center.

But exactly what that meant was unclear.

Patrick Harris, the charter captain and owner of the sailboat *Ventura*, was enjoying the solitude of his morning when American Flight 11 came out of nowhere and flew overhead. His deckhand saw it first and yelled at Harris to look up, but Harris was facing the wrong direction and only caught a glimpse of it. "I turned and just caught the tail of an airplane disappearing into the North Tower. For a split second it was completely silent but suddenly there was a loud *whump!* and a large balloon-shape fireball erupted from the north side of the building and was sucked back in within a second or two."[3]

Struggling to believe what he saw, Harris nonetheless composed himself. He wanted to alert someone, so he reached for his marine radio and switched it to channel 16, the emergency channel monitored by Staten Island. Harris took a breath and tried to reconcile the improbability of what he had seen with the reality of the smoke and flames that were now billowing from the North Tower. "I could not bring myself to say it," he said, speaking of a jet crashing into the building. Rather he toggled the mic and said something along the lines that there had been a tremendous explosion at the World Trade Center.[4]

The Coast Guard needed more information.

"It looks like a plane has hit it," said Harris, hoping that was clear enough. The North Tower was burning, he said; flames were consuming multiple floors.[5]

Up the Hudson River, the morning crew change was about over when someone on the docks started frantically waving their arms trying to get Captain Ed Metcalf's attention. Metcalf broke away for a moment and went outside to see what was going on. "I looked down south and saw a heavy volume of smoke pushing from the North Tower of the World Trade Center," he said. Metcalf had no idea what was causing the smoke —a bomb he thought—but he figured sending a fireboat down there was a reasonable thing to do so he ordered Jim Campanelli, the pilot of the *John McKean*, to get underway. Campanelli hurried out of the station, down to the docks, and into the wheelhouse. He started the engines then switched on a panel of electronics that included radar, GPS, a fire department dispatch terminal, and radios of all sorts. Metcalf asked Campanelli to take the fireboat down to the seawall and put her in near Liberty Street just past the North Cove Marina near the base of the North Tower.[6] Then, as head of fire operations, Metcalf grabbed his turnout coat and jumped on board. "Let's go," he said.[7]

Enroute, Metcalf used his binoculars and radio to broadcast situational updates. In the shorthand of firefighting, his most important message may have been the simplest: The fire in the tower, he said, was already three-sided.[8]

The breeze that morning kept the air fresh and the temperature mild as the New Jersey state troopers prepared their cabin cruiser for departure. As they did, their routine was interrupted by someone running down to the docks. "They told us a plane hit the tower," said boat captain DeMarino. "That was a big problem." Without wasting a breath, the troopers cast off and accelerated down Newark Bay toward the Bayonne Bridge where DeMarino banked left and sped under the arced span. "Once you make that left under the bridge, you have a clear view of the towers," he said. And what he saw was smoke. He pointed the boat down the center of the Kill Van Kull and raced forward with every bit of speed he could get until they were out in the river near the buoy that marked the end of the channel and the open waters of New York Harbor. DeMarino cut a clean line across the brown waters of the Hudson River, a path across the river he'd sailed so often he could do it with his eyes closed. But there was no closing any eyes today. As the tower sent thick waves of black smoke billowing into the sky, DeMarino banked the patrol boat toward the North Cove Marina.[9]

Back on Staten Island, with the bright sun and smooth seas, Perez expected an uneventful day, a thought that was interrupted by the clanging of the emergency alarms ringing through the station. "I assumed it was an accident," said Perez of the burning tower, but his training said otherwise.[10] Perez gathered his crew and raced to *41497* and got underway. He pushed up the throttles on the twin 300-horsepower outboard engines and carved a frothy white line across the harbor, the hull of his response boat slapping the surface of the water, his crew hanging on as he raced toward the area on the tip of Manhattan called the Battery.[11] In and of itself, the smoke did not create a bona fide nautical emergency, nor did it necessitate a response from the Coast Guard, but caution dictated otherwise. The smoke was blowing to the east away from the harbor, but it could easily blow the other way, and if it blew over the harbor, ships might be blinded and sparks could set fires causing a true nautical emergency. Moreover, if the smoke was the result of a major explosion, debris would have been blown into the harbor, which would create a serious hazard to ships.

Plus, this was not just *any* building.

CHAPTER 8

"We are gearing up, psychologically, for a major MCI."

8:49 a.m.

THE SMOKE BILLOWING FROM THE TOWER STOPPED NEW YORK CITY IN its tracks. Across Manhattan, people dropped what they were doing and pointed toward Lower Manhattan. Cabs pulled over and drivers got out. Men and women, most of them dressed in short sleeves or light jackets, came out of bagel shops, delis, and coffee shops and looked. One and two gawkers quickly became five and six people deep. "Everyone was staring at the tower," remembered one witness in her digital archive. "No traffic moved on the street. People were standing outside their cars. Lights changed; the Walk signals changed—without a reaction. Drivers turned up the volume on their radios for everyone on the street to hear the announcements."[1]

"I was on 04 Henry, a hazardous materials ambulance," said EMT Jonathan Moritz, Battalion 4, FDNY EMS. "We had heard the boom [of the first plane hitting] and had a thousand people waving to us and pointing to the World Trade Center."[2]

Alarms continued to clatter across the boroughs as more first responders raced to the scene. Before jumping into their fire engines or ambulances, extra bottles of water were stuffed into pockets, bites were taken out of the leftovers from breakfast—one medic even put on lipstick, it was just habit. Ambulances, police vans, fire engines, ladder trucks, unmarked cars with flashing red and blue lights raced nose-to-tail down to the World Trade Center, their sirens and horns echoing through the canyons of the city. "We could see a stream of emergency vehicles speeding down from uptown, lights flashing and sirens wailing," said a survivor in her digital archive. "The fire engines, ambulances and police cars just kept coming, in groups of two and three."[3]

The fire department assigned the towers three alarms, then multiple alarms. In Staten Island, Manhattan, Brooklyn, the Bronx, and Queens, the police opened lanes for emergency vehicles to speed toward the towers while simultaneously closing off cross traffic that would slow them down. "They had corridors open for us," said Louis Giaconelli, Engine 33, FDNY, a firefighter who was the driver on one of the rigs. "We picked up a few police cars in front of us or vans and we made it down there pretty fast."[4] Ten, twelve, fourteen emergency vehicles raced nose-to-tail. They came through the tunnels, over the bridges, and through the heart of Manhattan —the FDR, Broadway, the West Side Highway—but not everyone knew how to get there. Some of the drivers from the outlying boroughs were lost or missed their staging areas. EMT Brian Smith, EMS FDNY didn't know his way around. "I'm not very familiar with Lower Manhattan," he said. "It's not like Upper Manhattan where there are numbers. That's easy. It's a little tougher down on the low side if you don't really know your way around."[5] Lower Manhattan is a jigsaw puzzle of streets that run on confusing diagonals, some no wider than a truck, others just two or three blocks long and then, maddeningly, they end. When push came to shove, a truck or ambulance simply fell in line with whatever siren-blasting emergency vehicle rocketed past them.

Data terminals inside the ambulances and emergency vehicles clattered out messages. Staging areas. Assignments. Units. Secret Service agents in WTC 7, personnel from the New York Office of Emergency Management, and the Port Authority police force all went into motion. First responders armed themselves physically but also mentally.

"All my training in terrorism, hazmat, and confined space rescue started to kick in," said Deputy Medical Officer Glenn Asaeda, Medical Affairs, FDNY.[6]

He headed Downtown.

"I was gearing up, psychologically, for a major, major MCI," said Assistant Chief Jerry Gombo, Operations, EMS, FDNY.[7]

He, too, headed downtown.

Ramos and Loutsky, call sign 01 Charlie, and Orlando Martinez, call sign 01 Adam, were on the scene.

Firehouse 10 responded.

Rescue 2 responded.

40 Bravo responded.

40 Adam.

Rescue 4

Squad 288

A map would later be drawn showing the convergence of ambulances and fire engines on Lower Manhattan. So numerous were the responders that it would look like a starburst with the towers as the center point and lines radiating out some twenty miles from ground zero.

At 8:49 a.m., CNN broke into their regularly scheduled programming to begin what would become continuous coverage of the attack on the towers. It was accompanied by the first live camera shot of the burning North Tower to hit the airways. ABC television followed suit at 8:50 a.m.

Inside Firehouse 10, Captain Mallery of Ladder 10 paced the apparatus floor, listening to the radio and trying to get a feel for what was going on outside. Not that it was entirely necessary. "Civilians [were] coming in [with] burns [and] broken bones [and] cuts and bruises the next thought was oh shit this can't be good," said Mallory in his interview. "[Then] I hear [a lieutenant] of Engine 10 over the radio . . . he said 'give me 10-40 and give me every ambulance you've got.' Those [were] his exact words."[8]

One by one the MCI preplans for the World Trade Center that were filed away in the digital memories of the computers used by the city's emergency resources were put into effect. But on September 11, there was no preplan to mount a rescue of Lower Manhattan by the sea.

Sirens blaring, lights flashing, and nervous energy coursing through their veins, New York's finest and bravest were going to war.

But no one knew there was a kink in their armor.

"I wanted to surround the lower tip of Manhattan, and the Battery Park area, with fireboats."

8:54 a.m.

MANHATTAN IS AN ISLAND SURROUNDED BY A NETWORK OF BAYS AND rivers that form one of the busiest ports in the world. More than 4,000 ships enter the harbor each year, not to mention the dinner cruise boats, ferries, and tugs.[1]

The island lies roughly on a north-south axis with the Twin Towers at the southern end. Familiar landmarks such as Times Square, Broadway, Central Park, the Waldorf-Astoria, the Empire State Building, the tightly packed neighborhoods of the tony Upper East Side, are all well north. It is at the southern tip of Manhattan—the end jutting into the harbor—that one finds the residential area of Battery Park City, the Battery, and the promenade with its ticket kiosks, docks, landings, and boarding ramps for the various dinner cruises and sightseeing boats, including the Statue of Liberty cruises.

Ferry terminals dot Lower Manhattan with boats plying the harbor to and from the bedroom communities of Long Island, Staten Island, Sandy Hook, New Jersey, to Jersey City, Hoboken, and Weehawken. "Many people don't realize, as I did not realize, that lower Manhattan's docks are bustling with commuters, not to mention tourists, in the mornings," said a commuter who routinely used the Long Island ferry. "There is a continuous flow of ferries in and out of the numerous slips lining the southern tip."[2]

On average, 91,000 people used a ferry every day to commute into Manhattan.[3] Names like NY Waterway, Seastreak, NY Fast Ferry, Fox Navigation, and other ferry operators were as familiar to commuters as were the names of the subway stops. They could find a seat, unfold a newspaper, and watch the spray from the bow of their boat giving little thought to the trip across the water. It was fast and convenient, and on a beautiful day like September 11, 2011, the view from the boat was scenic.

But on this day those same boats would save lives.

Around the harbor the feeling of an easy workday framed by blue skies and calm seas quickly disappeared into the smoke. Boat captains were talking to first mates, mariners were gesturing to their crews, vessels were beginning to move. The *John McKean* was sailing toward the seawall. Trooper DeMarino was headed toward the smoke.

Coast Guard responder Carlos Perez reached the channel between the Battery and Governors Island and slowed down. The North Tower loomed large in front of him, a thick stream of black smoke trailing to the east with visible flames flickering across a half-dozen floors. Perez knew his next steps had to be measured so he trained his binoculars on the grassy area behind the seawall, then down to the railing, then back to the towers themselves. He saw people running across the park and down the streets toward the harbor. Some seemed to be headed toward him, some toward the Battery, while others were breaking off and headed toward the Staten Island Ferry Terminal. He couldn't see the base of the tower or, for that matter, anything more than the upper floors, so he couldn't get a feel for the situation in the plaza. The towers were too far back, plus there was a haze of smoke in the air that was obscuring his visibility.[4]

Perez scanned the water for survivors as well as debris that could sink his boat as he moved toward the tip of Governors Island.

The New York City Police Department's elite Harbor Unit was perhaps the first rescue boat to arrive on the seawall. A well-trained air-sea rescue team, the Harbor Unit was designed to respond to emergencies on the waterways using rescue helicopters based at Floyd Bennet Field on Long Island and a half-dozen emergency response boats docked next to the Brooklyn Army Terminal. The pilots were trained in sophisticated flight systems and the tactical employment of a helicopter in aerial rescue, hoists from the water, and law enforcement. Their boat crews were trained in everything else.

James Cowan, Harbor Unit Scuba Team, NYPD, 39 years old, was a scuba diver on the team. He was trained in water rescues, underwater search and rescue, and was capable of diving into in the tangled wires and sharp edges of a downed airliner or squeezing into an underwater pipe the size of a small man, "In our unit, we keep three divers on the boat and two divers in the helicopter at all times," said Cowan. "[After the plane hit] we were right near the North Cove Marina looking to set up the triage area."[5]

In the air above him, one of Cowan's teammates, Officer Steven Bienkowski, 37 years old, was circling the towers in the rescue chopper. Bienkowski's chopper had a sling and harness to hoist people in a rooftop rescue, but the situation looked bleak. "People saw the helicopter and I'm sure many of them were thinking we were going to be able to save them," said Bienkowski. "In fact, we weren't able to do anything. We were as close as we could possibly be, and we were still helpless, totally helpless." The heat from the flames was generating dangerous thermals, and the heavy black smoke that was curling over the lip of the tower was blocking from view 80 percent of the roof. "People were hanging out the building gasping for air. Some were jumping," remembered Bienkowski. "It was just so much more horrible than anything your mind could have ever conjured up."

Bienkowski looked down to the harbor. "Our guys were down there, the scuba launch," said Bienkowski, meaning that at the very least they could transport the injured by boat.[6]

And for that there would be plenty of demand.

Across the river in New Jersey, US Coast Guard Chief Boatswains Mate James A. Todd was having breakfast while his boat was being refueled. Todd, a 14-year veteran with the force, was officer in charge of the Coast Guard tugboat USCGC *Hawser*, a 65-foot harbor boat that was at that moment berthed at the Military Ocean Terminal in Bayonne, New Jersey. Todd had a clear view of the towers some 2 miles across the harbor, although he gave it only a passing thought until he saw a smudge of black coming out of the North Tower. Todd knew that meant trouble. He ran down to the waterfront to the offices of the Aids-to-Navigation Team and borrowed some extra seamen. Next, he recalled his crew. "We knew we had a job [to do] even before we were contacted," said Todd. True to the motto of his service, he made ready to sail.[7]

Over in Brooklyn, FDNY Captain Alfredo "Al" Fuentes shot off orders as he raced down to the docks and fireboats operated by the Marine Division of the New York City Fire Department. A burly man, Fuentes had recently been installed as commander of the city's fleet of nearly a dozen fireboats. His largest were some 130-feet long and weighing 334 tons, and had a crew of seven. They drafted water from the river in enormous quantities—just one of them could pump out as much water as a half-dozen land-based engines combined. Because of that capability the fireboats were frequently called to fight fires on land. "Our fireboats can get in close to the Manhattan shoreline," explained Fuentes. "The pilots and officers know the waters well, their depths, their currents, and the best places to berth."[8]

As smoke billowed into the sky, Fuentes ordered his boats to cast off and head toward the towers. There they would augment the *John McKean*, of Marine 1, which was already underway. The fireboat *Kevin Kane*, of Marine 6, was hurried into service from the Brooklyn Yards, as was a second fireboat, *Firefighter*, of Marine 9 based on Staten Island.[9] Fuentes held Marine 9 in reserve in case there were other waterfront emergencies, but as the crisis took shape, it was quickly released, along with *Smoke II*, a small tender that was ordinarily used as a spare.[10] "I wanted to surround the tip of Lower Manhattan and the Battery Park area with fireboats because the West Side Highway and the FDR drive would probably be impassable," explained Fuentes in his autobiography. "The fireboats could be used to supply river water to augment the water supply for the land units operating at the World Trade Center."[11]

Little did he know at the time, though, that he was putting in place assets that would be remembered as much for their job fighting the fires as they would be for the scores of lives they would save.

Including his own.

CHAPTER 10

"There were people running everywhere."

8:55 a.m.

In 1988, the average New York City ambulance arrived at the scene of a medical emergency in a little over eleven minutes. For someone clutching their chest in the vice of a heart attack or gasping for air as they choked on a piece of meat wedged down their throat, eleven minutes was a death sentence. That improved when EMS merged with the New York City Fire Department—they added more ambulances and better dispersal patterns—and the response time dropped to nine minutes.

On September 11, the first ambulance was on scene in 90 seconds, but it ran head on into dense crowds of people running uptown. The office workers in the North Tower streamed down to the streets and headed away from the building. Clerks and commuters in the lower concourse did the same. Anyone who saw the blood or heard the cries joined them. This included office workers in the South Tower, the one that hadn't been hit. All together they numbered in the thousands as they overwhelmed the sidewalks and spilled into the streets. "[The scene was] packed with people," remembered one firefighter of the congestion his fire engine encountered as they went downtown. "There were actually people gridlocked in the street, thousands of people. The apparatus actually had to slowly plow the people out of the way so we could respond."[1]

"I can't really describe it," said EMT Alwish Moncherry, EMS, FDNY. "It was just hell. People were just pouring out. Thousands and thousands of people just coming out. And everybody seemed to have been injured in one way or another. Triaging patients, that's all we could do."[2]

"The scene was hectic," agreed EMT Jody Bell, Battalion 4, EMS, FDNY. "There were people running everywhere. There were units flying everywhere. There was debris falling. It was just the worst." Bell drove his ambulance down the West Side Highway and parked at West Side and Vesey where he and his partner got out. They were overrun. "The horror on the people's faces," he said. "People were running with second-degree, third-degree burns, half their hair burned down to the scalp. People had broken arms. They were holding limbs. It was a bad scene."[3] Many of the injured were unable to comprehend that help was at hand and some of them were so frightened that they tried to shake off the medics even as they attended to their wounds. "They were in such a state of shock that they didn't know what was going on any more than you did, and they just wanted to get out of there," said paramedic Kenneth Davis, Battalion 22, EMS FDNY. He tried to calm people down, reassure them, funnel them to the ambulance, but he had little success. "Some people, as you were grabbing them, they didn't want to sit still for anything. So, you were just grabbing their clothes and using their clothing as bandages and just saying 'okay, fine, hold this and keep going,' you know, 'don't go back that way.' It was just sheer madness."[4]

EMTs Martinez and Puma were unable to get through the crowds to their staging area so they pulled off at Church Street and Vesey to attend to victims they saw on the road. It was as if they were the only ambulance in the world. "As soon as we opened the doors up, we got overwhelmed by patients just coming over to us for help," said Martinez. "People were bleeding, tripping, minor injuries, some major, we had some second-degree burns run up to us initially."[5] They triaged as fast as they could, sometimes four or five patients at a time, minimal treatment but effective, then put the most critical cases in the back until not an inch was left vacant. When they had a full load, they raced off to Beckman Hospital, worried that they'd lose a man they had with second-degree burns who was developing respiratory problems.[6]

Loutsky and Ramos were also overrun with patients. "They looked terrified," said Loutsky. Using the back of their ambulance as a triage collection spot, they began splinting broken bones, closing lacerations, and cooling second- and third-degree burns—but there simply were too many victims. They grabbed the radio and called for backup, then went back to work patching the torn anatomies of the patients who surrounded them.[7] "We were inundated," sighed Loutsky[8] Paramedic Manuel Delgado, Office of Medical Affairs, FDNY agreed. "We had more patients than we had ambulances. We were stuffing four and five people in an ambulance at this point."[9]

—◦—

EMT Ernestina "Ernie" Nyquist, St. Vincent's Manhattan EMS, Unit 02 Victor arrived and wanted some clarity. Nyquist knew that in any MCI, seconds were precious and an accurate understanding of the situation was vital. The North Tower was in flames and showering down deadly debris that was turning the base of the tower into a kill zone. The lobby was in shambles and in parts charred black from the flames of the jet fuel. The burned and injured were stumbling out; some bodies lay still and were smoking. She didn't need to be told it was bad—the visible carnage said all that—but how bad was it? How close had the victims been to the impact zone? She wanted to understand the situation. "They brought us to a guy burned from head to toe. I said to him, 'I know this is going to be a strange question, but I have to know what's going on in those buildings. For everybody's safety, can you please just tell me where you were.' He looked at me and said, 'I was in the basement of the North Tower.' I said, 'My God, these people are coming out from the basement. What is going on in that building?'"[10]

"The elevators were infernos from the jet fuel," explained EMT Louis Garcia, St. Vincents Manhattan, Unit O6 King, in an interview after the event. "The pressure from the explosion blew out the elevator doors on the main floor. Whoever was walking by those elevators [in the North Tower] was burned or had multiple trauma injuries." Garcia parked his ambulance on the West Side Highway under the North Pedestrian bridge that connected the north end of the World Trade Center to the World Financial Center. He and his partner jumped out and began treating and triaging as fast as they could but they were inundated with injuries that required immediate medical care. They packed the back of their ambulance but once again, there were more patients than ambulances. "We transported six patients to St. Vincent's [but we] had to leave people behind because it wasn't safe [to put more in the ambulance]," said Garcia. One victim they had to leave behind was a terribly burned women for whom there was little they could do given that their ambulance was already overloaded with critical patients. "Her back was badly burned. She had no hair left. No eyebrows left. She was sitting down, like in a squatting position, and her skin had peeled up and was crisp," said Garcia. "She sat there and looked up at me, and I felt terrible. I took a sheet, covered her and poured water on her to cool her down."[11]

By midday, some 350 patients had arrived at NYU's Downtown Hospital, which was not more than a half mile away, while another 300 presented at St. Vincent's, about a mile away. In addition, some 75 critical care patients were on the way or currently being treated at other hospitals not counting the 19 burn patients who were or would soon arrive at Cornell's Medical Center, Manhattan's primary burn center.[12]

"We were trying to save as many people as possible," said Nyquist.[13]

Some 744 patients would be admitted to hospitals uptown.

But not everybody ran uptown. Some of the injured ran the other way.

Many of them ran to the water.

CHAPTER 11

"There were bodies strewn all over West Side Highway . . ."

8:59 a.m.

INSIDE THE NORTH TOWER THE FIRE GAINED STRENGTH AS IT BURNED through the floors, consuming corporate real estate like it was kindling. Of the scores of elevators that ordinarily traveled the giant tower, most of them were damaged, jammed, burned, or otherwise inoperable.

Up near the roof, or nearly so, desperate faces crowded the narrow windows, the smoke and heat at their backs, a 900-foot drop in front of them, their eyes searching the ground and air for something, anything to get them out of there. Office workers broke windows and heads appeared through the openings. Some frantically waved gesturing for help, others leaned out to gain one more inch separation from the heat. All too often the grim choice between succumbing to flames and jumping is suddenly resolved with a final leap. It was a sight seen from the ground and from neighboring buildings, often with striking clarity and unwelcome detail. "I looked up, and I saw a man in a business suit go flying by the window," said a witness in her digital archive who watched from across the street on the 34th floor of the World Financial Center. "I still remember that he had brown tassel loafers on, and the tassels and his tie were floating upwards as he fell."[1]

On the streets and in the plaza around the tower, death was accompanied by loud explosions as bodies hit the pavement. "We got out of the ambulance and started getting our equipment together," remembered EMT Scott Beloten. "I looked up at the tower and saw people jump and got fixated on it. You didn't realize they were coming 600, 700, 800 feet. I watched a person just sail across Liberty Street, right into the parking lot across the street, 100 feet away from us. He landed on a car. . . . It was horrible."[2]

Body parts and red clumps of clothing were scattered around the base of the tower which was disturbing enough, but it was a blackened hand that got to EMT Alex Loutsky. Loutsky was in the plaza when he came upon the body of a jumper that was largely intact. "The hand was charred black in a grasping position," he said, recalling the moment. "I could see how the person had been grasping the building —not wanting to jump, but not wanting to be incinerated. 'Should I jump, or should I burn?' It must have been a tremendous agony. This person was found dead due to the fall—every bone broken—but the hand was charred black." Loutsky was a highly trained, experienced emergency medical provider. In his years of service, he had seen his share of terrible injuries. "It's not so much what you saw as what you [imagined] that they went through," he admitted. "It's an agony to me. Very difficult."[3]

Peter Wells lived in an apartment building two blocks away. He went up to the roof of his building for a better view. "[There] were huge flames and smoke pouring out of the North Tower," he remembered. Worse was what he could see around his feet. "There were pieces of the building—and pieces of flesh—all over the roof."[4] Gary Welz, another resident, saw the same carnage from his apartment building. "There was blood on our roof and body parts on some of the ledges and balconies. It was gruesome."[5]

SWAT team member and NYPD Captain Sean Crowley was at the base of the tower. Crowley had been on the force for 15 years.[6] He had seen people die before, some of them in the most horrible of ways. "I've cleaned up people run over by trains but probably one of the most disturbing things I saw that day were those people jumping from the towers," he later said in an interview. "These were regular happy-go-lucky people. These were people like you and me, people who worked hard every day. They went to work that morning, and now they are jumping out of windows 100 stories in the air."[7]

From the 17th floor of the World Financial Center, one eyewitness evacuated his building only to walk out on the street head-on into the carnage on the ground. "What I saw blew my mind," he later wrote in the digital archives of 9/11. "There were bodies strewn all over the West Side Highway, as well as body parts."[8]

EMT Peter Ashby, Division 1, EMS FDNY, tried to fit the sight of the body parts, destruction, and flames into a narrative that made sense of it all. "I thought somebody launched a missile from the East River or over the Hudson," explained Ashby. "We were in a war zone."[9] He was wrong of course, but he was right too. The towers were tall, majestic, indestructible—icons of America's might—and yet here one was burning uncontrollably. "I had the feeling we should get out of Manhattan altogether," said one survivor. "[I felt] that we were at terrible risk."[10]

Jonathan Segal, the commuter from New Jersey, evidently agreed. "There was potentially no safe place to be," he wrote.

And on that point, there would be no argument.[11]

CHAPTER 12

"I knew right away we couldn't put the fire out."

9:00 a.m.

FOURTEEN MINUTES INTO THE CRISIS, MULTIPLE FIRST RESPONDERS HAD been assigned to the North Tower; fire engines and ladder trucks were racing downtown and parking shoulder-to-shoulder, with more rigs yet to come.[1] The New York City Police Department cordoned off lanes for emergency vehicles as Port Authority police began closing down parts of the transportation grids in and out of the Twin Tower complex. NYPD Emergency Services Units—an elite police team capable of complex, technical rescues—had arrived, as had Haz-Tac units, the latter a tacit recognition that a structure as complex as the World Trade Center was little more than a witch's brew of industrial toxins. Specialized trucks were also on the scene and scattered about the base of the North Tower. There were the school bus-like, twelve-patient EMS Major Emergency Response Vehicles (MERVs), some EMS Logistical Support Units (LSUs), and at least one Mobile Command Post with an array of communications equipment packed inside.

Manhattan hospitals were fully staffed; most had canceled their elective surgeries and nearly all of them had recalled their off-duty nurses and physicians.[2] Survivors with minor injuries were told to walk under their own power; the critically injured went by ambulance. As patients arrived at area hospitals they were sent to one of three areas, two of which, the Yellow and Red areas, were manned by teams of surgeons in operating scrubs ready to evaluate a patient and wheel the ones who needed immediate surgery into an operating room.[3]

West Side Highway and Church Street, the primary evacuation routes, were congested but open. With sirens screaming and lights flashing, ambulances raced uptown, every inch packed with patients. One ambulance overheated and ground to a halt. Others came close as they strained under their loads.

The National Pharmaceutical Stockpile was mobilized, ensuring a ready supply of key medicines for a mass casualty event.[4] Mutual assistance pacts with neighboring hospitals were activated, opening beds in Upstate New York, New Jersey, and Connecticut. The Hackensack Medical Center's state-of-the-art Mobile Intensive Care Communication system was activated 54 minutes after the attacks, alerting the Mobile Intensive Care units at New Jersey hospitals within a 500-mile radius of New York City to the crisis. In Ewing, New Jersey, the police activated the state's Emergency Command Center. Ambulances, mass casualty units, field communications trucks, and EMS crews responded from cities as far inland as Paterson, New Jersey.[5] In Jersey City, the closest and largest city to New York's Lower Manhattan, the fire department of Jersey City followed suit by activating a mutual aid pact with the Port Authority of New York and New Jersey. Liberty State Park just across the river from the Twin Towers, was closed and converted for emergency use.[6] More trucks and ambulances flooded the streets. Further south, University Hospital in Newark went into emergency mode and got ready to receive patients from Lower Manhattan. In an instant, the streets of northern New Jersey lit up with bright flashing lights as the air filled with the scream of sirens.

On the harbor, the waterways offered options no one had on land. Dozens of boats from the various emergency response teams were now underway or arriving near the base of the tower. The commercial captains plying New York Harbor were focused on the stream of smoke. Radios in their pilothouses crackled to life with calls asking for information—what's going on, what had happened in the North Tower? So little was known.

Across the harbor at Caven Point, the ships of the Corps of Engineers were being readied to give assistance. "Everybody went to their boats," said Joe Meyers, one of the captains. Engines came to life in clouds of blue smoke; the harbor waters began to churn with frothy bubbles as propellers began to spin. The patrol boat *Hocking*, a 66-foot scout boat for the larger collection vessels, eased away from the docks, as did the *Gelberman* and her sister ship, the *Driftmaster*. Liz Finn looked down at her charts. On this day, the driftwood and debris could wait. She plotted a course for the North Cove Marina.[7]

New Jersey trooper DeMarino made it across the river and was abeam the entrance to the North Cove Marina. Unlike the sprawling 520-boat marina at Liberty State Park near Jersey City, the North Cove Marina, the main marina in Lower Manhattan, was exceedingly small. It could berth 50 or so boats, most of them small sailboats and pleasure craft, with only a few larger vessels near the mouth of the breakwater. DeMarino's launch could get into the marina, but as a seasoned mariner at the helm of a 45-foot boat, the opening through the breakwater worried him. If things went wrong, getting out would be a problem. The opening was too "narrow," as one historian later put it, and the proximity to the burning North Tower was a problem. "It's just a few hundred feet away," said DeMarino. If the tower toppled, he and his shipmates would be crushed or blocked, and if that happened, the rescues they were trained to perform would be for naught. No, rather than enter the marina, DeMarino inched his boat along the seawall while he and his fellow troopers decided where to put in.

Then they saw the injured.

The fireboat *John McKean* steamed down the Hudson River quickly closing the 20 city blocks from its berth at Pier 53 and West 14th Street to the seawall near the World Trade Center complex. Marine 1 Captain Metcalf reported in and explained his situation by radio as well as some general updates on what he could see of the tower. "From the river, because of our unique vantage point, we had a pretty good view," he later said in an interview. They made their way past the North Cove Marina and began to slow down not far from where DeMarino was idling offshore. Pilot Jim Campanelli picked a spot on the seawall and began his turn a few hundred yards out.

On West Side Highway scores of fire engines and ladder trucks were parked as columns of fresh firefighters marched toward the towers carrying rollups over their shoulders and pry tools in their hands. One witness saw a group of newly arrived firefighters walking single file in their bunker gear toward the burning tower. "The bravery and image of these men at that time will never leave me," he later said. "Everyone was running away from the carnage and they walked forward, determined to do their job. Amazing people showing amazing courage."[8] Many of the trucks had ridden "heavy," meaning they deployed with extra firefighters. The attack had occurred during the morning shift change, which meant two shifts of firefighters were in the firehouses when the alarm was broadcast. In the charged atmosphere of multiple-alarm fires, staying behind was impossible, which meant that a rig that normally deployed with three or four firefighters rode downtown with six or seven or even eight.

Chief Goldfarb and Mary Merced parked on the West Side Highway and walked toward the tower. From the base, the sheer verticality of the World Trade Center made it nearly impossible to gain any real perspective on anything 80 stories up. "Basically, [you're] looking straight up a vertical cliff, two vertical cliffs, and you're seeing the bottom of some smoke and fire and you see debris or whatever, but I don't think you [had] a full appreciation of the extent of damage," said Goldfarb.[9] He was right, of course. The towers were too tall to know what was happening where the plane hit, and the fire was too big. Firefighter Edward Kennedy, Engine 44, FDNY, was headed toward the tower. "I had the hose on my shoulder and my mask on and, of course, I'd never seen anything like it," he said of the North Tower fire. "I'm looking up and I knew right away that we couldn't put the fire out."[10]

New York City Chief Fire Marshall Louis Garcia was also on the scene. "I have never seen more than one floor going, [and here] you're talking about multiple floors, [not just part of a floor but] the entire floor, from west to east, north to south," he said in his interview. "That's a lot of fire."[11]

Chief of the Department, Daniel Nigro, FDNY, knew they'd never put it out. "In my high-rise experience, we've had success putting out partially involved floors, not 10 floors. I don't think any of us on the scene had any intention of putting out 10 floors."[12]

Citywide Tour Commander Chief Joseph Callan felt the same way and explained what that meant: "We [were] not going to be extinguishing the fire," he said. "What we were going to do is assist in evacuating the building."[13]

Fully dressed in bunker gear, and carrying pry tools, rollups, and oxygen tanks, a firefighter would begin the ascent loaded down with some 60 pounds of gear, pounds that would grow in weight with each step. Each floor would be climbed, checked, and cleared in a classic search-and-rescue protocol. When the firefighters finally got a half dozen floors below the flames, the hoses on their shoulders would be used to secure a boundary zone. In the North Tower that would mean they would have to ascend roughly 70 floors straight up. Such a climb would be an extreme test of human endurance against the unrelenting pull of gravity. "As the companies were coming in, we were giving them assignments based on the distress calls," said FDNY Deputy Chief Peter Hayden, First Division, FDNY. Hayden was a veteran on the force and had served as chief of safety from 1995 to 1997. A search and rescue was old school to him. "There were numerous distress calls coming in from the dispatcher and also coming in directly to the lobby of people trapped in elevators, people burned in different areas of the building, people needing wheelchairs and unable to get downstairs. Absent specific distress calls, we assigned battalion chiefs over a range of four to five floors with companies to search those floors."[14]

But it was grueling. Ten floors up, stop and rest. Ten more floors, stop again. Firefighters were soon soaked in their own sweat. Groups of five and ten firefighters sat down to rest. Chest pains were reported between the tenth and twentieth floors. A woman coming down from the 29th floor passed the firefighters. "Around the 25th floor, we encountered the first of a steady line of fire fighters who looked winded and extremely hot and tired," she recorded in the digital archives of 9/11. "They were fully outfitted in their firefighting gear plus carrying extra fire hoses, air tanks, face masks, and cutting equipment."

She kept navigating the stairs, officer workers on the right, firefighters on the left, the injured down the middle. "I looked at the firefighters and noted their age as being between mid-twenties and mid-thirties with the exception of a few 'seasoned' individuals. I wanted to say something to them to encourage them. I put my hand on the shoulder of one of the firefighters and said, 'you guys have got a lot of heart.' He smiled and said, 'thank you.' I thought I saw the others straighten up a little and walk with a little more purpose." It was an encounter that would be repeated time and again, grateful survivors inspired by the bravery of the firefighters driven by a sense of duty to ascend toward whatever inferno lay ahead.[15]

And most had 50 more floors yet to climb.

Inside the South Tower, the one that had not been hit, office workers were receiving scant, if not confusing, information and as a result, only a partial self-evacuation was underway, some workers choosing to leave, others staying at their desks thinking—*hoping*—that the tower was okay. Those that stayed were nervously sifting through their options, their heads filled with possibilities but little certainty; those who left arrived at ground level to find a surprisingly organized array of first responders already in place. They were funneled away from the towers, most of them uptown to safety.

But many more remained.

CHAPTER 13

"With the second plane in, I knew this was no accident."

9:02 a.m.

IT HAD BEEN A MORNING OF STAGGERING VIOLENCE.

And it was far from over.

A second jetliner, United Airlines Flight 175, was at that moment a missile packed with human cargo headed toward New York City.

Tom Sullivan was on the deck of the *McKean* when he saw it. The plane flew over his head, or nearly so. The *McKean* was against the seawall ready to disembark Metcalf so he could go inland to report in. Sullivan thought the jet was doing some sort of low-level fly-by damage assessment, which fit the picture, but he was wrong. "[It flew] between the Statue of Liberty and Staten Island," said Sullivan. "It was coming barreling in and descending . . . we were like 'what the . . . , we knew. I said to myself, 'this is the beginning of World War III, it's got to be.'"[1]

Carlos Perez didn't know anything about war. He was in the pilot-house of *41497*. He was busy—he had his binoculars trained on the waterfront and might have missed the plane except that one of his crewmen yelled out in surprise, *"There's another plane! Look out the port side!"* Perez quickly turned his head and caught sight of the 767 through the cabin window. A second later, it slammed into the South Tower. As accustomed as he was to tragedies at sea and the loss of life, he and his crew were too shocked to speak. Hundreds of innocent people had been slaughtered in the blink of an eye. "We had a long moment of silence," said Perez. "A long moment of silence."[2]

Unlike American Flight 11, which flew down the Hudson River and was seen by only a handful of people, United 175 flew over the harbor and was seen by hundreds of people. Lyn Flynn at Caven Point saw the jet. The park rangers on Ellis Island saw the jet. It flew and raced across the water, which gave them an unobstructed view as it flew past. One observer thought it was a firefighting airplane like the ones used out west to put out forest fires, arriving here in New York City to dump water on the burning North Tower.

Jim Parese saw the plane from the pilothouse of his ferry the *Newhouse*. "We were just about off Governors Island," he said. "At that time, we watched the plane [and] how it just glided right into the second building. At that point we knew it was no longer an accident." Parese picked up the radio and requested permission to hold his passengers on board and turn back to St. George. "We didn't think it was a good idea dumping a couple of thousand more people in Manhattan in that situation," said Parese. "A police boat responded to us. [He] told us to take them back." No one could recall when a Staten Island ferry had ever turned around, not on a beautiful day with calm seas. Parese began a slow sweeping turn, his wake carving a half circle across the harbor.[3]

NYPD officer Bienkowski was in the helicopter circling the World Trade Center in hopes of finding a way to execute a rooftop rescue. Bienkowski was seated near the left rear window. The terrorists nearly hit them. "We were on the southwest side of the South Tower, and I glanced over my shoulder and there came a United Airlines aircraft right at us, a little bit underneath us," he said. "And I do mean a *little* underneath us." So close did it fly to the helicopter that from the seawall Sergeant Cowan, his teammate in the unit, thought they would collide. "[It] came in so tight on them that the pilot took evasive action and pulled up and the plane actually flew under them before striking the building."[4]

An eyewitness on the 34th floor of one of the buildings across the West Side Highway saw it up close. "All of a sudden, out of the smoke, I saw a United Airlines jet appear. I thought my eyes were playing tricks on me, because it was so close that I could see passengers at the windows. They looked terrified, and some of them were pulling down their window shades rather hastily. Then it banked very hard, seemed to accelerate, and it ran into the tower."[5]

—◆—

United Airlines Flight 175, a transcontinental Boeing 767, banked over the New Jersey farmlands and turned in toward New York City. With sparkles of the bright sunlight reflecting off its smooth skin, it headed toward the South Tower. At the controls were terrorists trained as pilots, products of the best American flight schools, accurate in their flying abilities, intent on terror, able to navigate across thousands of square miles of airspace and hit a target several hundred feet wide. They accelerated the jet to a speed that was at the very outside of the plane's flight envelope, hitting some 546 miles per hour not more than 800 feet above the ground. The jetliner was loaded with more than 80,000 pounds of explosive jet fuel and 65 innocent souls.

At 9:02 a.m., Flight 175 slammed into the South Tower hitting the south face of the building between the 77th and the 85th floors killing hundreds instantly. An enormous fireball blossomed into the sky and a violent explosion ripped out huge sections of the building. Debris rocketed outward and rained down on the plaza below. "I looked up and I just saw the top of World Trade Center go up like a lit candle," remembered an EMS technician who was at the far end of the plaza. "Everything just lit up and everything just came down on the street. It was just raining steel."[6] Jonathan Segal, the commuter from New Jersey who was in the 10-and-10 firehouse saw it too. "I watched fire rain down and could see bodies cartwheeling out of the holes in the side of the building along with fire and metal," he said. "There was a great deal of screaming and panic at that time."[7]

Unlike the jetliner that hit the North Tower, which hit it square in the middle, United 175 hit off center, near the edge of the South Tower, which allowed more energy to pass through the building and more debris and burning fuel to surge out into the sky on the opposite side. "(I) could feel the heat from the explosion through the glass in our windows," said a witness. To give some perspective, he added that his offices were nowhere near the South Tower. "Our offices are about 10 blocks from the Trade

Center site."[8] Tamara Drummond EMS NYU Downtown Hospital was too close for comfort. "Somehow I lost sight of my partner because she was triaging on one side, and I was triaging on the other," said Drummond. "The next thing I knew, I heard this loud crash. It was the second plane running into the South Tower. All of a sudden there were huge chunks of debris raining down on us. Fiery pieces of metal. A big piece of the plane's fuselage fell to one side of me. The plane came in from the south and when it went through the building, the stuff that came out rained down on us on the northeast side. The pieces of debris were the size of desks. . . . It was chaos. People were being trampled, grabbing at you, screaming and yelling."[9]

EMT Jonathan Moritz was in the plaza and was caught in the middle of it all. He began pulling people to the side, afraid they might be trampled or hit by debris. "We looked up and the entire [South] Tower was turning into a fireball," he later recounted. "The plane came from the [south] side and blew everything out toward us."[10]

The number of dead and injured soared. Lieutenant Michael Donovan, Engine 290, FDNY, arrived a moment before United 175 hit. He got out of his truck east of the tower on Church Street between Liberty and Vesey. "We couldn't see it because it was blocked by the buildings," explained Donovan as the second plane hit the tower. "We heard the plane briefly, [then] the earth shook, the buildings shook, a tremendous fireball [erupted] overhead. I thought there was a bomb or an explosion. [It was] a tremendous fireball, [with] flaming debris, pieces of the airplane, fuselage, landing gear, pieces of the building. People started running. We started running down one of the streets." As he ran, Donovan saw that it was too late for some of those who tried to escape. "There were people dead in the street that obviously you couldn't help them," he said. "There was flaming debris coming down all over. It was just a matter of who [did and who did not get] hit with the debris."[11]

NYPD officer Ralph Balsi retired from the force to become the director of security for the World Financial Center. Balsi was on the North Pedestrian bridge helping with the evacuation when the second plane hit. A fire truck pulled up below him and a fireman got out. "He had his helmet on, but he got hit with a piece of steel, a steel beam, and it killed him instantly."[12]

Todd Maisel, a photographer, dodged the debris as best he could. "There were body parts and luggage scattered on the ground—a human hand pointed at me on the pavement," he remembered. The things he saw described a small version of Dante's *Inferno*. "Jagged parts of the plane were strewn about, one spear-like piece having pierced the hood of an auto," he said. "Cars were burning in the parking lot and firefighters were attempting to put them out as small pieces of debris rained down from above. On Church Street and Dey, I saw a [police officer] helping a man [who was] suffering burns to his face and back. He handed off that man to medical crews and ran back to the buildings to see who else he could help. That was the last I saw of him."[13]

Despite these dangers, Captain Jay Swithers, Health Services, FDNY, started triaging on the spot. "Patients were just coming out of the wood-work; some badly injured, some being gathered, being carried by civilians, some being carried by civil servants," he said. "One man was brought over in a wheelbarrow."[14]

The engine bay of the 10-and-10 firehouse was like a field hospital. A dozen victims were arrayed on the floor, some with lacerations, some with broken bones, some with terrible burns on their bodies. "Some of them were standing—those that were capable of standing or sitting—[they were] holding bandages on themselves," said Firefighter Lieutenant Sean O'Malley, FDNY Engine 10. "Two or three people were on the floor on a backboard. A male civilian was in a sked, a collapsible stretcher. I think they were treating him for a broken pelvis. There were the EMS paramedics and a civilian who apparently had some first aid training who was assisting them."[15]

EMT Brian Smith was almost certainly one of the medics that O'Malley saw. Smith had deployed to the site but had become lost in the maze of streets in Lower Manhattan. He asked a police officer where EMS was staging. "Nobody really had a clear sense of what the heck was going on," said Smith. "But he said to me, 'Listen, I don't know where they are setting up staging but they have some people that are at the 10-10 house' and he said, 'maybe you could do something over there." Smith headed over to 10-and-10 and did what he could but in truth he had enough injuries to fill the emergency room of a small city hospital.[16]

CHAPTER 14

"People were streaming out toward the ferry."

9:04 a.m.

THE SECOND PLANE LEFT LITTLE DOUBT IN ANYONE'S MIND THAT THE burning towers were terror, pure and simple. Said Dennis Smith, a firefighter: "We knew things had radically changed—from 'Oh, what a horrible accident,' to 'Oh, my God, they're trying to kill us.'"[1]

EMS Chief Gombo agreed. "With the second plane in, I knew this was no accident,. Two planes—that's much more than coincidence. In my mind, I switched from accident to terrorism."[2]

Sergeant Cowan of the NYPD Harbor Unit had the presence of mind to call the offices of the Liberty Island ferry and tell them not to take people to the Statute of Liberty. The statue itself was a likely target, he worried. For that matter, anything that would make a "statement" could be a target. "We were sure [there would be] a third plane and if it wasn't going for the Statue of Liberty it could have been headed for the UN which was being evacuated simultaneously."[3]

Patrick Harris, the captain of the charter yacht *Ventura* who called in one of the first reports of the attacks, was among the first captains to evacuate survivors from Manhattan. After American Flight 11 crashed into the North Tower, Harris left his boat to get a better view of the burning tower. It was a fire at this point, a terrible fire caused by an unimaginable accident but a fire nonetheless. Harris walked a considerable distance from the North Cove Marina through the glass-and-steel pavilion of the Winter Garden Atrium, across the West Side Highway, down the entire length of Vesey finally reaching the far corner of the World Trade Center at Church Street. He was at that corner when the second plane hit the South Tower and a fireball erupted out into the plaza. Harris turned and raced back to his boat. "I had to literally run and dodge people," he said of the panic that followed. "I needed to get the boat out of [the marina] because its my livelihood." But as he raced to his boat, Josh Hammitt, his first mate, came up frantic for his family. Harris told Hammitt to go back into the melee, find them, and bring them to the marina. Hammitt did and returned with his wife and brothers. [4] They set sail. "Two boats had already left, which was lucky for us," said Harris. "We needed the maneuvering room." A masterful yachtsman, Harris managed the throttles on the engines as he carefully negotiated the confines of the marina and made it out into the Hudson River. He idled the yacht for a moment then decided to take his passengers over to Hoboken where he could refuel. As one of the first boats out, he had little difficulty crossing the river. "There was no traffic to speak of in the harbor," said Harris. "It was still early."[5]

But it built quickly.

A senior operations manager for NY Waterway, the largest operator on the harbor, was in Hoboken, New Jersey, when he saw the smoke. He had enough experience to know he would be needed in New York, so he jumped on a ferry and crossed over to the World Financial Center terminal near North Cove. "Whenever there is an incident in the area—PATH breakdown, the last bombing of the WTC—we get bombarded with riders," he said in his digital record of the day. "When I got to the terminal, people were already streaming out toward the ferry. Many were quite panicked. My first thought, [though misguided in hindsight] was to keep calm, and to establish a sense of normality." But the lines were already too long so he reverted to protocol. "Normally when there is an incident, we put out garbage cans and collect the tickets and cash up on land to keep the flow of people moving. So that is what I did." It sped up the lines—he was selling tickets faster and moving things along—but he had a nagging feeling that something wasn't quite right. "At that time, we were not yet aware of the seriousness of the situation," he remembered.[6] Lacking the authority to board passengers otherwise, and not close enough to see the dead and dying, it took a few words from a policeman to give him clarity. "Finally, a Police officer came over and told me to let the people on for free. I told him that I did not have that authority. He told me he did, and thereby authorized it. I thanked him profusely." [7]

Liberated to do what was right, new ropes were positioned and people were funneled to the boats. Some firefighters passed by as he was setting up so they spontaneously pitched in. "As we walked, we were watching the New York Waterway ferries come over from New Jersey," said firefighter Robert Norris, Engine 202, FDNY. "[The ticket takers] were starting to [put up] makeshift ferry entrances for civilians who were coming over to [the boarding area]. Some were screaming, crying, some injured, some not. There were a lot of people [who were] injured so we independently started helping people who looked as if they needed help because as a unit we were firemen but we were without tools so we just kept assisting civilians and just ferrying them onto the ferries to get out of the area to go toward New Jersey."[8]

The second plane changed everything on the harbor too. The boat captains knew it was terror, and it was terror unlike anything they'd ever seen before. The smoke and flames meant people had been murdered, that people were injured, that people had to get out of there. And on that count, they knew the waterways were as good as any road when it came to getting people to safety. Ships began to move.

Kim Newton, an employee of Sea Streak, a ferry company operating from Highlands, New Jersey, out in Sandy Hook, heard of the second attack when she received a call from one of her captains. She immediately went into action, shifting gears from day-to-day operations of a commuter ferry to rescue operations. "I would say within five minutes [of his call], we decided to mobilize," said Newton. To speed up operations, which largely meant gearing up turnaround times, Sea Streak moved their ferries to a central location, which streamlined refueling. Then, in anticipation that some of the passengers would have injuries, they put police officers and EMTs on the boats. "The first group of returning passengers were not hurt," she said. "Just stunned and shaken up."[9]

Good weather was good for business, or so the axiom went in the ferry industry. Arthur Imperatore, president of NY Waterway, had 22 of his 24 boats on the water when the attacks began. Imperatore was in New Jersey not far from his office in Weehawken when the second plane hit. He immediately hopped on one of his ferries and raced over to Manhattan to help. "We were there and on the scene," he later said in an interview, meaning his ferries were there, in the harbor, ideally positioned to get people off the island. His boats starting loading passengers from the terminals and even from the seawalls. "We just let people jump over the railings onto the boats," said Imperatore. "There was no one in charge yet, no central authority coordinating efforts at that time, so we just went ahead and did it."[10]

And so did others. Out on the harbor, boats of every kind began to move toward Manhattan. "The people [who] worked for [the ferry companies], everybody automatically did what they needed to do," said Paul Amico, owner of a company that erected piers and terminals around the harbor. "The captains, as soon as they heard [about the attacks], automatically came down [to their boats] just as fireman and police automatically came down into the city."[11]

Amico had been near Giants Stadium in New Jersey when he saw the smoke. "I was about five miles west of the Hudson River right near Giants Stadium. . . . I saw this smoke from the World Trade Center. I immediately went back to my shop, which is only another mile and a half away, grabbed my marine radio, life jacket, and headed straight for Lower Jersey City to hop on a ferry. I knew there was a fire; I knew that we had to do evacuation, we meaning the ferry company."[12]

The iconic tour operator Circle Line Cruises responded. One of their first acts was to get as many of their boats into motion as possible. They were eventually able to get six of their high-capacity sightseeing boats into service.[13]

The dinner boats that ran nightly cruises on the harbor started to mobilize, too, as did the Liberty Island sightseeing boats, the Long Island ferry companies, and the various high-speed ferries. "It's human nature," said Captain Kirk Slater of NY Waterway. "[You] see people on the sea-wall in Manhattan begging you to pick them up. You pick them up."

"It's just, everybody just wanted to get out, everybody was so desperate," explained a boat captain. "They're desperate because they don't know what's going on, and they're desperate because they know they have to get out."[14] The captains took on as many people as they could. "We didn't want to overload, but we didn't want to just take on the exact amount we needed," added one of the ferry captains. "We took as many as we could possibly take and [so long as we considered] that it was safe, then we went."[15]

Said Paul Amico, the builder. "We are comfortable on the water. Most of these office people are not, [so] we just had to do what we had to do."[16]

—◆—

Ken Summers, a burn victim from the North Tower, was one of the first to be rescued by the boats. His evacuation was a story that would be repeated time and again. Summers worked on the 27th floor of the North Tower. As was his habit, he got in early—sometime after 7:00 a.m.—and was at his desk until 8:45 a.m. At 8:45 a.m., Summers decided to take a break, so he went down the elevator and stepped out into the plaza for some fresh air. He was no more than ten feet out of the doors when American 11 hit the North Tower. He was met head on by a blow torch of burning jet fuel. "I had no idea of the severity of my injuries," said Summers. "[But] I knew I was severely burned." Dazed and in pain, he shuffled across the plaza to the West Side Highway murmuring calls for help. He somehow walked across the West Side Highway and found a bench. He sat down, his shirt scorched, his hair burned down to his scalp, sheets of skin hanging from his arms. "I had been sitting there about five minutes when I heard the increasingly louder whine of a jet engine," he later said in a speech.[17] It was United Flight 175.

Summers managed to get up and run and made it behind one of the buildings of the World Financial Center on the Hudson River side. Safely shielded from the debris but exhausted, he stopped. "A man named Steve Newman came up to me and offered to help," said Summers. Newman said that he grew up in a doctor's family and would help Summers get to a hospital. But how? Smoke and debris seemed to cover Lower Manhattan in every direction and the Twin Towers looked bad, which limited their options. They decided the fastest way out was by boat, a decision that may have saved both their lives. They turned and shuffled over toward the river, west, away from the towers, each step harder than the first, until they spotted yet another bench. Summers needed to rest.[18]

Jim Campanelli had the *McKean* against the seawall south of North Cover Marina but only reluctantly. "He was worried about chemicals and toxins in the air," said Captain Metcalf. Metcalf left the boat and hurried over the railing and headed toward the fire. He was racing to the command post to report in and let them know that the *McKean* was there and ready to supply water. More importantly, he needed to know know how they wanted to use his boats. "I wanted to know what our orders were," said Metcalf. He told the crew to lay out their tools and stay put until he returned.[19]

"We were [just then] tying up to the bulkhead," said firefighter Tom Sullivan of the *John McKean*. As ordered, Sullivan and the crew were putting out the tools they needed—spare masks, oxygen cylinders, ladders, a first-aid bag, cutters, nozzles, and so on—when Summers appeared. Firefighter Billy Gilman spotted him and climbed the seawall to help. Gilman hurried across the esplanade and started basic first aid —an oxygen mask, water to drink—but patting water on the burnt skin was too painful. "I asked them if they could take us to New Jersey on the fireboat," said Summers. "They replied that they were ordered to stay where they were. Steve and I informed them that we then must get to the ferry."[20] "We could see over in Jersey [that] there were ambulances [and] police cars assembling over there waiting to help the injured people," said Sullivan. Gilman walked Summers upriver to the docks of New York Waterway, which had a boat leaving at that very moment. The ferry was already crowded and there was a long line of people waiting for the next one, but the crowds took heart. "There were thousands of people trying to escape Manhattan and still everyone cleared the way," said Summers. "They parted like the Red Sea. They let us pass right up to the edge of the ferry dock. The ferry had just pulled away from the dock and when they saw me standing there, they nosed back in and Steve and I and several other people jumped on board."[21, 22]

Summers arrived in New Jersey and was loaded onto an ambulance and rushed to the Jersey City Medical Center where he was admitted. Summers later credited Steve Newman with saving his life, but Newman had his own perspective on that. Had he not helped, Newman believed he would have been caught beneath the tower when it collapsed minutes later. "This huge plume of smoke came down, weaving its way like a snake in and around the buildings right over where all those people were standing—where we had been standing—and right into the water," said Newman. Newman believed he would have been in the middle of the falling I-beams had he not helped Summers down to the waterfront. "Like I told him on the boat, I said he saved *my* life."[23]

CHAPTER 15

"You have to evacuate the injured . . ."

9:07 a.m.

THE SITUATION ON THE WATERFRONT WAS DETERIORATING. THOUSANDS of people were running from the towers, many of them with lacerations and burns, many of those now swarming the seawall. "It was just hell," said Tom Sullivan on the fireboat *John McKean*. "Burnt, cut up, people helping each other, carrying other people. They're coming to us for help. They wanted to get out of there anyway they could."

Sullivan's group had orders to prepare the fireboat to fight fires but instead they felt compelled to shift into EMT mode. "Firefighters are hardwired to save people and property," said marine chief Captain Fuentes. "You have to evacuate the injured."[1] They administered first aid and tried to ease the pain of burn patients then funneled victims up to the World Financial Center's ferry terminal. "There were some ferry boats, New York Waterway ferry boats (who) were taking people over to Jersey," said Sullivan. "(After administrating) first aid, we started putting (people) on ferries."[2] But the crowds were too much, the injuries were overwhelming. The crew of the McKean had a decision to make—were they to stay put as ordered, or get the injured to the doctors. In the end, it was automatic: As Fuentes said, you have to evacuate the injured. They got underway.[3]

It was thus that while Metcalf was on his way to the command post the crew of the *John McKean* decided to use the fireboat to get people off the island, and it came none too soon. "People [were] jumping on, they weren't waiting for assistance, just jumping on," said Sullivan. "It was low tide, so they had to jump down about 10 or 15 feet to reach the deck of the boat off this concrete wall. We were catching them, trying to help them get on. There was some mothers or nannies from the luxury apartment building at the seawall who had infants in their arms, and they were dropping the infants down to us. We were catching the infants. We had about four or five of them, wrapped in little blankets. We slipped them down in the crews' quarters. There're some bunks in the crews' quarters, there, four bunks down there. We had them all lined up. Had four of them lined up in a bunk, like little peanuts, they all lined up there. Then we helped the mothers down."

Donna Jensen jumped. She wasn't panicked. In fact, she was thinking clearly. She walked over to the railing and looked down at the *John McKean*. The deck was an intimidating 10-foot drop if it was an inch.

The firefighters yelled up to her "Jump, jump!"

"I did and they caught me," Jensen later wrote.[4] "One of the firemen—a few of them caught me—but one held on to me and he just hugged me." Jensen knew what the hug was all about. "He needed to do that," she said. "He just needed to hug." Perhaps she did too. Having narrowly escaped death, a hug was as good as a splint or a bandage on a wound.

Better, in many ways.[5]

Sullivan estimated that they had some 150 victims and evacuees on board. They thought about taking their passengers up the Hudson River to the docks that were near Manhattan hospitals, but no one knew what it was really like uptown. Had there been attacks? Were the streets closed? How long would it take? They turned and looked across the Hudson and saw the flashing blue and red lights of ambulances and police vehicles. "[We had] everybody on the boat," said Sullivan. "[So we] let the lines go and we headed to Jersey."[6]

◆━◆

In the charged atmosphere of two burning towers, thousands of New Yorkers ran toward the Whitehall ferry terminal to escape the island by boat. Captain Parese of the Staten Island ferry *Newhouse* was quickly at full capacity. "We [had a lot of] passengers on the boat," said Brian Walsh, safety manager for the Staten Island ferries of those initial loads from Manhattan. "We [had] them on the main deck and the salon deck and had everybody quiet down."

But it wasn't that easy. When the ferry reached its legal capacity, the deckhands closed the gates, but that stopped no one. "[As] we backed out, people were jumping from the aprons on to the boat," Parese later recalled. "One that jumped from the apron onto the hurricane deck then slid down to the next deck almost went into the water. Somebody confronted him and they said, 'What are you doing?' He said, 'I'm jumping for my life.' They were under the impression that Manhattan was being bombed. So, you can't argue with that."[7]

On September 11, the Staten Island ferries operated at near full capacity, but to reduce their exposure on the harbor as they crossed, the captains had one request of their engineers.

They asked for more speed.

"My job is the safety of my passengers, my vessel, and my crew," said Captain Parese of that morning.[8] And a big orange boat was an easy target.

—◆—

Back across the river, at the first sign of smoke, Mickie Slattery, the paramedic, had abandoned her morning coffee on the Jersey City waterfront and hurried back to stock her ambulance. She was on the critical care team for the Jersey City Medical Center, a 308-bed trauma center not more than a mile from the waterfront. As she worked on her supplies, the phones lit up in the hospital's communications center all with the same message—causalities were coming their way by boat, and New York was in trouble.[9] As if anyone needed any proof of that, one of the first patients to arrive in New Jersey was a frontline Hatzolah medic who was badly injured. Under ordinary circumstances, he would have been receiving basic life support with an IV in his arm, but he wasn't, which spoke volumes about the situation in New York. "[He] had two fractured legs," said Slattery. "He gave me his tourniquet from his glove pouch. I started his IV with his own tourniquet."[10]

A writer for the Dow Jones newswire hurried down to the New Jersey waterfront and saw the first victims arrive. "This one boat landed at the pier and these people rushed by me with a stretcher and on the stretcher was a fireman, burned badly and not moving. Not an inch. And I remember I looked at his hand, laid across his stomach, and I don't want this at all to sound callous, but it looked like a slab of meat, dead the way a slab of meat looks. There was another fireman behind him, and he came off the boat and he was kicking the rail, furious, yelling in just pain and frustration."[11]

A Jersey City photographer managed to get into the triage area. "There is a pier there and tugboats as well as other types of boats were being used to ferry people across," he later wrote. "All of a sudden there was a police boat that came tearing across the Hudson and when they pulled up to the pier, I heard yelling that there was an 'injured firefighter on board.' A stretcher was rushed down and the firefighter was removed from the boat and brought to the triage area. He was checked out [and] put on a heart monitor and then removed to a waiting ambulance. It started to sink in that there were perhaps hundreds or perhaps thousands trapped, dying or already dead about a mile from where I stood. I started to get a sick feeling in my stomach. I headed home and had to stop to get some baby food for my daughter and it was then that I almost lost it. [I] almost broke down right there in the store."[12]

The Jersey City waterfront was quickly crowded with injuries. "There were tons of civilians brought to Liberty State Park, which then was manned by the Jersey City Medical Center," explained Deputy Chief Medical Officer David Prezant, FDNY, in an interview after the crisis.[13]

The waterfront was much the same in nearby Hoboken, New Jersey. "We were anticipating causalities coming through trains," said Hoboken Fire Chief Tom Molta. "But they were coming by boats at first. The first ferry had 600 people." Chief Molta set up a triage area and ambulances soon lined the streets. They were nearly overrun. "We had about a dozen injured people on [our] boat," remembered a survivor who arrived in New Jersey.

There were lacerations, burns, and broken bones. And that was one ferry.[14]

CHAPTER 16

"Thousands of people were running toward the water."

9:09 a.m.

Pilot Rick Thornton of the ferry *Henry Hudson* was at the West 38th Street pier on the Hudson River and was about to head back to Weehawken, New Jersey, when the fireball of the second plane announced that they were dealing with terrorism. He immediately turned his ferry around and headed down river to the terminal at the World Financial Center. His intent was to board anyone who wanted off the island. It was "pure instinct," he later said, meaning no radio transmission, nothing official prompted it. Within ten minutes, his 399-passenger boat would be overrun with the injured and the scared.[1]

Ferries were now a lifeline, although nothing official had been said. "You just kept on seeing people coming," explained one of the captains who helped survivors down to his boat. "One woman was blind and had a seeing eye dog. Four men helped pass her down to a boat. They looked like zombies coming through the fog [but] you knew those were human beings."[2]

How could you deny them?

Richard Naruszewicz, the captain of the commuter ferry *The Finest*, was completing his morning ferry run, a 20-mile dash across New York Harbor from New Jersey's Atlantic Highlands on the Atlantic Ocean, to Manhattan's East River ferry terminals. He had a full load of commuters as he usually did—he could carry as many as 350 passengers—all with their briefcases, purses, cell phones, laptops, legal papers, business proposals, and perhaps even a manuscript that needed editing —one of his passengers was in fact a magazine editor. He made his first stop at Pier 11 and unloaded half his boat then sailed uptown to the 34th Street terminal for his second stop. It was there that he saw the second plane. Naruszewicz quickly called the office and discussed his options. They recommended that he turn around and see if anyone needed help back at Pier 11. Naruszewicz agreed. He keyed his public address system and spoke to his passengers. He told them they were going back to Pier 11 to see what the situation was and if they could offer help.[3] "The captain announced that no one would be allowed off the boat," said Susan McCabe, the editor who was on the ferry. "There was complete mayhem," said Naruszewicz of the scene when he arrived. "Thousands of people were running toward the water. We were the second boat to arrive. We let down the ramps and the people just surged on. We took on double the number of people we're supposed to, but we couldn't turn anyone away."[4]

New boats set sail. Ken Peterson, the tugboat captain for The Reinauer Transportation Company, watched the smoke coming from the towers from the company's docks on Staten Island. His tugs were in their slips, each painted in the company's signature orange and black with the well-known black diamond behind the smokestack framing a stylish R. Had it been a smaller building, perhaps a run-of-the-mill high rise, Peterson might have done nothing, but this was the World Trade Center and it was on fire and no telling what sort of hell was up there for the men and women inside. However little he knew about the situation or what sort of help was needed, he felt an urgency to go across the harbor. "We needed to do something," said Peterson. "We got all the captains together. We told them we didn't know what we were getting into, but we want to know if you guys will volunteer to go and take your crew and your vessels up to Manhattan. At that time, all four of the captains that were here said yes, they would go."[5]

Vincent Ardolino of *Amberjack V* was at home in Brooklyn watching the burning tower on TV. "My wife was there, and I turned around and I said, 'I got to go do something,' just like that and she looked at me and said, 'What are you going to do?' I said, 'I'm going to take the *Amberjack* up into the city and help.' She said, 'What if we're attacked again?' I said, 'Well, that's something I'll just have to live with.'" He kissed her goodbye and headed off to his charter boat, instinct alone telling him to go toward the smoke.[6]

Back on Staten island, Lieutenant Kenneth Moser at United States Coast Guard Station New York, ordered three more rescue boats into the water. Two rigid-hull inflatables and a second 41-foot utility boat like Perez's, cast off and raced toward Manhattan.[7] One had to be pulled out of the water. "We departed and immediately encountered a debris field," said Coast Guard Reservist Don MacDonald, Flotilla 12. "We took the engine out of gear and floated through the field." But it wasn't enough. Not a moment after starting the engine they hit a submerged object, which dented the hull of their boat. They were forced to pull it out of service.

—⁓—

Paul Amico was dealing with the crowds as best he could. New York Waterway's World Financial Center terminal, the terminal that was just a few blocks from the North Tower, had room enough for the everyday ferries, but that wasn't enough to handle the panicked crowds. The seawall was an option. Because the New York Waterway's ferries had stub-nose bows, they could nose in against the seawall and take on passengers from the front. The only issue then was height. From the top of the railing along the esplanade, the decks would be a long drop down for a survivor, as much as 10 feet at low tide, which was the situation on 9/11. Amico made it work. "Against the wall, [we] hooked up what they call a 'man over-board ladder,'" he remembered. "We hung them over the top of the railing along the wall. We started lowering people down onto the ferries. Once we had injured people on board, mostly firemen, we immediately released the ladder and the boat went back to Jersey. Then the captains would call ahead and let them know to have the ambulances ready and where they were coming in. Then we would bring in another boat."[8]

CHAPTER 17

"Improvise."

9:12 a.m.

THE FIRES IN BOTH TOWERS WERE RAGING WITH GROWING INTENSITY. Licks of flames visible from the streets spoke to the inferno inside. In the sky, the volume of smoke had increased exponentially. Inside the towers evacuations were well underway. The stairwells were crowded, the injured were moving down slowly and often overcoming great pain.

The thought that one might be rescued in the middle of an event of this magnitude was entirely unwarranted, yet within minutes of the initial attack, that was precisely what was happening. EMT responders were evening the odds, narrowing the medical crisis down from the impossible to the possible.[1] A total of 87 ambulances and their crews were on the scene or on the way, a staggering concentration of responders even for New York City.[2] One witness saw as many as 18 ambulances on the West Side Highway and Liberty Street alone; another counted 40 near the North Pedestrian bridge.[3] There were more here and there—clusters at the various corners that defined the perimeter of the complex—ambulances at West and Vesey, Church and Vesey, Church and Liberty, and so on.

Although it was unlike anything they'd encountered before, the patient load was not unmanageable. The base of the towers had been divided into sectors, the EMTs were triaging at a steady rate. "We have 2,300 EMTs, 800 paramedics, and almost 500 supervisors in our system," said FDNY medical director Glenn Asaeda. "We teach our EMTs, paramedics, and officers that they will always have to improvise."[4] Against the volume of patients, the EMTs had their training to fall back on plus the experience of working on victims of lacerations, burns, and asthma attacks—that, and a clear path uptown to the hospitals.

Chief Gombo, EMS FDNY, arrived at the base of the North Tower shortly after 9:00 a.m. He parked north of the tower and walked down Church Street to Vesey. In the crowds he saw several EMTs, presumably Loutsky and Ramos among them, before running into two officers on the scene, Captain Janice Olszewski, EMS Operations, FDNY, and Lieutenant Rene Davila Battalion 4, EMS, FDNY. Davila, was already triaging, as was Olszewski, who was a veteran on the force.[5]

Gombo asked Davila and Olszewski to take command of the northeast corner of the World Trade Center and set up a triage at Church and Fulton Streets, which they said they would do. Gombo then turned and entered the plaza at the base of the towers. What greeted him was sheer devastation. "We saw glass all over the plaza, plane parts on the ground, and pockets of different things burning," said Gombo. "There was a significant amount of [human] parts, including arms, legs, and torsos. In all my years of EMS experience, I'd never seen a disaster of this magnitude. Other than the cameras not being there, it felt like this was a movie shoot."[6]

Gombo walked through the debris into the lobby of the North Tower to check in at the command desk but discovered that EMS command had moved across the West Side Highway. It was just too dangerous to be here, he was told. Gombo agreed and took one look before he left. The once magnificent lobby of the North Tower was devastated. Windows were shattered, tiles were hanging from the thirty-foot ceilings like New Year's confetti, sheets of ornamental wall coverings lay crumbled on the floor. Around him, coming from somewhere outside, unexpected but loud explosive *"thumps"* marked the impact of jumpers. He left.

～

EMS Chief Goldfarb and Mary Merced found the new command post, which was located on the car ramp that led into the underground parking garage at 2 World Financial Center, a location on the West Side Highway roughly midway between Vesey and Liberty Streets. A number of senior EMS commanders were already there including Chief Walter Kowalczyk,

Citywide Chief, EMS, FDNY. Kowalczyk wanted to make sure the sectors were supervised. "Basically, I started to assume the responsibility of the EMS operations chief," said Kowalczyk. "I started, in the midst of the chaos, to establish some type of structure for the EMS operations. I remember deploying chiefs and officers to Vesey and West [Side Highway] and to Liberty and West [Side Highway] with the global direction of setting up EMS operations there." Kowalczyk partitioned the 16-acre complex into sectors assigning one to each of his senior officers. Olszewski and Davila were given the northeast sector and were triaging at Church and Fulton. He asked Goldfarb to take the northwest sector at the West Side Highway and Vesey, the area closest to the North Tower.[7,8] Deputy Chief Robert Browne, Division 4, EMS, FDNY, was assigned the southern sector near the base of the South Tower on Liberty Street between the West Side Highway and Church Street.

The meeting broke and Browne walked down the West Side Highway to Liberty where he found ambulance crews. "I got to the corner of West and Liberty, just underneath the foot bridge that crosses over," said Browne. "There were probably about three or four [FDNY] ambulances parked there, and all the personnel were out of their rigs with their equipment, but they were standing more toward the corner of —they were more toward the Liberty Street side, just off of West, and they seemed to be like all in amazement. They were all standing there, staring up, looking at what was going on."[9]

The head of Hatzolah (the volunteer ambulance service that serviced the Jewish community), Rabbi Mechel Handler, was there, too, and discussed the current situation with Browne. They agreed that they were positioned too close to the towers and should move the staging area back. "We set up staging areas for our ambulances and emergency vehicles at the corner off South End Avenue and Liberty Street," he said. Before the morning was over, Hatzolah would take some 140 patients to area hospitals.[10]

◆~

Despite the fear that permeated the air, things were starting to work. With Goldfarb on the northwest quadrant, Davila and Olszewski on the northeast quadrant, and Browne and Hatzolah to the south, patients were being triaged and ambulances were moving uptown. "The system was starting to fall together," said Lieutenant Davila. "Supervisors were arriving on scene. We had a good triage system operating fairly well."[11] Captain Olszewski agreed with Davila. At her location she was receiving a steady flow of patients, some with burns, many with lacerations. "We were trying our best to set up a traditional MCI area," she later said. "The cops were directing [patients] to our triage corner with all sorts of injuries; you name it: soft-tissue injuries, burns, smoke inhalation—just everything."[12]

Newly arriving medic Lieutenant Amy Monroe, Battalion 4, EMS, was assigned to the south quadrant. She had no doubt about the challenges they faced. "It was gonna be a big job," she said. "[But] I have to say, for the [scope of the] scene, it really was not that crazy. I thought everybody was really organized, professional."[13]

Not far from her, EMT Alex Loutsky was directing patients off-site as fast as he could. He was organized, thought Monroe, an EMT turned traffic cop in the midst of the chaos calmly moving people away. "I was the staging officer," said Loutsky. "My function was getting people out of there. I loaded [private and hospital ambulances] up as much as I could—up to six patients each—to get them out of there, because [the area] was unstable. For example, I said, 'Where you from?' 'Brooklyn.' 'Name a hospital.' 'LICH [Long Island College Hospital].'

'Go—that's where you're going.'"[14]

"That shuts down New York Harbor."

9:15 a.m.

A CITY POWERED BY ENGINES AND ELECTRIC RAILS HAD BEEN PLUMMETED into the dark ages. The trains, subways, and bridges, once a cacophony of speeding cars, honking horns, and screeching steel-on-steel, were now silent.[1] PATH trains from New Jersey had been stopped, the subways in and out of Lower Manhattan were halted. On the bridges, the traffic signs blinked messages that said they were closed to inbound traffic.[2] Indeed, within minutes, the FAA shut down all the New York airports.[3] City streets, normally bumper-to-bumper with yellow cabs and commuters were suddenly empty, save for the rifle shot of a patrol car with flashing blue and red lights.[4]

Police officers now surrounded vital sites like the United Nations, City Hall, and other federal buildings, weapons drawn and intentionally visible. "There was nothing on the Brooklyn Bridge," remembered EMT Bruce Medjuck. "There were just emergency vehicles."[5] The bridge, normally crowded with cars, was now shoulder-to-shoulder with evacuees.[6]

Walking.

Manhattan was locked down.

Around the harbor the Coast Guard had a list of more than 100 vital assets that were critical infrastructure or particularly sensitive and had to be protected against terrorists. These included rail heads, tunnels, power grids, the nuclear power plants and fuel farms, not to mention bridges like the Verrazano-Narrows Bridge, whose collapse would be catastrophic. "It blocks everything [if it is taken down]," said Admiral Richard E. Bennis, USCG. "That shuts down New York Harbor."[7]

Added to the list were the ships in the harbor itself. Many posed threats. There were as many as 100 freighters, lighters, and fuel barges loaded with gasoline or other volatile items transiting the waterways or docked alongside the innumerable piers that edge the waterfront of Manhattan. "We had a lot of dangerous cargo going up and down the rivers and in the port," said Rear Admiral Roy J. Casto, USCG. If any of them were attacked in a new wave of terror, or if they were already under the secret control of terrorists and ready to be used as bombs, the damage would be unthinkable.[8]

Potentially more disastrous—and more opportunistic to a terrorist—were the oil refineries. Up the Kill Van Kull, the channel between Staten Island and New Jersey, there were so many oil refineries that the channel was called "gasoline alley." Millions of barrels of refining capacity stood next to enormous storage farms holding as many as 130,000 gallons of finished fuels in thin-shelled tanks. That's not forgetting the nuclear power plant Indian Point, located 38 miles north of New York City on the banks of the Hudson River, where memories of Chernobyl ran just beneath the surface. Or that New York Harbor had the largest underground propane tank on the East Coast.[9] Hitting any of those targets would land a catastrophic blow on a city already reeling from two brutal punches.

At 9:10 a.m., Captain Patrick Harris, the Coast Guard Station Chief, took the ultimate precaution—he shut down New York Harbor. His decision was based on the second jet. "At that point," said Harris "we knew what we had."[10] Nothing came in and nothing went out. If a ship was underway, it was turned around and sent back to its berth.[11] A robust billion-dollar transportation hub connected to an international network of piers and cranes and semitrucks on the land and hundreds of ships was in minutes turned into a ghost town.

Harris contacted all the New York-area Coast Guard stations and ordered their 41-foot fast response boat and their Zodiac-like raiders into the water. Coast Guard Station New York, Sandy Hook, and Rockaway immediately responded. Next, Harris ordered patrol boats to form a barrier in the Atlantic Ocean blocking the entrance to New York Harbor at Ambrose Channel. Up and down the Eastern Seaboard mariners ran to their radios to offer their help. Coast Guard stations from Newport, Rhode Island, to the Chesapeake Bay in Virginia, got their cutters and harbor craft underway. To get to New York faster, smaller harbor craft were loaded onto flatbeds and trucked in.

Coast Guard vessels—in time, as many as 50 or more—were quickly positioned at key access points along the waterways or sent around the harbor to be visible shows of force.[12] Specialized and highly weaponized USCG Port Security Units arrived from Fort Eustis in Virginia and began patrolling the harbor. Camouflaged for wartime operations, their gunboats were painted with a grey slash instead of the usual orange. Cutters were requested and were stationed at both ends of the Kills protecting the refineries. Harris brought in the 270-foot United States Coast Guard cutters *Tahoma* and *Campbell* from New Bedford, Massachusetts. The cutters had two .50-caliber machine guns and an impressive 76-mm naval gun capable of barking 80 rounds a minute on their weather decks. If necessary, they could ram the rudder on a terrorist vessel or hit their bows to deflect their forward momentum.

———

Chief Boatswains Mate James A. Todd, officer in charge of the Coast Guard tugboat USCGC *Hawser*, had organized a crew and was one one of the earliest responders and was now underway from Bayonne. "We headed right for the buildings," said Todd. "We knew there would be a need for medical facilities to be set up and people to be taken off the island. We took some people off, passed out gas masks, and unloaded our water so people had potable water. They wanted to get off the island," he said, so they loaded survivors and evacuated them, likely becoming the first Coast Guard vessel to take people from Lower Manhattan.[13]

The tender *Juniper* arrived from Newport, Rhode Island, to join the patrols. An H-60 helicopter launched from Coast Guard Air Station Cape Cod to attempt rooftop rescues and was on the scene before 10:00 a.m.[14] A 32-foot fast response boat manned by the Coast Guard Strike Team in Sandy Hook was launched and raced to the North Cove Marina where it took up station. Other Strike Team fast vessels were trucked in from nearby Fort Dix, New Jersey. "I sent a coxswain, an engineer and a boat crewman," said Lieutenant Scott Linsky, Operations Office, USCG, explaining his actions that day. "But I also sent an EMT with each boat crew assuming we were going to be responsible for some medevacs."

Out at the Coast Guard station on Sandy Hook, the 110-foot cutter *Adak* was called to duty to take over command-and-control of Coast Guard vessels on the harbor. The ship's crew got the cutter underway sailing under the Verrazano-Narrows Bridge toward Manhattan, 25 minutes away. They arrived at noon—no more than an hour after the *Hawser* began evacuating people—and positioned themselves just offshore of the tip of Lower Manhattan. On the *Adak*'s bridge, Lieutenant Sean McKenzie placed a piece of plexiglass over a nautical chart with the intent of plotting the positions of all the Coast Guard's small boats in the harbor. The chart would soon be spotted with countless markings.[15]

Coast Guard Auxiliary units from Westchester County ran security patrols around the George Washington Bridge, while a second unit from Sandy Hook patrolled the choppy waters around the towering stanchions of the Verrazano-Narrows Bridge. Perez was at the mouth of one river, his counterparts at the other, their vessels there to halt recreational boats that might be underway and interfere with emergency vessels.

To those in the grips of the crisis, to those on land struggling to control their very real fears, the Coast Guard's presence represented the very might of, well, the United States. The orange stripes across their bows were soon visible up and down the harbor, many of them in motion for no reason other than to reassure people on shore. "We got those pursuit boats early on," said Admiral Bennis. "I would have them run from the George Washington Bridge [on the Hudson River] to the Verrazano-Narrows Bridge at speed, several times a day."[16] For show.

All in all, it was a textbook response to defend against the prospect of further attacks. The city was shut down. Emergency responders had reacted. Coast Guard assets had been mobilized. "We weren't taking any chances," said USCG Lieutenant. Bob Post, watch officer at the Vessel Traffic System.[17] Patrick Harris agreed. "All of our vessels immediately moved in toward the scene. Very shortly, we had launched everything."[18]

But Harris had one more command.

He ordered his ships to impose a 1000-foot security zone around the Statue of Liberty.[19]

They weren't going to get *that*.

"It just looked like too much, high-rise towers, free burning like that."

9:19 a.m.

NEW NAMES ENTERED THE LOGBOOK OF 9/11.

Deputy Captain Charles Wells EMS, FDNY, of the Brooklyn Division, was on the other side of Long Island when the first plane hit so he hadn't heard or seen anything, but he a bad feeling. A 24-year veteran on the force, Wells had been to his share of MCIs, so he had a good ear for such things, and they all had one thing in common: radio chatter. And he heard chatter.

An imposing man, Wells was driving on the Southern State Parkway in the direction of JFK International Airport listening to the EMS radio. "The citywide radio started becoming extremely busy with radio traffic," he later said in his debriefing interview. He swung his car north to the Long Island Expressway, taking it through Queens toward Manhattan. The chatter kept growing, the incident coming into sharper focus. He radioed his status—available—and was immediately assigned the World Trade Center.[1]

Wells arrived near the base of the towers and saw a fire unlike anything he'd ever seen before. "I parked, looked up, and started putting my bunker gear on," said Wells. "Usually I just put a jacket or pants on, but [that day] I put everything on. I even strapped my helmet to my chin, which I never do. I realized this was going to be something you never really dealt with before. It just looked like too much, high-rise towers, free burning like that." Wells checked in at the command post on the

West Side Highway and talked to Gombo and Kowalczyk. They told him they needed a boss down on the far side of the south quadrant, on Vesey Street between the West Side Highway and Church Street. Could he go down there and report on the situation? Wells said he could and set out on foot. "I proceeded down West Street, past the Marriott, to the corner of Liberty and West," he said. "When I arrived there, there were two or three FDNY EMS ambulances and about 10 to 15 [other] ambulances. They were all hugging the World Trade Center side of Liberty and West. I announced who I was and that I was assuming command of this particular corner as a medical treatment sector. I told everybody to get in their vehicles and go to the west side of West Street and Liberty and set up to receive casualties."[2]

—◆—

EMS Captain Karin DeShore, Battalion 46, arrived at her duty station inside the busy Elmhurst Medical Complex on Long Island at 5:00 a.m. DeShore had risen to the rank of captain in the demanding world of the New York City Fire Department's Emergency Medical Services, no small feat in and of itself, considering she raised three girls in the process. DeShore was a first-generation immigrant from Germany. "I came to America two days out of high school," she said. "I started out as a maid for $105 a month." She was impressed by the sight of a smart-looking ambulance that routinely came to a neighbor's house She asked how you got such a job and eventually was accepted into what is now the EMS service. "Remember," she said, "nurses paved the way for women in EMS."[3]

As noise drifted in from the television set in the nearby lunchroom, DeShore threw herself into her morning duties no doubt reviewing the activities of the overnight shift and checking resources for the upcoming day tour. EMT Lieutenant Spiro Yioras, Battalion 49, was assigned temporary duty with Battalion 46. He arrived from his station and let DeShore know he was checking out the Conditions 46 car. EMT Timothy Keller, the battalion's jokester, was walking the halls. Keller had a way of coming up with a funny thing to say in almost any situation, although you had to be on guard. He was "*Mr.* Keller," to DeShore, a formality of address that DeShore used with her crew, but Keller was different. She knew his game well and most days waved him off, albeit with a smile. That morning Keller put his head into her office sometime after the first plane hit and gave her the news. "An airplane has just hit the World Trade Center," he said. DeShore looked up and thought it was a prank.

He said, *no, no kidding.*

"Leave me alone," she said lightheartedly. "Get out of my office or I'll fire you."

"It's true," said Keller.

DeShore got up and walked over to the television in the lunchroom. "Sure enough," she later told investigators, "there was smoke coming out of the building." DeShore immediately recalled Yioras and took Command Car 825 down to the towers.

Enroute, the South Tower was hit, making their arrival well after 9:08 a.m.[4]

Lieutenant Roger Moore, Division 5, EMS FDNY, was at the EMS academy for some refresher courses when the alarm came over his pager. In a nanosecond, the academy was a cacophony of beeps and chirps as pagers and walky-talkies and Nextel's up and down the halls came to life. In the next nanosecond, the academy building essentially emptied. Moore hitched a ride downtown and got to the EMS command post on the West Side Highway not long after the second plane hit, but as he waited for orders, he was forced to cool his heels.[5]

It would nearly cost him his life.

On Staten Island, rounds were well underway at the Staten Island University Hospital when pagers and Blackberries twitched to life. FDNY chief medical officer Kerry Kelly looked down at her device and read the message. It was the World Trade Center. She apologized to her patient and excused herself. Dressed in hospital blues, and wearing flimsy sandals, Kelly checked herself out of the hospital and raced down to the site. "My job is to take care of injured firefighters," she said by way of explanation. Her first stop was at the 10-and-10 firehouse at the corner of Liberty and Church Streets. She needed a helmet. Little did she know that she would soon need a boat.[6]

Little did anyone know.

"The tower might come down in the harbor."

9:21 a.m.

ELLIS ISLAND WASN'T PARTICULARLY WELL-SUITED TO TRIAGE PATIENTS. It has no hospital. There are no EMS stations or doctors and nurses. It's a national park, visited by hundreds of thousands of people a year. It does have a few desirable attributes, though, some that are particularly valuable. For one, Ellis Island is exceedingly close to Manhattan and, because it has a constant flow of ferries bringing in tourists by boat to see the immigration center, it has excellent dockage. For another, Ellis Island is connected to New Jersey by a bridge over which patients could be sent to a regional trauma center. Not to mention it has wide open grassy areas on which cots can be arrayed for the injured.

Ellis Island was, in fact, well-suited to the task of staging the injured on 9/11.

Sometime after 9:08 a.m. the national park's staff on Ellis Island received an urgent call from Manhattan telling them to get ready to receive patients. That wasn't entirely a surprise. Ellis Island had been designated an escape route by the Secret Service should a president need a swift way off Manhattan. That had never happened, but the memory of that designation welled up in the minds of the staff when the call came in telling them they were going to triage for Lower Manhattan. Several steps immediately followed. Nonessential park employees were evacuated by boat off the island. Those who remained were either security guards or people who had basic medical training.

To prepare the island, the outdoor lawns were divided into three sections. One area was given over to the medics who would perform the initial triage on injured arrivals. A second area was set up for the walking wounded or the evacuees who simply needed a kind word, clean T-shirt, or just a chair to sit on. A third area was more or less the quartermaster's corps station. This area was assigned the task of stockpiling and delivering supplies like water, diapers, cups, and so on to the other two areas.

By 10:00 a.m., the lawns were swarming with volunteers putting out folding chairs, portable toilets, and every manner of table and cot. New Jersey EMTs arrived with stethoscopes around their necks and cutting shears in their pockets. On the land side of the bridge that connected Ellis Island to the mainland, a line of ambulances stood ready to transport victims to the Jersey City Medical Center.[1]

Back in Manhattan, new problems arose. The aviation unit of the NYPD had a bird's-eye view of the burning towers and, while there was no hope of mounting a rooftop rescue, they did see something, and it was troubling. While the math was imprecise, it seemed that if a tower fell, it could, at least in part, land in the harbor. It wasn't out of the question. Dozens of firefighters felt the towers might tip over or fall sideways —1,300 feet being enough to reach the water. The helicopter crews felt compelled to radio Coast Guard operations with their impressions. Coast Guard commander Daniel Ronan, chief of Waterways Management Division, did his own math and agreed: It was certainly possible for the towers to fall sideways and hit the water, which meant that the boats on the harbor were at risk of being hit by a dangerous wave—a small tsunami if you will—that could swamp them. To prevent that, Ronan ordered USCG vessels to back off from the island and turn their bows toward Manhattan so they could ride out whatever happened. "Because of the police report that the second tower may come down into the harbor, we ordered our boats to stand back," said Ronan. He also told his commanders to be prepared for "a massive waterborne evacuation," perhaps the first official word that a formal evacuation might be initiated by the Coast Guard.[2]

High up in the towers, 1,800-degree flames burned. The trusses, which support the floors, were slowly weakening, bending inward almost imperceptibly, but just enough to throw off the exacting interplay of dynamic tensions required to keep upright a giant steel, concrete, and glass tower nearly one-quarter of a mile tall. Compounding the problem, other beams were bending outward and large sections of the vertical columns that encased and strengthened the outside of the towers had been severed at the impact zone. The towers were mortally wounded, and they were failing, although few expected a total collapse. In the memories of the firefighters, no one had seen such a tall high-rise come down. A partial collapse of a few floors, yes. A five-story building, yes. But nothing like the total collapse of a building and certainly not 110 stories tall. The towers were strong, impenetrably solid. Indeed, the architects who designed it years ago anticipated that a fully fueled jetliner would someday accidentally hit it and engineered it so it would scarcely twitch.

And yet, the unseen was speeding it toward an end. The towers were crowded with firefighters inside and medics outside, and were approaching catastrophic failure.

Time was running short.

"That's your evacuation plan— everybody goes south."

9:41 a.m.

AROUND THE BASE OF THE TOWERS, THE AIR WAS CHARGED WITH A sense of urgency and the streets echoed with the shrill sound of sirens. From the upper floors, those struggling with their injuries were now reaching ground level. By 9:30 a.m., the evidence suggests that approximately 5,000 of the 6,000 occupants of the South Tower had already evacuated. That was roughly true of the North Tower as well. The steady stream of people on the streets meant lives saved, but those remaining were the difficult cases and the clock was ticking.[1]

Viewers across the United States were glued to their television sets. More than 80 million people in the United States alone watching the attack from home, plus millions more who were in their offices and were crowded around TV sets. Fox, CBS, ABC, NBC, and CNN saw their viewership jumped seven-fold.[2] Some stations simply went off the air.[3] Out of respect.

❧

Assistant Commissioner Stephen Gregory was at the south end of the World Trade Center walking around the base of the South Tower when he realized that he had no fire engines. Gregory called dispatch to get a list of the units that were assigned to the South Tower. He jotted them down—Ladder 118, Engine 42, and so on—then waited for them to arrive. Nothing. "We weren't receiving any companies," he later explained in his debriefing. "It appeared that the companies that were responding were coming north to south and that [meant] they were all grabbed at 1 World Trade Center, the furthermost north building." He saw a solution. Gregory called dispatch and asked them to transmit an alarm for a box near the mouth of the Brooklyn-Battery Tunnel. This would bring in companies from Brooklyn who, by necessity and proximity, would cross the East River down in the southern quadrant. Minutes later he heard the reassuring sound of sirens and saw the engines speeding his way. "The companies, in a short period of time, they started to come [to the South Tower].⁴

One problem was solved; a thousand more were pending.

Charlie Wells was walking down the West Side Highway near the base of the South Tower when he ran into Karin DeShore. Wells asked DeShore to gather up some EMTs and follow him down the street. The air was smokey, and the sky was filled with deadly missiles of glass bursting off the heat-weakened windows and crashing to the ground. As they hurriedly walked, DeShore tried to keep her crew under overhangs, tight to the buildings where they were sheltered. "I had the rear; Chief Wells had the front," she recalled. "I was trying to keep them moving and trying to move left [close to the buildings] because once you got them out from underneath the buildings, [although] they weren't getting hit by bodies, but the debris just kept coming [down]." She navigated the sidewalks as best she could but it was hard to see everything that might kill them, so much was going on all at once. "There was billowing smoke and [the] people kept pouring out of the building," she said. "There was chaos."⁵

While the timeline is unclear, there were new reports of people stuck in the lobby of the South Tower, including a woman in a wheelchair, perhaps a few others. Wells asked DeShore to select two EMTs to bring them out. DeShore picked the only two who had helmets, EMTs Jennifer Beckham and her partner Bonnie Giebfried, both of Flushing Hospital Medical Center, Unit 52 Frank. Giebfried, the senior of the two, had

87

been a multisport athlete in high school but more to the point came from a family of first responders. "I grew up literally next-door to a firehouse," she said. Beckham had the same background in that respect; although only 24, her life in some aspects had always orbited around the Smithtown, New York, firehouse near where she grew up. "We'd go there," said Beckham "even on Friday nights and hang out."[6] In short, being an EMT was in their DNA.

Now they faced a burning tower with lives on the line. Beckham continued the story: "[FDNY EMS] Capt. [Karin] DeShore came over. Apparently, they had a person, a victim, in the lobby [of 2 World Trade]." The plan they hatched was to go into the tower, bring out the patient, hand her off, then go back in if there were more. They began walking toward the building but were stopped midstride. It was DeShore. "She was yelling at us," said Giebfried. "She wanted us to put a long board on the stretcher, then she called out again when the straps were dangling. It delayed us but ironically, it probably saved our lives."[7]

Things fixed, Beckham and Giebfried hurried into the South Tower where they discovered a largely empty lobby crossed by thick fire hoses and littered with shattered glass. "We went in the lobby, going, 'Where are all the people?'" said Beckham. Unbeknownst to either of them, just a few floors below them, hundreds if not thousands of office workers were running through the corridors of the underground shopping mall headed north and evacuating through the stairs near WTC 7.[8]

Through the smokey haze they saw their patient, a handicapped woman on a scooter. "We put her on the stretcher because the [scooter] wouldn't make it outside with all the hose across the lobby," remembered Beckham. Using sheer muscles they carried her out. Two other women were there and followed them, a mother and her daughter. They navigated the debris and emerged from the tower and all five went across the West Side Highway to a grassy spot under the South Pedestrian Bridge. It isn't exactly clear what time it was when they got out—there were no time stamps on any reports or journals—but it was certainly within minutes of 9:59 a.m., the moment when the South Tower came down. Later, DeShore would worry that she had sent her two EMTs to a certain death.[9] In fact, she saved their lives. "She delayed us when she had us tidy the straps and so on," explained Giebfried. "We were delayed going in which meant we lost time going in and coming out and getting the woman over to that grassy knoll. By the time we had taken her off the stretcher and were preparing to go back in, the tower came down. Had she not slowed us down in the first place, we would have been inside."[10] Instead, all five lives were saved.

Beckham and Giebfried were certainly among the last of the first responders to leave the South Tower alive.[11]

EMS Chief Robert McCracken was the operations chief for the FDNY's EMS division. McCracken was known for giving voice to abstract concepts of safety during emergency responses—utilizing one's instinct to navigate confusion and one's five senses to stay alive—as well as practical matters like not bunching up when responding to a fire.[12] McCracken arrived on scene in the south sector via the Brooklyn-Battery Tunnel and immediately drove his car north toward the command post on the West Side Highway. He got no further than Rector Street. "We were running over body parts," he said in an interview. "Chunks, flat pieces of skin, no skulls attached to [the bodies]."[13] He parked his car and walked into the chaos and immediately took command firing off orders like bullets as he walked north. McCracken ran into a group of firefighters and told them to redirect any of his late-arriving ambulances over to South End Avenue and to keep them off the West Side Highway and Liberty Street. It was safer over there, he said. He worried that the towers were going to collapse, at least the top part of them. Said McCracken in an interview: "When you looked at the corner [of the South Tower], you said to yourself, 'It's like a table that somebody cut [a leg] off. It's gonna crush down. The weight of the [damaged floors of the] building has got to crush the [floors immediately below]."[14] To his way of thinking, the floors above the impact zone would eventually break off and collapse—not the entire tower, just the upper floors—and when they did, they would destroy anything at or near the base of the tower. "My main objective was to get everybody off Liberty, get them off West Street," he later said. "I told everybody to get out of this corridor, get out of Liberty. They thought I was kidding. I said, 'Get out of Liberty because [2 World Trade] looks very unstable.' I wanted everything to face south on South End Avenue."[15]

McCracken continued north against the press of survivors headed south. The air was thick with grit and punctuated by the loud *thumps* that marked the jumpers. Groups of evacuees shouldered their way past him. "As long as the walking wounded were moving, we bypassed them," he later told a reporter. "They asked where there were ambulances. We told them, 'South Ferry end, South Ferry end.'"[16] McCracken walked past several clusters of medics and first responders and made sure they had some sort of organizational structure. "I looked at a group of people and said, 'Any medics here? Good, you're in charge. You have medical control. You supervise this group until I get a boss.'"

Eventually, McCracken came upon a group of ambulances, some which were FDNY, some of which were independents, but twenty or so of which belonged to Hatzalah. He tracked down his counterpart and colleague Rabbi Mechel Handler. Handler briefed McCracken on the situation. Ambulances to the north hadn't been able to get through to the south because of obstructions on West Side Highway, said Handler: "Numerous fire apparatus [were] blocking West Street [and] did not allow them passage [down] to the South Tower," he said.[17,18] McCracken nodded then told Handler that he was concerned about a partial collapse and the consequence of that.[19] "If there was going to be any transport, they weren't going to cross Liberty and they weren't going to go north," said McCracken. "Everything was going south. So, I told these guys, 'That's your evacuation plan—everybody goes south.'"

"Where?" said the drivers.

"To the [Staten Island] ferry," he answered. "We have to get out of this area."[20]

Go south. In hindsight, it was a stroke of brilliance. Unknown to anyone, as the crisis deepened, hundreds of thousands of survivors would be cut off from the rest of Manhattan.

Lower Manhattan would be their way out.

And the way out would be by boat.

"All of a sudden, you hear boom, boom, boom."

10:00 a.m.

AT 9:59 A.M., THE END WAS ANNOUNCED WITH A SERIES OF SHARP explosions and a ring of dark smoke that blossomed out from the sides of the South Tower some 700 feet above the ground. Some 500,000 tons of steel and concrete, clad in the familiar grey pinstriping of the 240 exterior steel columns, came crashing down. It took twelve seconds, give or take, to destroy what had taken six years to build.[1] On September 11, 2001, against a clear blue sky and soft winds, the1,300-foot-tall South Tower fell to the ground. Later analysis would show that the exterior walls bowed outward allowing the heat-weakened floors to collapse inward and then down. As the floors fell one on top of the other, a mountain of pressure built up, gathering in intensity and compressing more smoke, debris, and force, as each successive floor gave way.

Twelve-ton steel beams tumbled out and into the sky showering down to the ground killing, crushing, and destroying anything in their way. A 24,000-pound New York city fire department fire engine was driven through four floors of pure concrete. It was later found at the bottom of the underground parking garage, crushed and mangled deep beneath the World Trade Center. Sheets of façade speared the ground and now stood as brutalist sculptures as if crafted by the devil himself. A dozen or more cars and fire engines were crushed by the falling beams. Fires erupted here and there, each of which would ordinarily call for a run. Today they just burned.

As the tower pancaked to the ground, a tsunami of smoke and debris surged out from the base and rose more than 100 feet high into the sky as it raced over Lower Manhattan driven by a shockwave that hit the city with a wind blast that was later estimated to be 70 miles per hour. The NY Waterway's terminal on the Hudson River was hit, the boats in the North Cove Marina were nearly capsized, the Staten Island Ferry Terminal and Pier 11 on the East River were all slammed. Nerves, already frayed, were now shot. "The ferry rocked wildly," said Donna Deming, a passenger on the Staten Island ferry. "I didn't know if I should jump out the window of the ferry or get off the boat and run north for cover."[2]

Ferry captain Naruszewicz was returning to Pier 11 when he saw the South Tower collapse. "I was in the wheelhouse. The sound was incredible —like 50 sonic booms. I went deaf for a few minutes. The ferry shook from side to side. There was a thick cloud of smoke and dust. It was coming in through the air conditioning ducts, so we shut off the ventilation system. I wet my T-shirt and put it over my nose and mouth and kept going."[3]

EMT Jody Bell was strapping an injured woman onto a stair chair when the tidal wave of debris hit him. "I was damn near ready to jump in the river," he said. "I was holding the railing, looking back, as this thing's coming toward us. The debris went well into the Hudson. It almost went to Jersey."[4] EMT Frank Puma, Orlando Martinez's partner, was at ground zero dealing with the first set of patients at his ambulance at Church and Vesey. "All you heard was the sound of the steel starting to crumble," said Puma. "Then all of a sudden you just hear 'boom, boom, boom, boom,' like the building starting to pancake on itself. I started running."[5]

Captain Crowley was near the base of the tower surveying the fire. He heard the roar and quickly turned and ran up under the North Pedestrian bridges that crosses the West Side Highway near the World Financial Center. "We actually saw cars flying through the air," he later said. "We saw I-beams, 8-ton I-beams coming at us end over end like toothpicks."[6] Newspaper photographer Todd Maisel was near the tower when it collapsed: "Concrete and steel were raining down all over the place."[7]

Chief Daniel Nigro realized that running might not do him any good at all. At the time, Nigro was rounding the east side of the South Tower walking on Church Street and inspecting the damage when the collapse began. He looked up and saw a section of the exterior wall coming down at him. He was so close that he had to crane his neck to even see it. "I didn't think I could get out of the way in time," he later admitted, and he had every reason to believe that.[8] A fireman in 40 to 60 pounds of bunker gear would at best move in slow motion. "You couldn't run too far in bunker gear," agreed Battalion Chief Joseph Pfeifer, FDNY, Battalion 1.[9]

Those on the New Jersey side of the river could scarcely believe their eyes. "The view across the Hudson River was awful," wrote Steve Featherstone, a reporter from Jersey City, New Jersey. "I could see in one sweep the entire stretch between the Empire State Building and the Verrazano-Narrows Bridge. The smoke cloud was tremendous. It now enveloped the entire tip of the island south of the World Trade Center. The tower became a dark avalanche of exploding debris, originating from nowhere, cascading in great arcing plumes toward the street below, consuming itself until there was nothing left but a boiling brown cloud of ash and dust that rolled in every direction, sweeping onto the river and wiping away all traces of Manhattan south of City Hall. The rumble immediately followed . . . sound waves rippled through the riverbed and up the pilings into our feet. No one could live through that."[10]

"I didn't see how anybody could be down in that part of Manhattan and still be alive," agreed another witness to the collapse. "All I could see were things falling. Anyone on the streets down below would have to be killed by all of that."[11]

Donna Jensen was one of the thousands who ran to the river, not that it solved anything. Jensen lived in a building a few hundred feet from the towers. She wasn't panicked, at least not at first. She left her apartment and was on the esplanade hurrying alongside the river when the cloud caught up with her. She sifted through her options in milliseconds. "It must have been twelve stories high, this billowing wall of solid brown," she later said in an interview. "I realized there was nothing I could do, I couldn't run any further. . . . I knew it was going to hit me." Jensen saw a bench on the esplanade and knelt down. "Just before I closed my eyes, I realized there were people actually sitting on the park bench that I was kneeling next to, just sitting calmly, looking out at the river. I'll never forget the backs of their heads just sitting there. I knelt down, closed my eyes and it hit me. I could feel the debris hit me. I could feel the roar."[12]

EMS Chief Mark Steffens, Division 1, FDNY, was standing against the rail by the Hudson River near the Statue of Liberty ferry terminal not far from Donna Jensen's location. By some accounts there were hundreds of people around him, all fleeing the smoke, the collapse, the dust. He hadn't been there long—in fact, 30 minutes earlier he had been at home getting ready for his day when he saw the burning towers on TV. He raced downtown and before he knew it, he was next to the harbor facing an immense cloud of who knows what. "The thing blew over [me]," he said. "I felt heat. I felt all kinds of debris and stuff hitting my body." Steffens walked blindly through the darkness back to his command car and flicked a few switches and in that instant became a beacon of hope for those around him. "We turned on the emergency lights," said Steffens. "[My car] became a causality collection point. All the EMS people [who] were running down West Street; they collected by our vehicle."[13]

Commissioner Gregory was looking at the command board on Liberty and West Side before heading toward Albany Street. That's when the tower came down on him. He ran. "Looking back over my shoulder, I realized that I wasn't able to outrun whatever was coming. I went up against a chain-link fence. I got down on one knee, I put my hands over my head to hold my helmet on so I wouldn't get hit in the head with anything, and [I] just proceeded to get clobbered with all kinds of debris."[14]

Paramedic Neil Sweeting, Division Coordinator, Division 6, EMS FDNY, was running from the advancing debris cloud, but it wasn't the shockwave or the mountain of debris that stopped him in his tracks. It was a broken bone. "There was a woman on Vesey Street between the Financial Center and the complex, and she got hit with something. She just went down like a shot," remembered Sweeting. "She got up and tried to run and just collapsed again. You could see that she had snapped her leg, her ankle, like right at the TIB-FIB. It looked like when horses snap their hoof. Her foot was just flopping." Ignoring the obvious dangers, he and a paramedic from Cabrini Hospital turned around and picked her up and carried her down Vesey Street toward Battery Park. They reached the promenade along the Hudson River when the shockwave hit them. "I'm 6-4 and 240 pounds, and it knocked me down like a rag doll, ten feet away, down the street."[15] He didn't know the name of the woman he helped. He didn't know the name of the paramedic who helped him.

In a sense it was unimportant.

How anyone kept their sanity was the unwritten miracle of the day.

⌒

Death accompanied the collapse, and in many cases it was mercifully swift: the knife-like edges of a massive heating duct, the spear-like finality of an I-beam, or a quick end from a plate of glass. "When the towers came down, if you were in the [the towers], you were unfortunately lost, you were gone," said FDNY medical director Glenn Asaeda. "For those who happened to be outside and survived, we began to encounter waves of people with fractures because people ran into things and fell over each other. And a lot of the survivors—previously uninvolved, innocent bystanders—now had severe [injuries]."[16]

Paramedic Jack Delaney, director of the EMS service at New York Presbyterian, was in a group of EMTs working the area around the base of the South Tower when he was caught in the collapse. Delaney was in fact a 20-plus year veteran with New York Presbyterian. He had started his morning as he usually did, with a cup of coffee and a few minutes admiring the tugboats on the East River from the EMS deck of the hospital. He was not only respected for his work but for his advocacy of support groups to help paramedics deal with the stresses of the job. He had 23 of his people responding to the crisis.[17,18] "As we were running, the smaller debris started landing around us, then the larger debris started falling around us—I-beams and that type of material," he said in an interview. "By the time these HVAC ducts and everything were coming down, we were really looking to take a dive [under something to protect us]. One came down and just totally decapitated [someone running with me]."[19]

Rabbi Handler, the senior official for Hatzolah, also dealt with death. "We later discovered that many firefighters and rescuers were killed by heavy metal I-beams and falling debris and glass that descended upon then," he said. He gave an example. "The Hatzolah coordinator that I had been talking to moments before the building collapsed, ended up with 60 stitches in his head and many broken bones. Another firefighter, who was next to one of our members, was sliced in half by a plate of glass."[20]

⌐~

Knowing where to turn, when to run—*when it was safe*—was impossible. A map of the debris field would later show a spread of heavy items as far as three blocks from the base of the South Tower and steel columns as far away as the Winter Garden in the World Financial Center. For those caught under the collapse, choices had to be made in the blink of an eye. Said survivor Donna Jensen: "Every few seconds I had to make a decision. Should I run or should I brace myself here and would that be my fatal mistake? Because there was no in-between."[21]

Paramedic Steven Pilla, Division 6, EMS FDNY, was triaging patients across the West Side Highway near the Winter Garden. He had helped a woman with a broken leg, then took care of a fire chief with a broken shoulder, and finally treated a Port Authority police officer with falling blood pressure. When the tower came down, he was stuck. "I looked to the right and the plume was coming toward us," said Pilla. "I looked to the left and I said I can't go that way because of the buildings," he continued, remembering how he was boxed in. "I can't go this way, to the right, I can't go left. I hope my helmet works. That's all I've got left."[22]

Father James Hayes was helping patients at the Millennium Hotel when he was trapped by the collapse. Sandwiched between the debris and a plate-glass window, he dove for cover under a car and curled up in the wheel well. It was the debris that hit him hardest. "All the metal, the concrete, the pellets of white, light fabric from the walls; there was just a stream, a waterfall of brown, black ash," he remembered. "It just came down and came down and came down. It was like a waterfall that didn't stop for eight or nine minutes."[23]

No doubt people asked themselves why me? Why was one person dead and another spared? Firefighter Lieutenant. Gary Wood, Ladder 131, FDNY, was staging in the Marriott when the collapse occurred. "There was no place to hide," he said. "We just hit the deck wherever we were. It was literally 30, 40 feet [that made the] difference."[24]

Chief Pfeifer thought the margin for survival was even less than that. "A foot here or there made a difference, as we know now," he said.[25] Or more like inches, said paramedic James Creedon. He was near the South Pedestrian Bridge across from the South Tower when he was blown off his feet. "One lieutenant dove under a fire truck; he was okay. Another person dove under the same truck and his legs were crushed by a beam: He didn't survive," he said. "It was a matter of the building tilting half a degree this way, not the other—a matter of luck as to whether you lived or not. . . . People right next to me were killed by falling debris, and it didn't require a girder to fall on top of you: A stone the size of your fist falling from 800 feet could kill you easily." Creedon suffered burns and lacerations including debris that was embedded in his back, although it didn't stop him. He went on to help evacuate women and children down to the North Cove Marina. [26]

"It looked exactly like an avalanche coming down the street."

10:02 a.m.

AS DEVASTATING AS THE SHOCKWAVE WAS, AS INJURIOUS AS THE DEBRIS, it was the smoke cloud that brought rescues to a complete halt. This thick mixture of pulverized cement and other debris blocked out the sun and blanketed the World Trade Center in a deep and utterly disorienting blackness. The smoke seeped into every hole and crevice and swallowed up buildings and people alike. It was a fast-moving, 70-foot high storm front of debris and darkness with a curved leading edge, not unlike a dust storm. Tom Fitzpatrick, deputy commissioner of the fire department, likened it to a scene from a Cecil B. DeMille movie. "It reminded me of the 10 Commandments—when the great cloud [came] down on the street."[1,2]

People tried to escape the cloud, but it was moving too fast. "We were right near the North Cove Marina when the first tower collapsed," said one survivor. "It looked exactly like an avalanche coming down the street to you. There were hundreds of people running toward us."

The cloud ultimately covered anything within a mile or so of ground zero. Day turned day into night—darker even than night, like being underwater in a muddy river, said one survivor who was searching for a way to describe something that was entirely outside the human experience. Paramedic Karen Lamanna, Battalion 14, EMS FDNY, was parking near the North Pedestrian Bridge at West Side near Liberty. Her partner jumped out to organize their emergency gear when they thought better of where they were and backed up their ambulance. As they did, the tower collapsed, and they were in the smoke. "It [was] not like any darkness I've ever seen before as far as nighttime or anything," said Lamanna in her interview. "You couldn't see anything. There was no daylight. You couldn't see anything out of the windows [of the ambulance] at all. All we could hear is everything falling on the top of the ambulance, [on top of the] the hood."[3]

"It was dark, it was black, it was just deadly silent," remembered Captain Howard Sickles, commanding officer, Battalion 45, EMS FDNY. Sickles had been staging across the West Side Highway in front of 3 World Financial Center when he was caught up in it. "I really thought I was dead. I started talking to myself and then [EMT] Roger Moore in couple of seconds moans and tells me to shut up you're not dead."[4]

In their interviews, most of the medics said they lost all sense of direction, even their sense of physical orientation. Some thought they were buried only to bump into a tree or a car and realize they were on a street. One person said he was in a tunnel, but he wasn't. Deputy Chief Medical Officer David Prezant, FDNY, thought he had been entombed. "When I got up, it was completely black. It was blacker than midnight," said Prezant. "The only thing that I could think of at the time that could explain this was that I was still buried."[5]

EMT Thomas Bendix didn't think he was buried, but he had no idea where he was. He heard voices—*anyone here? Anyone have light?* Bendix had a light. "I took my small flashlight out and turned [it] on and the guy that was talking, grabbed my hand immediately, because I guess he was standing right next to me and then we waved the flashlight around asking if there was anybody else near us. You could hear a couple of voices near us, but most of them said they couldn't see the flashlight, even though they sounded like they were about 2 feet from you."[6]

Dozens of cameras caught the image of the debris cloud sweeping over Manhattan. Some show their lens filing with speckles of dirt and then day turning into utter darkness. Survivors and rescuers alike bumped into the sides of buildings, into lamp posts, into cars. They tripped on sidewalks, stumbled over beams that were at their feet. Captain DeShore ran up the grassy knoll to the safety of the South Pedestrian Bridge not far from the collapsing South Tower. She had her back to it all when she felt the smoke and debris sweep over her, the air dark and gritty. Her eyes filled with the thick particulate matter, she choked with each breath. The air swirled with blowing debris, paper, bits of steel or aluminum, chunks of concrete, and drywall. "I thought it was a major explosion," said DeShore. "I didn't know the building was collapsing. I had no clue what was going on."[7] Thoughts of survival, thoughts of family and life and death raced across the coils of her brain even as her training kicked in. "I felt beyond alone," she added. "I kept saying to myself within me 'I don't want to die. I don't want to die.' I just felt like the darkness, the loneliness, and being alone was the worst thing I ever experienced in my life."

EMS Captain Mark Stone, commanding officer, Battalion 8, FDNY, saw his life flash before his eyes. "I saw my two kids. I saw my father who passed away," he said. "I said to myself my god, that's it, it's over, because it was black, and it was silent. Then I hit the ground. I got an excruciating pain. So, I said to myself, 'you are not dead because there is no pain in heaven.'"[8]

Familiar landmarks had been replaced by jumbled steel. Soot and smoke obstructed the horizon. So much had changed, so much was unfamiliar. The senses could scarcely keep up, quantify it, dissect it. "It was a moment of disorienting shock," said one of the first responders. "North seemed south. Left seemed right. The simple act of drawing breath became a struggle, because the air was thick with dust and black smoke from raging fires. The stillness was broken at times by stray bullets exploding from the heat [but] there were very few cries for help."[9]

Everything was coated in the gritty powder. A flicker of a car fire or a red stoplight became a hazy beacon. Survivors emerged, their bodies slammed by the shockwave, many of them having been tossed through the air like rag dolls then coated head-to-toe by the powdery cement mixture, terra cotta soldiers armored in dust, monochromatic, stunned. "My blue uniform had turned completely grey," said Captain DeShore.[10]

Around the base of the tower, no one really knew what had happened. Had there been some terrible explosion, as DeShore speculated? Had the top of a tower broken off? The live television feeds into the homes of millions of Americans told a story that no one knew at ground zero. At ground zero there were no answers, just a once bright sun on a perfect September morning dulled to a rusty brown. Instead, there was an awning covered in blood and was dripping red. There were bodies, here and there, or things that looked like bodies. "I was walking in a daze," said paramedic Sweeting, who had been helping the woman with a broken leg when he was slammed by the shockwave. "There weren't a lot of walking wounded. There really were more just people stunned that were walking around. For the next 10 minutes, 15 minutes, nobody knew where to go, what to do and where to start. I remember asking one of the Port Authority cops what exactly happened, because I didn't know the whole magnitude. I didn't know anything at this point," said Sweeting. "I didn't realize the towers had come down completely. I thought it was just the area above where the planes had crashed. I didn't realize they had come all the way down. I said, 'No, no, just above where'—and he's like, 'No, I'm telling you, they fell completely.'"[11]

The idea of a complete collapse was so alien, so unimaginable, that it occurred to almost no one. Said Jack Delaney of the moment the South Tower came down, "We were probably 1,500 feet away from the building." When it collapsed, his immediate reaction was to run *into* the tower, so alien was the idea that this steel goliath could come down. "That would have been my safe haven," said Delaney. "If I were closer to the front entrance of the building, I would have run into the lobby. There was no concept of the building coming down."[12]

But it did and now no cars, ambulances, or fire trucks were on streets that moments before had been bumper-to-bumper with first responders arriving and desperate survivors escaping. It was dark, silent. "The South Tower had just collapsed," said fire fighter captain Jay Jonas, 6 Truck, FDNY. "This was a difficult piece of information to process. I had never heard of a high-rise building collapsing before. It gave me a sick feeling."[13]

CHAPTER 24

"People kept coming down to the seawall just looking to get away."

10:12 a.m.

OUT ON THE HARBOR, THE BOILING CLOUD OF DUST AND DEBRIS REDUCED visibility to zero creating a navigation problem not unlike sailing through a thick fog or navigating black seas on a moonless night. Ordinarily, a boat captain would simply turn on their radar and navigate relying on their instruments, except for one thing: This cloud was not fog, which was a known weather condition, nor was it a moonless night when the sky and the sea merged into one black nothingness. This was different. Nobody had any idea what was *in* the cloud much less how bad it might get or how much heat it contained. Could one penetrate the cloud without hitting a wall of airborne bricks or blowtorch-like heat that would peel off their skin?

Some likened the unknown dangers of the cloud, and the fearless response of the boat captains, to soldiers going into combat. "The guys who went over [to Manhattan] through that cloud of smoke and debris—without even hesitating?" said Mike O'Toole, an engineer on the Staten Island ferries. "[They just] flipped on the radar and went right into a war zone."

Armed with only a seafarers sense of duty to assist a boat in trouble, the mariners made the decision to sail headlong into the unknown. Captain Russell J. Bostock was on the ferry the *Bravest*. He was completing a run up the East River with a load of morning commuters. "When we docked at Pier 11, it was completely black from the smoke. There was no visibility. We came in by radar."[1] The crowds surged forward as the deckhands tied off. "Some people had no shoes because they had run out of them. Some had no shirts or were using them to breathe through. We brought some people down to the Highlands that were actually going to North Jersey, but when they boarded in New York, they just wanted to get the heck off Manhattan," said Bostock.[2]

A survivor recorded the scene in a digital diary. "Pier 11 is a hub for a number of commuter ferries. As a boat, hopefully mine, was pulling up, I could see down Wall Street. There was a huge roiling dust-brown, reddish cloud coming toward me and the pier. The barge started rocking and very quickly the great cloud was upon me." From somewhere above them, they heard another jet. People ducked. It was later determined to be a US military aircraft arriving on scene, but the sound only served to exacerbate fears. "I was certain that my time for heaven had come."[3]

Paul Frank, captain of the tugboat *Resolute*, navigated the smoke as he approached Manhattan. "That was something that I won't forget which was low dark, acrid black smoke," he said, "It was like there was a big chimney in Manhattan. When we were pulling into Pier 11 the dust was unbelievable."[4]

It was a story that was repeated time and again around the harbor.

— ᴥ —

NYPD's Harbor Unit was alongside the Battery. They had multiple rescue boats in the water and began boarding the injured, smoke or no smoke: "People kept coming down to the seawall just looking to get away, not knowing what was coming next," explained James Cowan. Their best bet, he decided, was to take the injured across the harbor. "We had ambulances waiting on Ellis Island."[5]

In the quick response patrol boat *41497*, Coast Guardsman Perez, tried to steer clear of the cloud altogether—after all, the safety of his crew was job #1. "It became so dark that you couldn't see anything," said Perez of the moment when he was forced to make his decision. "The rumbling was so loud that I couldn't hear myself yelling to my crew to hang on as we tried to outrun [it]." He steered the boat toward Governors Island, but the cloud overcame him. He was plunged into darkness.[6]

Peter Johansen, the senior operations manager for New York Water-way, was handling the crowds at the World Financial Center Termi-nal. Because his company's ferries loaded from the front, they could use their bow-forward design to load and unload passengers much like a landing craft from World War II—bow first, with engines churn-ing against the current. The cloud plunged the terminal into darkness, which under ordinary circumstances would have shut things down. "The debris flew right past us," he said of the cyclone of dirt and dust that swept over the terminal. Rather than cease operations, he simply repo-sitioned his boats. "We had to keep moving up the seawall to continue loading people."

Jim Parese, the captain of the ferry *Newhouse*, was docked inside the Whitehall terminal in Lower Manhattan when he was caught in the collapse. "It was zero visibility," said Parese. "You heard the building go down, but we were in the slip and [couldn't] see it. That's when we saw the cloud."[7] The rolling cloud of smoke swept over the terminal and seeped inside. "It [was] totally black outside and people keep pouring into the terminal," wrote one evacuee in her digital archive. "While the smoke [was] not yet filling the terminal, it was getting smoky. I am coughing, as are other people. I'm feeling tremendous fear that this place will fill with smoke and the crowds in here will panic. I try to get hold of myself. I talk to someone next to me. She is scared too."[8]

The ferry was packed with people desperate to evacuate when the cloud overcame them. "It became so dark that you couldn't see anything," said Parese. Perese would later describe the cloud as "some kind of mon-soon" or a "fog bank."[9] Either way, the situation suddenly turned for the worse. "The boat filled with smoke," he said. "People were crying so we just calmed them down, the mates and the deckhands went down there, calming everybody down." The best thing to do was shove off and get the *Newhouse* out into the harbor where, presumably, there was fresh air. Parese closed the boarding gates and cast off the lines and went into the East River, carefully watching for ships around him lest he have a colli-sion on the waters. "We were on radar," he said. Parese watched the blips on his scope as he came around and was pointed toward Staten Island. "It was like a nightmare in that smoke."[10]

Parese's deckhands walked among the passengers, asking people to get back in their seats, reassuring them that things were okay, that they were going to be alright. But nothing could match the calming effect that fresh air and clear visibility had on the cabin. "As we got to the south end of Governors Island we started coming out of the smoke," remembered one of the deckhands. "And that's when everyone pretty much calmed down. By the time we got to St. George, we dumped everybody off. We had at least 6,000 people on the boat."[11, 12]

But they were a much-changed boat load of people. Said Brian Walsh, one of the deckhands after sailing clear of the smoke, "There was no panic or anger. [The passengers] were mostly sitting in circles, holding hands and praying or crying." But they had escaped Manhattan.[13]

Trooper DeMarino could hardly load 6,000 people, but he could take on a dozen or so. He was just yards offshore when the first tower came down. He avoided the cloud of debris as best he could, then put in alongside the seawall and took on survivors, perhaps a dozen or so in all. He and his fellow officers, DSG Alexander J. Koopalethes and trooper Clark T. Motley, settled their passengers on the aft deck, then took a look at the condition they were in. In the main, they were a bloody mess. Among them, Brian Gestring, a master forensic scientist and medical examiner with the New York City's Department of Health. Gestring had been on West Side Street when the South Tower came down. He was hit hard. "I was walking next to an entire company of firefighters," he later recalled. "All of them got wiped out." He ran toward a ladder truck but was blown off his feet and thrown several feet. Gestring doesn't remember much after that. Someone carried him down to a boat where one of the New Jersey troopers lowered him onto the harbor boat, placing him inside the cabin next to the helm. Gestring was a mass of blood, his head sliced open, his hand mangled, glass piercing his face and eyes. He was in extreme pain and going in and out of consciousness. "Next thing I remember, I was on the boat. I forced my eyes open and saw a hand reaching down toward me. I saw the French sleeve with a yellow triangle on it. I knew it was a state trooper." It was, in fact, Joseph DeMarino, he would later determine. Said

Gestring: "He reached down and said 'Calm down. You'll be alright.' He was very reassuring." After that Gestring felt the vibration of the engines and the shock of the hull as the boat slapped the waves and sped across the harbor to the New Jersey docks where paramedics took them to the Jersey City Medical Center.[14]

His passengers safely offloaded, DeMarino spun the bow of his boat around and pointed it back toward Manhattan. He checked in with the dispatcher at his station. It was no more than a few minutes to cross the Hudson and he had plenty of gas. Despite the unknown and despite the risks, he knew he could pull some more people off the island. He told them he was going back.[15]

While there was no official record of such things, DeMarino's boat was surely one of the first harbor patrol boats to carry off the injured. That this is so can be documented. A local news photographer caught Gestring, the 6'5" medical examiner, being helped off his boat on the Jersey side.

In the background, only one tower was down.[16]

CHAPTER 25

"We had steel beams all around us."

10:22 a.m.

BACK IN MANHATTAN, IN THE DUST AND DARKNESS, VOICES FOUND voices, survivors connected with survivors. EMT Karin DeShore survived the shock wave and the debris and was now near the South Pedestrian Bridge sifting through what little information she had. The air was heavy; each breath was like pulling in handfuls of powdered cement. She looked around for something familiar, but everything was obscured by the dark, thick smoke. There was a silence.

A man's voice yelled out, "Is anyone there?"

"I'm over here," answered DeShore. "Please don't leave me."

They followed each other's voices until a hand found a hand and they connected, a stranger and an EMT, neither knowing the other but both eager for human contact. "We held onto each other like little kids," said DeShore. "By then, we were coughing, vomiting, spitting—we were trying to breathe, and it was total darkness and we couldn't see anything at all." DeShore and the man stayed together and walked blindly to the west trying to find a way out, not knowing where they were headed, or what they were heading into. "As we walked we stepped over bodies and body parts, half bodies," said DeShore. "I held his hand. I needed to hold his hand as much as he needed to hold mine."[1]

———

EMT Lonnie Penn, Battalion 20, EMS, FDNY, survived the falling I-beams and concrete slabs although he was clearly shaken by his near-death experience. He, too, took a moment to gather himself, to calm down and sort things out. He squinted through the haze and made out some shapes—one of them was EMT Bill Truocollo. "His leg was gashed," said Penn. "He had a lot of glass all over him, over his neck. He was cut up. I guess his adrenaline just kept him going."[2] Penn lent Truccolo a hand and together they made it out of the nightmare, eventually running into DeShore. "We all hugged," he remembered. Penn and DeShore looked themselves over. "I didn't have any obvious signs of injuries that I could see myself," said DeShore, "but other people were bleeding." Trucolo and Penn made DeShore's group four.[3]

Twenty-three minutes had passed since the South Tower came down. Across the collapse zone, small groups of EMTs banded together, one person helping the other, all coated in dust, confused, gathering themselves, certainly wanting to be anywhere in the world other than in the middle of this nightmare. Instead, they turned back into the devastation and looked around for medical gear so they could help victims. EMT Joe Jefferson found an ambulance relatively intact so he broke into it and grabbed some oxygen and bandages and other supplies, then began to help a group of some 20 civilians that he found. He moved all of them in the direction of the Staten Island Ferry Terminal.[4]

Charlie Wells drew on his years of improvising, too. He gathered some EMTs and had them fan out over the wreckage looking to scavenge anything that would be useful—bandages, splints, albuterol for asthma, masks, backboards, whatever. "We broke the driver's-side window, the butterfly window [of an ambulance], and then we could get in," Wells later explained. "We got a lot of stuff."[5] Coated in dust himself, Wells helped a group of nearly 80 make it over to the Hudson River waterfront.

DeShore's group continued to grow as they walked toward the water. "It just got worse," said DeShore, describing the injured people that attached to her. "[A] fireman was severely, severely injured. I had some female police officers who had severe cuts and lacerations and [other] people were just bleeding, by now maybe 10 of us." Their wounds required a doctor and sterile bandages but they were at the edge of the debris field in a witch's brew of destruction.[6] She could vaguely make out the bent and misshapen objects around her. "There was a police van in front of me," said DeShore. "It was totally destroyed; two feet to my right there was an overturned car. We had steel beams all around us. There were dead bodies lying everywhere."[7] They stepped over the beams, walked away from the fires and pile of debris and away from the horrific sounds of bodies exploding as they hit the ground. Above them, the North Tower burned. Although at the moment luck seemed rather distant, they stumbled through the door of a restaurant supply company and decided to regroup. Inside were two women who offered up dinner napkins, tablecloths, and linen to help treat the injured. DeShore went to work. "I kept telling them 'bring all the wounded in here you can find.'"

"Do you a have an ambulance?" someone asked.

"I have nothing," said DeShore.[8]

Nothing except tablecloths and napkins, which she cut up and used as bandages.

But with years of experience guiding her every move.

CHAPTER 26

"The group started jumping over the wall into the boat."

10:24 a.m.

Michael McKee of Bloomberg News reached the harbor, not that it helped, at least not at first. He ended up against the railing above the water. "[I was] trying desperately to stay ahead of the huge cloud of debris and smoke, but the Hudson River blocked [my] escape," he later wrote. When the smoke lifted enough to see anything, he saw vague figures and shapes moving through the haze, survivors struggling for a breath of clean air, feeling their way through the blindness of the smoke. "Grasping the riverside railing, dozens of people staggered, crawled, and walked through the smoke, with no idea where they were or where they were going, other than away," said McKee.[1] It was a modern-day version of the horror of trench warfare and the gas attacks of World War I.

One survivor thought she was going to die so she stuffed her ID into a pocket so her children could identify her later. The bow of a fireboat emerged from the smoke and she—and the crowd around her—had their chance to escape, although they weren't sure anyone would be allowed on board. "The group started jumping over the wall into the boat," wrote a friend of hers who knew of her experience. "She said people were hurting themselves in the jump, but she jumped in also. She was afraid the firemen would make them get back out, but, instead, it immediately hauled them across to New Jersey."[2]

FDNY EMT Freddy Burgos, Battalion 14, headed to the harbor after triaging some victims but everything was so distorted that he had trouble navigating his way forward. "I remember falling on my face a couple of times," he said. "I kept tripping over body parts. They were covered by dust, [and] I couldn't see where I was going." Burgos went back to his ambulance to get some oxygen tanks. On the way, he looked into a crushed ambulance to see if anyone needed help. He saw a severed limb. "I kept saying to myself, if something else comes down, I'm going to jump in the water." Despite the lack of landmarks, Burgos finally got his bearings, something he credited to his wife. "I knew [the Hudson River] was there," he said. "My wife works at [the] World Financial Center. So, I knew the water was there."[3]

—

Despite the 10-foot drop to a boat, despite the current and the depth of the water along the Battery, the fear of what might be next was so strong that people risked the waters and jumped directly into the harbor anyway. It was yet another problem for the boat captains to solve. "We were yelling for people in the water to answer us," said one of the officers on a NY Harbor patrol launch. "There were dozens of people in the water. Luckily, a New York city fireboat was tied up on the seawall. Most of the people were able to get over to the fireboat, where some fellas with ladders and ropes were pulling people out."[4]

Brian Fitzpatrick, Ladder 22, FDNY, thought jumping into the harbor was a deadly mistake. "I wound up by the railing by the water. I remember there was a bunch of senior [firefighters] there and they were getting out of their bunker gear and they were getting ready to jump in the water because you could see ferries out in the distance waving us on," he said. "They said, 'Get out of your gear. We're going in the water.'" But Fitzpatrick had experience with the deadly nature of currents and tides. "When I was younger, I used to work out in the Hamptons on people's boats and I remember currents. I knew the currents down [in the harbor] would just kill us, you know, they'd find us in South Jersey. So, I just buried myself in the fence and hoped for the best."[5]

The current that Fitzpatrick feared did nearly kill one survivor. A woman had jumped into the river and was carried downstream into the bow of the fireboat *McKean*. The firefighters thought she'd be pulled under, so they hurried to rescue her. "This woman hanging on the bow was getting pushed between the bow of the boat and the bulkhead," said firefighter Tom Sullivan. "We threw her a life ring—we were throwing everything we could at her to keep her floating—[but] she just couldn't hold on." The problem had to do with the *McKean*'s design. The *McKean* was a big fireboat, 129 feet long with a 12-foot freeboard and an upward rising bow. The crew leaned over the side and created a human chain to grab her, but she was unreachable. Sullivan yelled to her saying, "Take a deep breath. Breathe. Just a second, we'll get you out." Voices shouted from one crewman to another. Engineer Greg Woods worked as a weekend lifeguard. He dove in. Engineer Gulmar Parga dove in. "Greg had her around the waist," said Sullivan, but he had no leverage except what he could gain by kicking his feet, and that would only go so far. The firefighters tied off a ladder and one of them stepped down and reached out a hand. Woods gave it a good hard scissor kick and lifted her up just enough to be reached. He did it again and she got yet another hand on the ladder, and then a knee. "Then it was like slow motion, said Sullivan, she only had to go 8 or 10 feet. But she got up high enough where she had her whole body on the ladder, and we could reach down and grab her and pull her in."[6]

CHAPTER 27

"[It was] a lot of chaos, a lot of people running around, a lot of screaming, a lot of people asking for help."

10:26 a.m.

A WOMAN BY THE NAME OF JOAN FILSON WAS ATTENDING A CONFER-
ence in the Marriott's Grand Ballroom on September 11. The luxurious,
22-story hotel was sandwiched between the Twin Towers. So dissimilar
were they in height—two Goliath's over a solitary David—that one could
wonder why such a small hotel would even be built. But the Marriott was
far from small—in fact it was one of the larger hotels in Manhattan with
room for 1,000 guests plus many more who might be attending meetings
or conferences there.

The night before, Filson had walked over to the North Tower and
taken the elevator up to the 107th floor and walked around the Windows on the World restaurant. She took in the spectacular view of the
city, a seemingly endless carpet of lights sparkling through the light rain,
a vibrant city stretching out beneath her feet. "We walked around the
bar, stepped outside on the balcony, admired the night view, and peered
down," she later said in an interview. "I would think that we were among
the last people to leave Windows on the World alive."[1]

The next morning, at 8:59 a.m., life forever changed for the 900-
plus Joan Filsons in the Marriott when American Flight 11 slammed
into the North Tower raining massive steel beams, structural facade, and
fiery debris down on the hotel. Part of it was crushed and one of the

jet's 3,000-pound landing gear assemblies crashed through the roof and ignited deadly fires.

Because the Marriott was connected to the towers it was a natural staging area for arriving firefighters who would get their orders before mounting rescues inside the hotel as well as the towers. "There were a lot of companies in the lobby," remembered firefighter Mark Ruppert, FDNY. "It was full, maybe a total of 75, maybe 100 firefighters."[2] Matthew Harttree, a guest at the hotel, was caught in the chaos of the damage and made his way down the stairs through the debris of the first attack until he reached the mezzanine level. There he stopped. "I just remember looking down from the top of the stairs toward the lobby," said Harttree. "It [was] filled with firefighters and law enforcement."[3]

He turned and continued out of the hotel, and not a moment too soon.

—∼—

New Jersey State Trooper Joe DeMarino headed back across the river toward the devastation. The situation was markedly worse than it had been on his first trip over. The South Tower was down, the North Tower was engulfed in flames, and people coated in dust and blood were scattered pell-mell across the width of the curved esplanade between the North Cove Marina and the World Financial Center. "They were in bad shape," said DeMarino of the people he could see. "They were cut up pretty badly. Blood, stretchers; it was a mess."[4] Firefighter John McGinty, Special Operations Command, FDNY, was on the esplanade and described what looked like a war zone. "[It was] a lot of chaos, a lot of people running around, a lot of screaming, a lot of people asking for help," he said. "It was all mayhem."[5]

Unfortunately, the best way to help people off was to do the last thing DeMarino wanted to do, that is, to take the patrol boat into the North Cove Marina and use their docks. DeMarino was still concerned about the tight confines of the docks and being so close to the North Tower but he also saw no other way to evacuate the injured, so he pushed up the throttles and motored through the breakwater, his engines churning just a notch above idle, his eyes sweeping the surface for debris, his launch motoring past a porcupine's quill of boats and slips.[6]

In the haze, he tied off and looked up. He could hardly believe his eyes.[7]

⟞⟝

As Karin DeShore's group of survivors sheltered inside the restaurant supply company, four more victims arrived, making it a group of ten. But DeShore was uncomfortable in the building and wanted to get her people out. She looked at her patients. They were a pitiful lot, injured or bleeding from multiple lacerations that were, for the moment, staunched by napkins and strips of tablecloth cut into bandages. What they really needed was a hospital. "After I bandaged everybody up and everybody was sort of calm, I went outside to see what I could do," she said. She looked around. Through the haze she saw the North Tower above her, fire and smoke billowing from the top with more ferocity than ever before. They were too close, she thought; the tower was burning and it could be unstable. She went back inside and addressed the group. "I told them, 'I can't force you to, but I don't know if we are going to be safe here.'"[8]

She suggested they move farther away, receiving no argument. They went back out and walked through the dust and debris and haze, past bloody body parts, walked through the World Financial Center and into the curving esplanade that faced the North Cove Marina. Wrapped in bloodied napkins and caked in powdered cement, DeShore's ragtag group of survivors came up to the edge of the docks and looked down.[9] They saw DeMarino. "Just then, a small Jersey boat—it was Jersey police officers—entered this little marina," DeShore later recounted.

That's when DeMarino looked up.

It was as if he was watching a movie about the walking dead.

⟞⟝

The New Jersey state troopers weren't the only rescue boats using the North Cove Marina. New York City Fire Department's Marine division was on scene or had boats underway including the *Kevin Kane*, which had Captain Fuentes on board. "As we were at the tip of Manhattan, the second plane flew over us," said Fuentes. "Until that moment I was more concerned about what we needed to do for this type of fire. But when we saw the plane hit the tower, I grabbed my aid and said 'We're under attack.'"[10]

The *Kevin Kane* docked in North Cove Marina to offload Fuentes so he could report to the command center. Fuentes knew the firefighters would need every bit of water he could supply and, if not that, they might need his boats to evacuate people or bring in supplies. He ordered the crew of the *Kevin Kane* to stay there until he got back. "I told them to stand fast," said Fuentes. He hustled through the smoke toward the North Tower where he found Chief Ray Downey, Special Operations Command, FDNY. No doubt Fuentes told Downey his fireboats were at his disposal, but that wasn't all he said. "Give me a company or two and get me up there to help put this thing out," he added.

"No, Al," said Downey. "Stay here with me. Give me a hand."

Downey and Fuentes were old friends. Downey knew Fuentes would want to go inside the tower and fight the fires—any firefighter worth his salt would want to—but Fuentes was the commanding officer of the fireboats, and that changed things. Downey might need those boats, so going into the towers was out of the question. But a little help? That wouldn't take long and Downy was shorthanded. There were firefighters staging across the street and Downey didn't know if they knew where they were supposed to go. "Ray sent me over there to check on them, to make sure they had orders," said Fuentes. Downey had one more request. "Al, tell them to be careful with secondary devices," he said, as Fuentes headed across the street. Fuentes yelled "Okay" over his shoulder.[11, 12]

A Staten Island ferry noses into the Whitehall Terminal on Lower Manhattan. The Governors Island ferry terminal is to the immediate right while just up the East River is Pier 11. To the left is the Coast Guard building with its three piers, then the green spaces of the Battery and the Hudson River. WIKIPEDIA

A view of the North Cove Marina, the World Financial Center, and the esplanade. A New York Waterway ferry is maneuvering around the terminal at the World Financial Center. Note the close proximity to the base of the World Trade Center. WIKIPEDIA

A street-level view of the North Cove Marina. The sailing vessel *Ventura* can be seen in the foreground. The captain of the *Ventura* was one of the first persons to notify the Coast Guard of the attack. The Twin Towers are about a block to the right. AUTHOR PHOTO

The wide-open lanes of the West Side Highway as seen present day, looking south toward the South Pedestrian Bridge. The Twin Towers would be to the left. The North Pedestrian Bridge was identical to this one. When it collapsed, it blocked West Side in both directions effectively cutting off Lower Manhattan from the rest of the island. AUTHOR PHOTO

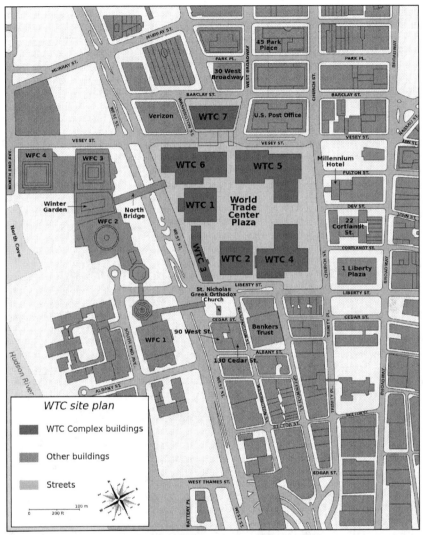

The World Trade Center. North is to the top, the Hudson River is to the left. Note the names of the streets that immediately border the 16-acre site. These four streets were essential to the evacuation of victims in the event of a Mass Casualty Incident (MCI). To a varying degree, all would become impassable. COURTESY FEMA

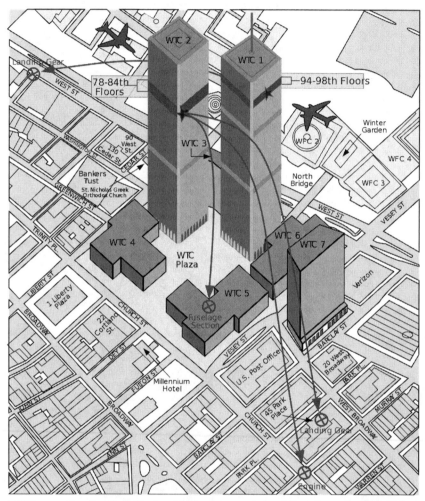

FEMA map showing the attack and where large parts of the planes landed. This view is looking south toward the Battery. COURTESY FEMA

United 175 hit the South Tower, raining fire and debris down toward the first responders around the base. WIKIPEDIA

A view of the cloud of smoke and debris that followed the collapse as seen from a NYPD helicopter. COURTESY NYPD

Ground zero. Rescue workers scavenged anything that was useful.
COURTESY LIBRARY OF CONGRESS

Hatzolah EMTs assisted the NYFD EMS crews. A total of eight EMS responders
died that morning. COURTESY LIBRARY OF CONGRESS

Survivors escape Lower Manhattan as seen along the Battery.
COURTESY DEPARTMENT OF TRANSPORTATION

Lower Manhattan as seen from the Hudson River. The smoke is blowing east toward Brooklyn. Note the boat headed into the smoke along the seawall.
COURTESY DEPARTMENT OF TRANSPORTATION

A Staten Island ferry departs Lower Manhattan with a load of evacuees. The Staten Island ferries carried 50,000 to safety.

The US Army Corps of Engineers vessel *Gelberman* is seen responding to the crisis. A ferry and a dinner boat are in the background. North Cove Marina.

This photo shows Manhattan's seawall during the boat lift. Note the two fire-boats, center and center right, and the NY Waterway ferry, to the left.
COURTESY DEPARTMENT OF DEFENSE

Rescue vessels along the seawall in Lower Manhattan. The captains had to keep their engines turning to counter the currents. NY Waterway evacuated more than 150,000 survivors that day. COURTESY DEPARTMENT OF TRANSPORTATION

A Seastreak ferry seen alongside the 34th Street docks. WIKIPEDIA

Tugboats cluster along the seawall. COURTESY DEPARTMENT OF DEFENSE

Evacuees wait in line along the seawall. The picture was taken after the second collapse. WIKIPEDIA

Abandoned strollers, Battery Park City. COURTESY DEPARTMENT OF DEFENSE

On the tugboat *Nancy Moran* as she heads to New Jersey. WIKIPEDIA.

New York as seen from a Coast Guard quick response boat in the harbor. Note the vessels nosed into the seawall. Lower Manhattan.
COURTESY DEPARTMENT OF DEFENSE

The Coast Guard cutter *Adak* arrived from Sandy Hook, New Jersey.
COURTESY DEPARTMENT OF DEFENSE.

The pilot vessel *New York*. The windows surrounding the bridge offered an unobstructed view of the ships in the harbor. Harbor pilots on the *New York* acted as
air traffic controllers for the numerous civilian vessels that responded. WIKIPEDIA

Coast Guardsman Perez sped across New York harbor on a 41-foot utility boat like this. COURTESY DEPARTMENT OF DEFENSE

The US Coast Guard cutter *Hawser* was one of the first Coast Guard vessels on the scene. COURTESY DEPARTMENT OF DEFENSE

US Army Corp of Engineers vessel *Driftmaster* seen during a recent rescue. The Corps sent numerous vessels from their docks at Caven Point, New Jersey.

Liberty Landing Marina, New Jersey, far right. Note the bridge over to Ellis Island, background left.

Manhattan was closed to inbound traffic. Ferries and boats evacuated some 272,000 people off the island, making it the largest single-day boat lift in history. COURTESY GEORGE W. BUSH PRESIDENTIAL LIBRARY

An aerial view of the wreckage of the World Trade Center. The North Cove Marina is to the top center. Also visible is the South Pedestrian Bridge. COURTESY NOAA

"The building was a quarter-mile high, and we were way too close."

10:28 a.m.

THE AVERAGE HOUSEHOLD WATCHING TELEVISION HAD INFINITELY MORE information on the situation at the World Trade Center than the first responders at the base of the towers. Firefighter Christopher Fenyo, Engine 60, FDNY, tried to make sense of the attacks but accurate information was nearly impossible to find. "We had really no concept of the damage on the east side of 2 World Trade Center," said Fenyo of the South Tower. "Many people felt possibly explosives had taken out 2 World Trade, [so] officers were gathering companies together and the officers were debating whether or not to go immediately back [into the collapse zone] or to see what was going to happen with [the North Tower], said Fenyo. "The debate ended pretty quickly because [the North Tower] came down."[1]

At 10:28 a.m., the 1,368-foot-high, 500,000-ton giant of steel and concrete fell in and on itself, pancaking down to the ground with an eruption of I-beams and a tornado of wind, dust, and debris. "We were standing in the corner of West Street and Vesey Street, and I heard that rumble again, that roar, that thunder, and I said dear god, I almost died once. God can't be letting this happen to me again," said EMS Captain Mark Stone. "1 World Trade Center was falling on my head."[2]

"[S]omebody ran past us screaming, "The building is falling!" said Battalion Chief Pfeifer. "I heard the steel falling. I was waiting to be crushed. The building was a quarter-mile high, and we were way too close."[3]

"You heard a big boom," said paramedic Neil Sweeting. "(Then) it was quiet for about ten seconds. Then you could hear another one. Now I realize—it was the floors starting to stack on top of each other as they were falling. It was spaced apart in the beginning, but then it got to just a tremendous roar and a rumble that I will never forget. We started running. People were diving into the back of ambulances that were open and on the hoods of ambulances, cars. Anything that was moving, they were trying to get into. There was one ambulance, there must have been 25 people piled into the back of it: firemen, policemen, civilians, EMS. It was just incredible. I remember the MERV bus with the ramp that it had going up the street. The guy didn't even stop to unhook the stairs of the ramp, and everything was dragging down the street."[4]

Familiar landmarks were now largely gone. Many survivors had no idea where they were, particularly those long-time commuters who fell into habits and rarely explored the financial district around the towers. One woman found herself in front of the Liberty Café, which helped her get her bearings. After that, she found it impossible to orient herself. "Head toward the water, we were told," she said in her digital archive. "Me, being from New Jersey, and having had spent 5½ years working in that building, (I) had no idea where to go! My PATH train took me right inside, and I spent almost every lunch hour, working or eating in the building. Sure, I'd been in the surrounding area but that was it! With the PATH down, I had no idea how to get home. So, like hundreds of others, I stood on Greenwich Street, 2 blocks away, just staring with disbelief, watching the smoke, watching the people jumping."[5]

"At that moment, a million different questions seemed to run through my head," said another survivor. "Should I evacuate and take the ferry off of the island? But which one? Staten Island or New York Waterways? Were any other parts of the city being hit? Could this really be happening? I decided the only thing to do was direct my attention to what was unfolding in front of me."[6]

No one wanted to cool their heels, not in Lower Manhattan, not anywhere near it. What was next? More attacks? More violence? More death?

The harbor represented safety and the possibility of escape. It became a vortex that drew people toward it, creating crowds of survivors at the ferry terminals and along the seawall. There was nothing formal, nothing official announced yet about an evacuation, but witnesses remember seeing police officers in their blue uniforms and firefighters in their turnout coats directing people out of the high-rises near the Twin Towers. Nannies and children were fed into the stream of people elbowing their way toward the boats. "Along the river, the pace was slow and frustrating, with survivors and injured alike crowded shoulder-to-shoulder on the sidewalks," as one survivor noted in the digital archives. "At some point, near Battery Park, we could barely make progress against the weight and depth of the crowd."[7]

Donn Monroe was due to leave New York after spending several days in the Marriott for business. He was shaving when the attacks began. He got out of the hotel alive and made it to Battery Park and the fence between the grounds and the river. He saw a boat and didn't hesitate. "I was right in front of the first ferry, and someone helped me climb the fence with my luggage and get on that ferry." He spent the night in New Jersey renting a room in a rundown hotel.[8]

Fuentes and Downey locked eyes for a moment in silent anger. "Al, we just lost a lot of guys," said Downey after the first collapse. "Where are the fighter pilots?"[9] To their left, the gilded ornamentation of the Marriott's entrance was mixed in with a pile of steel and large sections of concrete that had cut open the hotel like a can opener. Cars were burning in the street, dust coated everything. Through the smoke they saw eight or so firefighters and half as many civilians in the all-but-destroyed hotel lobby. They heard cries for help. "I'm going in to give them a hand," said Downey, pointing toward the Marriott. "Stay outside and let me know when I can safely send them out."

Downey was asking Fuentes to be his signal man, to let him know when it was safe to send out survivors, a standard firefighting protocol to avoid being hit by falling debris.[10] "We used hand signals," said Fuentes, who stood in the street. "I gave them the signal but only one of the eight came out." Fuentes signaled again and again—*It's safe! It's safe!*—but no one came his away. Firefighter Mark Ruppert was in the lobby of the hotel when the second collapse occurred. Ruppert had taken off his turn-out coat, shed his tank, and put his tools down. "It was hot," he remembered of those minutes before the second collapse. He got something to drink, then went to the bathroom, looked around the lounge area, only to hear the sound of the second collapse.[11] "We just hit the deck," said Ruppert. Around him, what the collapse of the South Tower had sparred, the North Tower was now shredding: Walls split open, ceilings exploded downward, floors collapsed, and more firefighters and civilians perished.[12]

"There was no time to run," said Fuentes, who was caught on the street. "[All I could do was] just get ready for the impact."[13] Fuentes braced himself as much as he could then was buried in a pile of steel girders.[14] He had multiple broken ribs, a punctured lung, a broken hand, broken fingers, a severely fractured skull, and was foaming blood from his mouth. Incredibly, his was alive. Just as incredible, his radio still worked and, although he couldn't move anything else, he could move his right hand and with it he pressed the transmit button. It was one of the "super radios," the extra powerful kind you were given to run a marine division.

"I'm trapped here in the collapse," he broadcast.

"Where are you?" came the response.

"The west side," he answered, his voice weakening.

"The west side of Tower Number One or Tower Number Two?"

"Tower one . . ."

But in the sea of rubble, everything looked the same.[15]

❦

DeMarino hadn't liked the small opening into the marina, and he sure didn't like being so close to the North Tower, but here he was in the North Cove Marina, a place he avoided his first time over. There was simply no other way to mount a rescue, so he went in and tied off.

The DeShore group started down the steps to his boat. Once she got alongside, she had to get everyone over the gap between the boat and the docks without tumbling into the water. On a good day, boarding a boat can be awkward; on this day it was just one more obstacle to overcome. "We carried everybody down," said DeShore. "The elderly ladies got on; the fireman was put on board, and the police officers, and the EMS person—maybe 10, 12, 14 people got on the boat." Everyone except DcShore. DeShore had done her duty—everyone had been patched up and were safely onboard a police boat headed to hospitals in New Jersey—but she herself seemed paralyzed, unmoving, as if the last of her energy had been drained from her body. One of the troopers yelled at her to get on, but she was uncertain. "I'm still standing there trying to figure out what my next move should be when the same sergeant says, 'shit, it's coming at us.' I didn't see what was happening behind me but knowing of all the explosions, I just jumped on the boat, closed the door with my left hand, and just sank down to my knees. Whatever it was, it just came right at us again."

The second collapse propelled a fast-moving shockwave that surged through the gaps in the buildings of the World Financial Center and exploded over the boats with unchecked force. DeMarino's harbor patrol boat was tossed around like a cork, slamming his evacuees from one side to the other as it jerked and rolled, coming perilously close to capsizing. "I was just resigned to die," said DeShore.

"We were hit hard," said DeMarino. "It blew my glasses off my face." Luckily, they were still tied off to a cleat on the docks.[16] "That is about what saved our lives," said DeShore. "This force came at us and hit us with everything. The boat was attempting to overturn [but] it kept [being yanked back] against the pier."[17]

By instinct, DeMarino threw the engine into gear but the boat jerked back to the docks. *What the heck?*

One of the troopers yelled at him: "Get the fuck out of here! Get the fuck out of here."

Things were happening quickly. Up on the esplanade, shapes were racing through the smoke, one of whom was firefighter Michael Cain, fire marshall, FDNY. Cain saw DeMarino's boat and quickly recognized the problem. "The Jersey State Police had a launch in the [North] Cove Harbor," he said in an interview. "He was trying to pull out, but the bow line was still attached to the tie; you know, where they tie the boat up."[18]

Risking his own life, Cain turned back. He ran down to the docks and worked his fingers on the bow line until he untied the knot. "They had wounded people on the boat," said Cain, as if he needed any explanation.[19] DeMarino quickly threw his engines into gear and this time went free, only to discover another problem. "I didn't think we were going to make it out of there," he later admitted. "I couldn't see where I'm going."[20] The cloud had plunged the marina into darkness.

With 13 years of ship handling powering his moves, DeMarino turned into the cloud. "We were starboard to the docks," he said. "I just spun the boat to the port and bumped something and just spun it again." He nudged the boat forward looking for anything until he saw what looked like an opening through the breakwater. "I was threading a needle to get out," admitted DeMarino. "I hit something, turned it to the seawall at the entrance and put a good dent in the boat."[21]

"He did a hell of a job getting out of that situation blindly during the second collapse," said EMT Lonnie Penn who was with DeShore. "He got it backed up, did a little bump, hit the wall, and then swung it right out. I mean blindly because you couldn't see anything. The soot was hitting us already from the second collapse. Just covered the boat. Fortunately, we made it out of there. We just escaped with our lives. It was close, very close."[22]

Still, DeMarino had evacuated another load of survivors. "As we finally got out of this small opening of that marina, you could see the light in New Jersey," said DeShore. Once they were on the open water, DeShore turned her attention to an injured fireman in the back. "I went down into that small cabin. The fireman on the long board had come off the long board and was just lying there. He was bleeding profusely." DeShore saw some of his hose fittings scattered about. She picked them up and put them aside as she leaned over him. "He still had his helmet on and he was laying in his own blood and he says to me just, 'I'm all right. My name is Bob,' so I said to him, 'My name is Karin,' and we just held hands till we got over to Jersey."[23]

Al Fuentes was still buried in the pile. He didn't know what else he could do so he kept talking. Less than a minute ago, he had been waving people out of the Marriott; now he was in terrific pain and buried in debris. He was partially covered by pieces of the tower, but he could see the sky, which was good because it meant he could be found. He kept toggling the mic. *Where are you?* they would ask. *West side, near the Marriott,* he would answer. It was a good reference point if the Marriott looked like the Marriott, but visual cues were few and far between. "Over here" or "near the Marriott" were vague points in an indiscernible landscape of distorted and mangled debris. "There were fires and smoke everywhere around us," remembered FDNY lieutenant Tom Haughney. "He had part of the facade from the building across his back in addition to all the rubble." Haughney and firefighter Jack Flatley, Rescue 1, were among the first to find him.[24] Firefighter John Colon was there too. "He had frothy blood coming out of his mouth and was having difficulty breathing," Colon later wrote. "All I could do at this point was hold his hand and give him encouragement."[25] It helped, but Fuentes needed more than a strong hand and good bedside manners. He needed oxygen, a backboard, a doctor. He needed an emergency room, and fast.

One of the firefighters left to find something to carry him on—a Stokes basket or a long board—while another went looking for a way out. Both had success. "One of the men came back with the stokes," remembered Colon. "The other returned with the good news that he'd found a way to transport him through one of the buildings and to the safety of a New York City fireboat."[26] But to get to the fireboat the rescuers had to navigate the slippery and unsteady piles of steel and debris, work their way through the damaged lobby of the World Financial Center, then muscle their way across the wide esplanade down to the fireboat, all by foot and with a terribly injured 240-pound patient in a Stokes basket. A half-dozen firefighters lifted Fuentes. They carried him toward the marina, one set of arms to another, their muscles straining to get him up, over, and down the mounds of steel, catching their breath as they could, but none of them stopping. "It took nine of us to carry Al out," said Colon."[27]

Lieutenant Terry Jordan, Marine 6, FDNY, had command of the fireboat *Smoke* and was near the base of the Brooklyn Bridge when he heard

Fuentes on his radio. "Let's go," he said to the boat's pilot, Scott Hansen. Hansen raced *Smoke* up the Hudson River to the North Cove Marina. "We're going to see things that you never thought you would ever see in your life," said Hansen to his crew. "We'll just have to ignore that and do our job."[28] They docked in the North Cove Marina just minutes before the rescuers appeared alongside with Fuentes. "We reached the gangplank that leads to the fireboat," said firefighter Haughney. "It was narrow at that point, only two of us could fit and carry the stretcher. We got him to the side of the fireboat and some of the crew from the Marine Unit pulled him aboard. They placed him on the back of the fireboat and took off. We were exhausted."[29]

But deciding where to go wasn't so simple. Hanson debated going up the Hudson River to a drop-off point near a Manhattan hospital or perhaps over to Brooklyn, but the destruction and chaos ashore bothered him. He saw the flashing red and blue lights across the river in New Jersey. "What are those lights?" he asked.

"That's a triage center," came the reply. In fact it was Jersey City, one mile away, two minutes by boat.

"That's where we're going," said Hanson.[30]

Said Fuentes: "The docs later told me I had twenty minutes to live. Had we tried to go to Brooklyn, I might not have made it."[31]

Hansen spun the fireboat around and pushed the throttles to the max. It was mere minutes across the river to New Jersey.

The rescues continued. Gregory Fried, executive chief surgeon of the New York City Police Department, didn't want to be taken off at all. Fried had been assessing the wounds of a seriously injured firefighter on the west side of the World Trade Center when he got caught in the second collapse. "I rolled into a ball and hit the ground. I was laying there waiting to be killed," he said. "I figured I would be chopped in half, or I'd lose a leg. I can't tell you how long I was down. But then it stopped. I wasn't dead. But I was really hurting." Fried was a veteran surgeon who for the last 21 years had seen to the physical traumas of one of the largest police forces in the world. He trained other surgeons and was on call day and night, which was why he came down to the World Trade Center as soon as he heard: These were his patients. "One of the requirements of the Police Surgeon [is] to be available for 24 hours for serious injuries sustained by police officers," he wrote in his autobiography.[32] Now he was injured.

Half buried and hurting, Fried managed to free himself and make it down to the sidewalk along the Hudson River where two police officers came to his side, one of whom was NYPD Captain Sean Crowley. "We gotta get you out of here," said Crowley. Fried would have none of it, telling Crowley that he was a doctor and could help the people back there. Crowley wasn't easily dissuaded. Crowley was 15-year veteran and head of the security detail assigned to the city's police commissioner. He had an air of authority, so he insisted that Fried leave. But Fried saw a problem with evacuating. "Guys, there's nowhere to go," he said. "The rubble down there is waist high. We can't get anywhere. The fire engines and ambulances [are] all destroyed."[33]

Crowley couldn't argue with that, but he had a solution. He got on his radio and called for a boat. Said Fried: "They radioed the harbor guys, the scuba guys, and suddenly they're right there nosing up against the seawall."[34]

"Dr. Fried was bleeding from his nose and mouth and he was covered in what looked like cookie dough," continued Harbor Unit member Jim Cowan. Cowan got out a ladder and positioned it between the boat and the top of the seawall. Drawing on a reservoir of strength he didn't know he had, Fried started across the gap. He crawled backward, inching his wrecked body down one rung at a time. "If you asked me to do it today, I'd probably faint," Fried later admitted.[35]

Cowan helped load a few more walking wounded onto the launch, a woman with a baby and some others, then they raced across the Hudson toward the Jersey City Medical Center. "I love the harbor boat. I've been on it a million times," said Fried. "I realize that if anyone can help me make it, it'd be these guys." But it almost didn't work. "I remember lying there on my back in the harbor boat," said Fried. "I'm lying there feeling my pulse when suddenly it disappears. I knew things were pretty bad."[36] In fact, his blood pressure dropped so low that when he arrived, the New

Jersey medics couldn't find a vein into which they could insert a needle to feed him lifesaving IV fluids.

In the confusion, Fried would be listed as deceased.[37]

⌐⌐⌐

Despite the risks, DeMarino was by now taking his boat back and forth across the river, five to seven minutes in each direction. "Easily we did 20 trips," DeMarino later recalled. "We had people with missing fingers, limbs in bad shape, civilians, too."[38]

One of his patients was NYPD officer Lieutenant Joseph Torrillo, director of Fire Safety Education. "The one officer's head was split open and blood was everywhere," remembered DeMarino of his passenger. Before the collapse, Torrillo had been working in the south sector trying to keep newly arriving ambulances away from the towers. He knew that fresh crews would have low situational awareness, which would put them at risk, so he had positioned himself on the West Side Highway near where the Brooklyn-Battery Tunnel emptied into Lower Manhattan. "I prevented all of the ambulances personal [sic] from parking in front of the World Trade Center complex," he said. "I knew that within a couple of hours the tops of the buildings would start to come down."

His diligence nearly cost him his life. As it turned out, Torrillo himself was too close when the South Tower *did* come down. In the ensuing shower of debris, he was hit and suffered broken ribs, a broken arm, and his skull was fractured. "I didn't think I was going to survive it," he later said. In pain, and in the pitch black of the cloud, he crawled along the ground feeling the heat from the fires around him, fearing they would burn him to death. He drifted on the edge of consciousness, willing himself to stay awake lest he burn to death. Incredibly, he was found by two EMS techs who helped him out of the debris and put him on a backboard. "Next thing I know, I'm on the deck of a boat," he said. "Then all of a sudden I heard people screaming, 'here comes the other building.'" He remembers the boat rolling as day turned into night. He was faceup on the backboard as the debris hit and began to pummel him. "There's a seat belt that holds you down. Somehow my finger hit the release button." Torrillo tore off the collar around his neck, pulled off the straps holding him to the backboard, then felt his way around the back of the boat until he found a door. "I dove headfirst down the staircase and I ended up in the engine room of the boat. The next thing I know, I'm in the emergency room of a hospital."[39]

Captain Fuentes reached the New Jersey side of the river and was raced to a hospital. The crew of the *Smoke* now had a save which gave them incredible energy and boundless hope. They immediately turned around and motored across the river back to Manhattan. "Since Al turned up quickly, we expected to go back and find others just as quickly," said firefighter Jordan.[40]

Jordan was right, but not in the way he meant it. A small group was found, in the stairwell of one of the towers, but nothing like what he meant, at least not in the pile, not his brother firefighters and not under the 500-ton buildings. "Al was the only survivor whom I came across in the rubble that day," he said.[41]

CHAPTER 29

"They gave us water and comfort."

10:35 a.m.

THROUGHOUT THE DAY, ACROSS THE CITY, THE WELL OF GOOD SAMARI-tans ran deep, the unsung acts of kindness too frequent to count. The own-ers of a corner hot dog stand stood their ground even as frightened people swept past them. No doubt they were just as scared as anyone, and they were certainly covered with as much sweat and dust, but they had their carts and their carts were filled with bottled water and soda and, what with the attacks and the collapses and the injuries, maybe that was just what someone needed. So they stood by their cart leaning into the crowds and handing out a can of soda here and there as if they were a relief sta-tion alongside a marathon. One survivor ran past them and saw what they were doing, and it hit him, the kindness of it all standing in such sharp contrast the horror of the attack. He stopped and turned around. "He was confronted with hot dog vendors and what-not, giving all their water and soda away," said a friend who was with him and watched what he did. "They didn't run but stayed to hand out beverages. Dom stopped running and began assisting others in making it to safety. One image that he can't seem to erase [was] that of an elderly couple, unable to run very fast, look-ing horrified as the wall of smoke overcame them. He tried to run back to help them but couldn't find them among the smoke and chaos."[1]

Blocks from the tragedy survivors appeared as they worked their way home. "There were men in business suits, and some in khakis. There were women in skirts and dresses, walking barefoot or in shredded pantyhose, holding their shoes because their high heels hurt too much and they hadn't had time to grab their commuter running shoes," remembered a witness who saw one act of generosity as it unfolded. "I saw the ladies who worked in the manicure shop across the street from my building running outside with the flip-flops they put on their customers' feet when they've had a pedicure. Today, the staff was giving the flip-flops to the women who were barefoot. They were *giving away* the flip-flops."[2]

They weren't the only ones giving their livelihoods away to total strangers. The owners of a deli were outside their store handing out their inventory of bottled water to the walkers who passed by, some of whom had trudged across half of Lower Manhattan and were now soaked in sweat.[3] On another street, a survivor who had been forced to leave his apartment just blocks from the World Trade Center was walking uptown, coated in the grit of the collapse. He noticed a woman with napkins. "She was standing at the foot of Broadway," he later recorded in the digital archive of 9/11. "[She] was just another person facing the tide of people, [but] in her right arm she cradled bottles of Poland Spring water. In her left hand she held paper napkins. She was wetting the napkins and handing them to strangers to use as masks. I took one and have been grateful ever since. No idea who she was."[4]

Down in the Battery, the driver of a linen truck pulled over and began cutting up the sheets and towels he had in the back and handed them out to use as respirators or to clean one's face. Near him, two other trucks had bottled water. Both drivers stopped and opened their backs and handed out their bottles to anyone who needed one. They were seen by many but no one got their names.[5]

And so it went across the city. It scarcely mattered what direction a survivor walked or if they knew anyone on the way; the sense of community was the same. "We walked through neighborhoods that we would never walk through regularly," wrote a survivor. "People were coming up to us and asking if we were OK (we're covered in dust at this point). They gave us water and comfort. We see others helping people—a woman in a wheelchair giving directions and a bottle of water to two people; four people hugging in the middle of a street glad to find each other; police officers with their arms around people offering them comfort as well as direction. I realized at this point what my dad always said about the blackout of 1964 (he was trapped in the subway) that New Yorkers are people who put all differences aside when in a crisis."[6]

Dad had it right.

"The only way out [for the injured] was by boat."

10:41 a.m.

TWO PEDESTRIAN BRIDGES CROSS WEST SIDE HIGHWAY AT THE WORLD Trade Center, one at the north end near the North Tower and one at the south end near the South Tower. Both were impressive steel-and-glass structures some 400 feet long engineered to support the weight and movement of office workers on a grand scale. In addition to the 50,000 people who worked in the World Trade Center, another 90,000 visited the complex each day, for business or pleasure.[1] "The north bridge was the better of the two bridges," wrote Todd Burkun, a historian of places in New York that are now gone. "It led right into the beautiful atrium of the [World] Financial Center on the west and came right from the lobby of the North Tower of the WTC on the east. The north bridge was so popular there were often flea markets inside it with vendors lined up from end to end along both sides."[2] Tourists often walked the North Pedestrian Bridge just for the sake of doing it. And, for the office workers, a brown-bag lunch with a soft drink made the bridge a cozy pace to get away from it all.

On September 11, as the North Tower collapsed, so too did the North Pedestrian Bridge. West Side Highway, the primary evacuation route uptown, was now blocked.

Over on Staten Island, Deputy Chief Charles R. Blaich, FDNY, knew nothing about a collapsed bridge. In fact, he wasn't downtown at all but rather he was at home when he got a call from his brother William

Blaich, a firefighter whose station was in Manhattan, telling him they were needed. Together, they went down to the Staten Island terminal and boarded the ferry.[3] It was packed with first responders all anxious to get to Manhattan and help. For a moment, though, it seemed they would not.

They departed Staten Island and made their way across the harbor toward Manhattan. As their ferry neared Manhattan, it made a slight turn up the mouth of the East River. At that moment, the North Tower collapsed, which sent an avalanche of smoke and debris toward the ferry. The engines on the boat suddenly shuddered to a halt. "At about Governors Island, the towers came down," said Blaich in an interview. "The boat stopped; the captain could not see the terminal." Blaich and the others feared the captain would turn the boat around so the first responders protested—they needed to get ashore.[4] "Finally," said Blaich, "after urging the ferry captain to put in, we docked."[5]

The brothers split up and headed into the teeth of the catastrophe. William Blaich hurried to his station; Charles Blaich raced up the West Side Highway as far as he could, which was Liberty Street. There he climbed on top of a wrecked vehicle to see what lay ahead. The air was toxic and hazy; the site seemed to have three inches of grey powder covering everything, including numerous bodies and body parts. To his right was the flattened remains of the South Tower, while ahead was the massive pile of the North Tower. In between, he saw the North Pedestrian Bridge blocking the entire width of the West Side Highway, meaning his primary route north for the ambulances was shot. "North/south travel on this side of the WTC complex was impossible," concluded Blaich. "We couldn't move ambulances north or south and the only way out [for the injured] was by boat."[6,7]

Paramedic Marc Cohen, Battalion 22, EMS FDNY, agreed with that assessment. "I mean, there was no way anybody could get through," he said in his interview. "There was like a huge pile of debris now on the West Side Highway."[8]

Blaich sent his EMS people to comb the pile for anyone who was alive, and to search the edges and the voids. He told them to leave the dead for now, that their mission was rescue, not recovery. "[The] victims that they could see in the pile had I-beams through them and things like that," explained Blaich in his interview. "We just didn't have the time to invest in bringing out dead bodies. We were trying to find live bodies. We were tentatively directing the volunteers to start fanning out on top of the pile to see if we could make any spot rescues, if anyone was alive."[9] EMT Loutsky was one of the medics who helped. Remarkably, he had some success. "We went out looking for survivors again. There wasn't anyone on the streets, but there were people in the buildings, in the basements, hiding," he said.[10]

Now how to get them out.

—❦—

Deputy Chief Peter Hayden, FDNY, arrived on scene and he, too, climb on top of a vehicle. "I saw the rig. I got on top of the rig and I stayed there. And eventually we got a bullhorn, a radio. I had a bullhorn and we were able to get some type of order in the assignments and what we were doing." Hayden had a view of the towers, or what was left of them. "It was unbelievable, the devastation," he said of what he could see. "West Street didn't exist anymore. It was just covered in debris."[11] Firefighters were looking for direction, so he took the opportunity to address them. He asked for quiet. "I gathered everybody around me," said Hayden. "There were hundreds of guys and there was a lot of confusion. I had everybody take their helmets off for a moment of silence, and it calmed everybody down. Then, I said 'whether you're on duty or off duty, give them your name, your unit, and give it in to the chiefs.'" Hayden then handed out orders sending some companies to contain the fires at 90 West and others to an apartment building on fire in Battery Park City. "Keep the fire from jumping the street," he said.[12]

No one needed more problems.

"We started putting the women and children on boats to get them over to New Jersey."

11:00 a.m.

THE BOATS AND FERRIES WERE NOW, AS ONE SURVIVOR PUT IT, "(THE) last hope of getting off the island."[1] "All the roads were closed," said FDNY Captain Lou Guzzo of the situation. "The bridges were closed. The tunnels were closed, and the only way to get around was by water."[2]

The ferry's had their terminals but the others docked wherever and however they could. Many of the boats pulled into the North Cove Marina near the North Tower. Some docked at the Coast Guard pier on the southern tip of the island. Still more nosed in wherever they saw a cluster of survivors "[The boats] just kept going," said EMT Penn. "[They] kept going back and forth."[3]

But it wasn't working, not on a large scale. "It was chaos," remembered US Coast Guard Lieutenant Mike Day, Chief of Activities New York. "Every channel you clicked to, people were screaming 'Help! I need people over here! I've got someone hurt here!' Everyone was talking over everyone."[4]

Worse, passengers were at risk of drowning. "There was a small boat that was at the lower tip of Manhattan," said Lt. Day. "I thought the boat was going to flip over 'cause so many people were trying to get on. As I looked behind [it], there were just 10 [people] deep [waiting to get off the island]. That's what kind of gave us the idea [to organize an evacuation]."[5]

In a stroke of good timing, New York Harbor pilot Andrew McGovern was enroute to a port safety meeting in Manhattan, but upon hearing of the attacks, he turned around and headed to the US Coast Guard's Vessel Traffic Service Center on Staten Island and met with Lt. Day. Together, McGovern and Day came up with a plan to organize the blizzard of boats sailing toward Manhattan. Because civilian vessels were the only vessels with the lift capacity to mount a large-scale evacuation, and because the Coast Guard vessels would be largely focused on harbor security, they decided that they needed to have two voices on the radios, one that was well-known to the maritime community, and one that represented the authority of the Coast Guard. Lt. Day and McGovern agreed that the New York Harbor pilots would direct the movements of the civilian boats to and from the seawall, while the Coast Guard would do what they had to do—secure the mouth of the harbor, and control the movements of the dozens of USCG boats in the upper bay, on the East River, and up the Hudson River. New York Harbor pilot Jack Ackerman was their choice for the civilian voice, and Lt. Day would represent the Coast Guard.[6] "One of the advantages that the maritime industry people have over the Coast Guard is that we know most of the vessels that work in the harbor because we've been here all our life," said Ackerman, of the arrangement. "We kind of know the size of vessels, we know the capabilities of the vessels, we can understand where they can fit and where they can't fit."[7]

More to the point, said Ackerman of the chaos in the harbor: "This had to get better organized."[8]

That a civilian like Ackerman would be so directly involved in the management of a crisis of this magnitude had much to do with the hierarchy of the harbor. Of all the mariners plying the waters, harbor pilots were the most knowledgeable of the bunch. They were the ones who boarded passenger liners, tankers, and freighters out in the Atlantic Ocean and guided them through the shoals up the deep-water channels to wherever the ship was supposed to dock. Because they had to work in rain, sleet, snow, or fog, they had to be able to draw a map of New York Harbor from memory including every inlet, river, creek, and pier and the water depths across the entire network of waterways and twisting shorelines. To finish their license, a harbor pilot spent five years as an apprentice under another pilot until he had at least 1,000 transits in and out of the harbor.[9]

However sensible the plan was, it lacked one key element. To make it work, Ackerman and Lt. Day needed to be in sync with the flux of people ashore and the status of available boats on the harbor. They needed to get their eyes on the scene and for that to happen, they needed the near impossible—they needed a boat that would act like the control tower at LaGuardia Airport except it would be standing in the middle of the harbor in 60 feet of water with an elevated, 360-degree view. As it happened, there was one such a vessel. "I placed a call to the Sandy Hook Pilot station asking for the pilot boat *New York*," McGovern remembered.[10] A sturdy, stable 182-foot vessel with a bridge that was elevated above the main deck, the *New York* had windows uniquely configured to provide a 360-degree view of the harbor, plus it had a bank of radios on the bridge that operated on nearly every conceivable frequency, making it possible to communicate with vessels foreign and domestic, official and civilian.

Ackerman and Lt. Day boarded the *New York* and were taken into the harbor off the tip of Manhattan. Around them, the waters were the maritime equivalent of Times Square on a Saturday night. Boats were in motion, wakes crossed wakes, bows pitched up and down. "When we got up there, it was amazing to see the amount of maritime traffic that was in the area," remembered Ackerman. "We had tugboats up there, we had municipal tankers, we had water taxies, we had ferries." The *New York* moved parallel to the curvature of the southern tip of Manhattan bringing into view the docks and terminals as far up the Hudson River as the North Cove Marina and the NY Waterway piers. People were lining the shore up and down the Battery waiting for a boat to nose in and take them off. A procedure was initiated. "As [the individual boats] responded, they were asked to contact the pilot boat on channel 73, which they did," said Ackerman. "When they contacted us, we got their name of their boat, the size of their boat, the draft, how many people they thought they could fit on the boat, that kind of information. [We] knew the height of tug, how high the deck was, what wall he could get along side of so the people could step into the boat rather than have to climb down or climb up into a boat. And then using that information we were able to disperse them throughout the lower part of Manhattan. Our job was to direct the different vessels to different areas to move resources around the whole tip of the Battery from South Street Seaport up to and including the World Financial Center."[11, 12]

Once on location, Lt. Day radioed the Coast Guard administrative station on the tip of the Battery and asked them to send out a Coast Guard ensign, which he promptly raised on the *New York*. He also asked for Coast Guard caps, which he had the Coasties wear, all the better to reinforce, visually, that the Coast Guard was on scene. Having a system in place, there was one more step. Sometime between 10:28, and 10:45 a.m. Lt. Day broadcast a notice to mariners that would become the first formal notice that an evacuation of Manhattan was now officially underway. "We got on the radio and said 'United States Coast Guard aboard the pilot boat *New York*. All mariners, we appreciate your assistance.'"[13] According to other accounts, his message was slightly different. "All available boats," he broadcast. "This is the United States Coast Guard aboard the pilot boat *New York*. Anyone wanting to help with the evacuation of Lower Manhattan report to Governors Island."[14]

Either way, the call crackled over the airways and notice was sent.

Manhattan was being evacuated.

It was official.

And it was by boat.

"There are twenty-seven to thirty tugboats sitting there."

11:05 a.m.

THE IMPERATIVE TO EVACUATE BY BOAT WAS DRIVEN BY MORE THAN THE proximity to the harbor and the fact that so many vital streets had been blocked by debris. Power grids across Lower Manhattan had failed or were failing, a half-dozen office buildings were engulfed in flames; fire engines burned, ambulances lay crushed in the streets, medical supplies were wiped out. "We had nothing," said EMT John Rothmund, Battalion 22, EMS FDNY. "We didn't like the idea of having a triage here because we had nothing. We started putting the women and children on boats to get them over to New Jersey."

"No subways or buses were running. There was no running water, no electricity," said survivor Owen Burdick in his oral history. "The city around us was dead."

Standing against that seawall, the crew of the fireboat the *John J. Harvey* were loading the injured onto her decks. The *Harvey* was a floating museum, retired years ago by the FDNY but saved from the scrap heap by a volunteer group who used it for ceremonial purposes. It was a big boat painted in the distinctive red of the FDNY with monitors and nozzles pointed skyward ready for the next display of her powerful spray that arced over arriving ships.

When the North Tower's smoke started to curl into the sky, the team associated with the *Harvey* spontaneously got underway and took her down to the Battery to offer their assistance. "To make a long story short," said Huntley Gill, one of the volunteers, "by the time we got down to the Battery, both towers had collapsed. The Coast Guard were on channel 13, which is the channel that all the big boats use to talk to each other asking every vessel in the harbor to please go down to the Battery, go down to Pier 11 on the East River and get people off the island of Manhattan. By the time I figured we had about 150 people, which is about twice what we ever like to carry, we stopped people from getting on the boat. We headed back up the North River toward Pier 40 at Halston Street." There they offloaded their first group of survivors after which they turned back and came alongside the seawall again.

Battalion chief Dominick DeRubbio, Battalion 21, Field Communication, saw the fireboats being loaded with the injured. He went over to the crew and asked them to get a message broadcast on the radio. "I told the pilot in the marine company, 'Tell the dispatcher—any injured people, bring them to the Hudson River.'"[1] Officer Peter Moog, a New York police department technician, heard the message on the police frequency. EMS chief Robert McCracken was issuing the same order to anyone he saw, not by radio, but by word-of-mouth as he walked. *Go south. Get the injured to the boats.*

EMT Loutsky quickly made the transition from EMS responder to traffic cop. He went down to water. "I was directing people—the general public—onto ferry boats to Brooklyn, Staten Island, New Jersey. There were hundreds and hundreds of people. I did that for 12 hours; lost my voice," he remembered. "I wasn't doing any EMS; I was just working as part of an evacuation operation."[2]

⌣⌣

Tugboat captain Ken Peterson approached the seawall around Lower Manhattan. Peterson was a well-known fixture in the maritime community, having worked on the harbor for nearly two decades. "[W]e all worked together. As I mentioned before, we're a small . . . community. We all know who knows what to do and who's better at it. . . . I knew a lot of the other captains from being in New York Harbor for the last 18 years working on the tugboats and small harbor tankers through the harbor, and cleaning oil spills. It's that small of a community. Everybody knows everybody."[3]

Peterson had left his Staten Island docks with four of his tugboats and crossed the harbor only to run into at least twelve other tugs holding short of the Battery, idling their engines in the waters off the southern tip of Manhattan.[4] Peterson knew what that meant. The emergency boats were coming and going but they were police and harbor patrol boats. The ferries were coming and going and they, too, had tacit permission. After all, they had their docks, but the tugs were different. Any of them could easily and safely navigate directly into the seawall and take survivors, but it wasn't the sort of thing anyone wanted to do without the blessing of the Coast Guard. Peterson picked up his microphone. "I made the radio transmission on channel 13 to the US Coast Guard and said, 'There's 10 or 15 tugboats out here.'" Peterson told them he wanted their permission to go into the seawall and evacuate people. "A few minutes later they called back and said 'Reinauer, you have permission to get on the island.' I got on the radio and said, 'break, break on channel 13, this is Kenny Peterson. All of Reinauer boats—and anybody else—let's go and get the people.' And that's when we got on the lower Battery wall of Manhattan right by the Staten Island ferry."[5]

"We didn't know exactly what we were going into, once we got on-scene," said tugboat deckhand Mike Scanlon of the *Vivian Roehrig*. "My first experience? We started taking people on and the first passenger on was a woman, and she wasn't talking. She was crying and another woman was holding her. She asked if we could help. I said that's why we're here. She said she just lost her husband. Walking with him one minute and the next minute he's gone. I started getting caught up in her emotion. I told myself I need to calm myself."[6]

Wayne Carnis, the captain on one of the first tugs to get to the seawall, warned his crew to be prepared for the scene they might encounter. There would be injuries, he said, and very possibly people in the water. "I told them to get all the lifesaving equipment available on deck and be ready to activate the life raft—anything that floats be ready to throw it in."[7]

The Moran Company, another well-known and respected operator on the harbor, sent eleven of its tugs to the seawall. One of the evacuees heard a boat captain calling out the tug's destination much as a train conductor would do standing next to a train on the tracks. "I wandered in circles for half hour or so wondering what to do," she said. "I started east when I heard a tugboat calling out, 'Atlantic Avenue in Brooklyn, the *Miriam Moran* is headed for Brooklyn.' He kept calling this out over his speaker. I ran to it. He called out, again over his speaker, 'Don't run, we ain't leavin' yet.' I walked to it and got on. I was so thankful and finally relieved. I felt safer the further I got from Manhattan."[8]

But not everybody slowed down. As accommodating as the captains were, as reassuring as they tried to sound, no one wanted to be anywhere near ground zero. Most rushed the tugs as if they were going to disappear. "We all looked a little dumbfounded because people are just trying to climb over all the railings and just getting off the island," said tugboat captain Peterson. "[The only way to keep it organized] was to get cardboard or sheets, pillowcases, blankets, or something and have someone tape it onto the forward end of the tugs [with the tugs destination written in big letters]. We were doing 5th Ave., Brooklyn, Jersey City, Jersey Square. We felt like a regular taxicab business. We were saying, 'you're going [to that boat]. Where are you going? You go [to that boat].' By the time I would turn around, there are 27 to 30 tugboats sitting there. As one would move out all I would do is say, 'The McAlister boat come in here, he's moving out.' They would leave and call me back on channel 73 and say, 'Where do you want us now?' I would say, 'Just get in line and everyone slide down [the seawall].'"[9]

By 11:30 a.m., tugboats were shoulder-to-shoulder against the seawall, one tug bumping up against another, their bows so close that, as one captain from the Maritime Academy put it, you could walk up the river, going bow-to-bow. Engines churned to hold bows firm against the tide. The crews negotiated the waves coming in from the harbor and the shear vertical seawall of concrete and steel now ten feet to the railing. It was risky seamanship, but the captains shrugged it off. Said one, "Pushing the tug into the seawall was no different from facing the clifflike sides of a ship."[10] One captain estimated that at its peak, there were 27 tugs around the Battery and five others at Pier 11. Others put the number as high as 40 on the Battery alone. Whatever the number, pictures from that day show one thing to be true: Tugs were packed against the seawall like sardines.[11] "It was pretty awesome to watch," said USCG Chief Petty Officer Brandon Brewer, who was in the Coast Guard's building on the tip of Manhattan. He had an unobstructed view of the evacuation. "The tug crews built homemade signs and hung up sheets they had spray-painted from the railings so people would know what boat was going where. The captains and their crews were on the dock with the police officers and firefighters directing everyone on to the boats. I think it was very calming to people that they would arrive and be told where they needed to go almost right away."[12, 13] The Coast Guard also put people ashore. They, too, directed survivors toward the tugs and boats. One coastguardsman heard the people on a tug cheering in approval as they left the seawall.[14] By the end of the day, more than 5,000 people would be taken off the island by the harbor tugs.[15]

And so it went. Every vessel now had a point of contact on the pilot boat while on the land, nerved-frayed survivors now had the reassuring voice of a deckhand standing among them and a sign hanging before them.

It was the beginning of a ballet of sorts, one that was being choreographed on the water.

For the next ten hours, New York was about to see the performance of a lifetime.

CHAPTER 33

"Get the hell out of the city."

11:10 a.m.

EMS CHIEF ROBERT MCCRACKEN HAD BEEN THROUGH ENOUGH CLOSE calls to last a lifetime, but that didn't stop him. He was nearly killed in the collapses, entombed once, covered in dust and debris, but survived. In the dark fog of the smoke he even rescued one small infant and helped the mother and child to safety, then escorted another group of survivors out. By any measure, he'd done enough, but instead he went back into the pile. "I'm going to make sure everybody's OK," he said to one of the chiefs as they passed each other in the debris. He ran into other first responders, not many of them, or at least he remembered it that way, but each time he did, he told them to get their survivors down to the ferry terminal, that they would triage and transport from there. "I walked back and started searching all the stores. I saw people [who] made it into stores: [I said] 'Get out, I don't know what else is coming.'"[1]

McCracken turned toward the ferry terminal, but on the way encountered a large crowd of survivors who were reluctant to evacuate. "When I got down to Robert Wagner Park—by Battery Park—there were close to 1,500 people [there]," he said. "For some strange reason, this little piece of real estate had good air quality." Maybe it was the clean air; maybe it was the human need to find order in the midst of chaos, but they all wanted to go back to their apartments or homes, to clean up, pack, or feed a dog or a cat. In a word, they wanted to go north, back to the pile and into the debris. McCracken would have none of it. "Everybody kept saying, 'We got to go through [the smoke and debris cloud].' I kept saying, 'I don't know what's on the other side of that smoke. We're not going. We're staying; at least we're in a safe haven.'"

McCracken had someone radio for a boat and soon he had ferries and harbor boats up against the seawall—but again his efforts were met with resistance. "People were taking [their] time to say goodbye to their loved ones and [asking], 'Where are [the boats] going?' I tried to tell them, 'Listen, forget all that. We've got to get you out of here.' After we got most of them out, we had about 200 stragglers who still weren't getting on the available boats. The only way I could get to their emotions was by saying, 'People, you have to go now. You have no choice. You're stopping us from effecting another rescue. By us sitting here, negotiating with you to get on the boats, we cannot move forward."[2]

EMT captain Frank D'Amato, EMS Bureau of Communications, pitched in. D'Amato had been caught in both collapses. When the second tower came down, he was on the esplanade bordering the Hudson. "Everybody starts running south on this little boardwalk," he told an interviewer. "A lot of people were tripping and falling. I remember seeing like parents holding children in their hand like covering their mouth and trying to run with them."[3] Although he was covered in dust, D'Amato ran into McCracken and helped get the people on the boats. "At that point there was police boats, fire boats, tugboats," remembered D'Amato. "We started loading people onto the boats and the boats were taking people to Liberty State Park and Staten Island. It took us about 20 minutes to clear that area. After we cleared that area, an EMT pulled up in like golf cart and [we] jumped in and went to the Staten Island Ferry terminal."[4]

❧

The burning towers were news items, and reporters and photographers streamed down to the site. David Handschuh, a newspaper photographer, was driving down the West Side Highway when a fire engine rocketed past him on the wrong side of the road. Handschuh jerked his car out of his lane, jumped the median into the opposing traffic, and tailgated the rig down to ground zero. When he could go no further, he got out of his car and started taking pictures, ultimately walking as far as the Marriot, 100 yards from the base of the South Tower just as the collapse began. He tried to outrun it, but he was much too close. His leg was crushed, and he was half buried. Miraculously, two firefighters found him and carried him to a nearby deli that was trashed but not destroyed. But then the North Tower came down and more debris poured in including chunks blown through the broken front windows.[5] When the dust cleared and they could see, the police officers went out to find help.

Charlie Wells made it into the same delicatessen and helped himself to some water to wash out his eyes and mouth. He was tired. The collapses caught him head on, one blowing him through the door of the Marriott's Tall Ships bar where he had to dig himself out. After that, he helped nearly 80 people find their way to safety. "We brought this group out of the bar and directed them to the river," said Wells. "Fifty to eighty civilians or residents. We brought them out to Liberty and West and crossed them over to the World Financial Center. Then I went back into the Marriott bar and found more people. I had no communication. I just looked for other EMS people and more people to get them out."[6]

He went into the deli and started washing his eyes as he tried to regroup. "I went into their refrigerator and started pouring whatever I could find on my face," he remembered. "All of a sudden, a voice behind me goes, 'Buddy can you help me?' I turned around and there was the form of a person lying on the floor. I didn't see him when I climbed through the window. I said, 'Hey, sure. I'll help you. I'll get you out of here.' All of a sudden, he said, 'Are you Charlie Wells?' I turned around and it was Dave Handschuh, a New York *Daily News* photographer. He had a fractured tib-fib. He said three firefighters got him in the deli. I go, 'Your leg's broken,' and he goes, 'I can't get up.' I said, 'Okay, fine, I'll get you out of here, but we will be moving fast. I don't know what the hell happened.' I grabbed him and started dragging him out the door. There was nothing to splint him. I said, 'Just cross your legs and I'm gonna drag you out head first.' He screamed when we went over the lip of the broken door. So, he starts moving with me, and he says to me—he goes 'You know that one of the towers has collapsed.' So, I go, 'No, no I wasn't aware of that.' He says, 'Because I took a picture of it as it was happening. That's how I got caught up and then got blown around.' So, I go, 'All right.' A couple of firemen and a cop came over and we picked him up and moved him all the way to the marina." In fact, Chief Wells did make a splint. To ease Handschuh's pain, Wells made a splint from a few loaves of bread and wrapped Handschuh legs in the cellophane used to wrap a sandwich.[7] Said Wells: "We got him on a police harbor unit and that was the last I saw of him that day."

Handschuh was taken to Liberty Island where he was triaged and sent onward to a hospital in Bayonne, New Jersey. On his part, Wells started the long walk down the esplanade toward the Staten Island Ferry Terminal, his boots stirring up a cloud of debris as he shuffled his feet. He sent every person he saw to the boats. "People started coming [up to me]," said Wells. "They wanted to know where to go. If they were walking and there were no obvious signs of bleeding, we told them to keep walking to the marina. We said just go to the water. Just go to the—get on the boat, get the hell out of the city."[8]

More studied in his response was EMS Chief Kowalczyk. "In our minds," said Kowalczyk, "southern Manhattan was questionable from a safety perspective."[9]

But the message was the same.

Get the hell out of the city.

"Just like the *Titanic.*"

11:15 a.m.

THE MEDICS IN THE SOUTHERN SECTOR WERE ACCOMPLISHING THE impossible. However grave the peril, search parties were walking the perimeter, checking the voids, and finding more survivors. Others were continuing to direct people away from the collapse. Deputy Chief Robert Browne, Division 4, EMS FDNY, found a half dozen other EMTs around Albany and South End. Together they started funneling people to the boats. "There were hundreds and hundreds of people running down that promenade," said Browne. "All kinds of boats were pulling up. The fire boat had pulled up and docked, several other boats, a police boat, there was a tugboat there, there were civilian boats pulling up, and they were going to take them over to Jersey for us."[1]

"There was only ten of us, maybe give or take," said paramedic Karen Lamanna. "We started getting lot of people coming toward us having difficulty breathing and stuff in the eyes, so we started treating for that. Then it was decided we would start putting people on boats and get them out of there. We were sending them wherever [the boats] were going—Staten Island, Jersey City, wherever—just to get them out of there because we didn't know what was going to happen next."[2]

Browne saw a simple way to load the boats more efficiently. He took it upon himself to create a sort of triage-within-a-triage. "I got together the crews there," he said. "We would evaluate people before we put them on the boat because we wanted to put all the non-injured people on one boat, and we wanted to put the injured people on another boat." The clarity of that idea was astonishing, more so that no one had yet thought of it; one boat for the injured, one for the others. Said Browne: "We loaded hundreds and hundreds of people onto those boats that [way]."[3]

Firefighter Howie Scott, Squad 18, FDNY, followed Browne's strategy as he helped people evacuate. "All [those] boats were coming over from Hoboken now, all those ferries," he said "Anybody that was banged up, I got them on just one boat and got them out of there, and the other boats, we were just moving people [out of Manhattan]."[4]

More pockets of survivors were being found, nearly all of them sheltering in place unable or afraid to leave where they were. What was coming next? Where was I going to be safe? Best to stay in place, many of them reasoned.

EMT David Blacksberg, Battalion 31, EMS FDNY, found a group of ten or twelve civilians, he's wasn't sure of the exact number, but he wasn't going to lose a single one of them. He had them form a human chain and got them moving through the haze and debris toward the water. "One girl was telling me she was from the 63rd floor and another was telling me she was from the 84th," he later remembered, no doubt amazed at the impossibly long walk they endured down smoke-filled stairwells. "We were directing as many people as we could find. Injured, non-injured. We were putting people on the boats." Not everyone automatically complied. Some asked Blacksberg what would happen next, how would they get home from wherever the boast left them? "I told them, 'It [doesn't] matter where [the boat is] going. You'll always find a way home.'"[5]

Miracles were to be found in the clouds of smoke. A survivor named Michelle was a temp with a company in the World Financial Center complex of buildings. She saw the planes hit, the jumpers, the fires, the collapses. She was overwhelmed by the nightmare of it all, but pressed forward. She ran into a woman named Shira who at the time was helping a man with an injury. Michelle pitched in. She found some napkins and they patched him up and afterward they stayed close, and were caught in the collapse and darkness. "I remember Michelle saying, 'Shira, I can't see you—where are you?' I cracked my eyes open and they stung—I found her hand and held it. [I said] 'I want to go home and see my baby, Michelle.' 'You will,' she said, 'you're going to go home and see him.'"[6]

Just then, they heard a voice in the darkness. *Follow me! Join hands and follow me!* it said. "I will remember it as long as I live," said Shira. "I later told my family that it reminded me of something Jesus might say, were he here in flesh. 'Join hands and follow me—follow the sound of my voice.' We joined and we followed. He led us into a building across the street, all of us. It was clean, and the air was good. They had supplies, [clean] torn up rags, and cases of bottled water. We were given what we needed and asked if we were alright. I was never so grateful for anything in my whole life."[7]

The voice was almost surely that of paramedic Joe Jefferson, Battalion 26, EMS, FDNY. Jefferson had narrowly survived the first collapse by squeezing into a window well and making himself as small as possible, but even so, he was hit in the back by falling debris. When rational thinking was possible again, he tried to make sense of where he was. Around him it was as black as night, the air was thick with grit, and familiar references nonexistent. "I heard a couple of secondary explosions and some vehicles were engulfed in flames," he later recalled. "I go, 'this is not the place to be.' I grabbed my trauma bag and started feeling around. I called out for help a couple of times for myself then I realized I'm supposed to be the help." He mentally switched gears. "I started telling people 'come toward my voice, come toward my voice' because I knew I was on West Street. I didn't know exactly where, but I knew that if they were further [back] where the buildings were, they should probably come out toward this way and walk up toward the South Ferry."

In minutes, survivors began staggering toward him, surely Michelle and Shira among them. Jefferson looked them over for injuries, then had them form a group and together they started walking south until they were slammed by the second collapse. They ducked inside a building and sheltered again. While there Jefferson treated a leg injury and a few others. "After cleaning them up we did head count and we had like about 20 people," he remembered. "I told them, 'listen,' I said; 'Remember my name. I'm paramedic Jefferson and I'm going to get you guys out of here. There are some bathroom facilities here and there are some phones. If you want to make a phone call or something do that, and I'll be back in a couple minutes and were going to get you out of here. I don't know exactly how, but just stay put we're going to get you guys as far to safety as we can.'"

They did as they were told.

Jefferson came back to direct them down to the boats then went back into the destruction to see who else he could help.

— ❦ —

Across the collapse zone, survivors were cautiously making their way out, many under their own steam, most of them headed toward the water. Richard LoPresti, a survivor from the North Tower, made his way down the sidewalk and through Battery Park. He had no destination in mind save one: He wanted to get off the island. "We never made it. Tower 1 collapsed with the same furious sound as Tower 2." He said. "It looked like a volcano."[8] LoPresti survived the volcano and ultimately reached the harbor where saw the boats nosing into the seawall. "We saw Coast Guard, fire boats and the New York Waterway ferries from New Jersey come to rescue us. 'Women and children first,' I commented. 'Just like the Titanic.'" LoPresti recently completed bypass surgery so he was in no shape to climb a fence or jump on a ferry. "I had to be picked up fireman's style and placed on the deck. I was given first class treatment by the deck hand, checking on me later to see if I was all right."[9]

Julia Frey, an author and resident of Battery Park City, made it down to the waterfront and saw the mass of rescue boats and the people going over the railing to escape. "There were a lot of people clinging to the esplanade," she said in a later interview. "Ferry boats, tugboats, motorboats, fishing boats, sail boats, police boats were pulling up to the esplanade and breaking down the rails and people were climbing over the rails and being taken on boats."[10]

Matthew Harttree, the guest in the Marriott Hotel who paused to look down at the firemen in the lobby, made it down to the boats too. Like so many, he worried that there would be another attack. "I was in Battery Park City and somehow managed to walk all the way to the railing near the river. I was about to jump in because, simply put, I needed to get off that island." But a patrol boat from the New York Police Department was in the marina and an officer saw him leaning over. "Don't jump," he yelled. "Just come down here!" Harttree looked over and saw the police officer and followed his instructions. Good thing. He was slowly losing consciousness. "They put me on the boat, and I passed out for a bit," he remembered. "I was then taken to a drop-off point across the river, put on an ambulance, and taken to the hospital." He was admitted with a laundry list of injuries including cuts across his back, blows to his head, a hurt knee, and lungs filled with pulverized cement.[11]

NYPD lieutenant Tim McGinn, Commanding Officer/Barriers, was one of those unsmiling officers one sees manning the blue crowd control barriers at large events like football games and celebrity appearances —and around accident sites. But on September 11, instead of manning barriers, McGinn was helping people get over them. Between the first and second collapse, he organized a group of survivors he found sheltering in a building near the marina. As soon as the smoke cleared, he identified himself as a police officer and addressed them in clear, simple language. "We're going to evacuate," he said. "As soon as you come out the door, make a left and continue south on the esplanade to the South Cove Marina." He helped 30 or 40 people down to the waterfront that morning—he wasn't sure of the number—but he later recalled that they included an injured fireman, a dozen other assorted emergency workers, a woman who was pregnant, another woman who was elderly, and a third woman who was blind. "We sent them on their way down to the boats and to New Jersey," he said.[12]

One of the evacuees on the New Jersey side was too young to thank his rescuer but he gave them all a shot in the arm. The evacuee was a baby. A police officer carried the small boy off one of the boats. The child was struggling to breath and was fading in and out. Officer Elba Garnier D'Aiuto cradled the baby hoping for a small miracle. "He wasn't breathing when he came off the boat," said D'Aiuto. "I passed him to the EMTs and they were trying to revive him." She was later told the child made it.[13]

And that was the only thanks they needed.

One more life saved.

Todd Maisel, the newspaper photographer, had an eye for history. He was at ground zero looking for his friends and people he knew. "I wanted to find out who was still alive. I had a lot of friends who went into that building—firefighter friends, my neighbors in Marine Park, Stuy Town people, the cops, the people I had photographed before the building fell down. I started searching around until I found a firefighter, Kevin Shea, in the debris. He'd lost his entire company. He was the only survivor." Maisel yelled for help. "A lot of guys came over," he remembered. They needed a backboard, so Maisel took off to find one. "I found an ambulance but couldn't open it. I saw a second ambulance overturned, though, and was able to get the door open. I pulled the backboard out and dragged it back over to where Kevin was lying. The other guys loaded him onto it, and we all carried it out." Before they left, Maisel took a picture. The photograph shows a man prone on the ground unmoving, his body buried in the twisted, grey rubble, a fireman kneeling next to him and pointing west toward Albany Street, two EMS techs bending forward to examine him, and a police officer in the middle. They all look the same—distraught shapes covered in the grey soot of the collapse.

"We took [Shea] one block west into a parking garage where there were a bunch of people huddled," continued Al Kim, a MetroCare medic.[14, 15] "One of the women said she was a physician." It turned out to be Chief Medical Officer Kerry Kelly, the doctor who was with a patient in Elmhurst and had to leave when her beeper went off. Kelly bent over Shea and talked to him. "He [was] bleeding from his head," said Kelly. "He was complaining about his right lower abdomen, and it looked like part of his finger had been sliced off." Dr. Kelly comforted Shea, cleaned him up, but there was little more she could do. Around her there were injuries enough to swamp an emergency room even in a city the size of New York. One person had a broken leg, a firefighter named Mattie had a broken ankle, another unidentified firefighter had a head wound, and a firefighter named Richard Boeri had a deep laceration.[16] "My whole face was full of blood," said Boeri.[17] But neither Shea nor Boeri—nor any of them—were in any shape to do much more than get to a hospital, as if getting to a hospital was even possible. "They told us, the whole southern sector, you couldn't get to anything [going north]," said Boeri. But neither were they close to the boats. Luckily, they found an ambulance that was in working order. "So, we got [an] ambulance and drove straight west on Albany Street all the way to the river," said Boeri. When they got there, they saw a chain-link fence between them and a patrol boat. "We broke through the chain fence when the police boat pulled up. We [handed] Kevin on the backboard over the side railing and into the police boat. A few minutes later I ended up going on a police boat also."[18]

Most certainly that boat was one of the NYPD Harbor Unit Scuba Team's patrol boats. The scuba team had been navigating their patrol boats up to the seawall to help people wherever they were needed. "We had six or seven boats at that time transporting people back and forth [to Ellis Island]," said James Cowan.[19]

The captain at the helm loaded Dr. Kelly's group then spun his wheel to leave. Dr. Kelly yelled down from the rail, "Where are you taking the guys?"

Someone answered, "Ellis Island."

Kelly worried. Could the Statue of Liberty, maybe even Ellis Island, be next?

The boat crew shrugged it off. Maybe. Maybe not. But they had ambulances waiting at Ellis Island, that was for sure.

CHAPTER 35

"We have no communications with the outside world."

11:25 a.m.

EMS CHIEF JAMES MARTIN, BATTALION 53, FDNY, WAS AT HOME when the attacks began. He was alerted to the crisis by an aid who called and briefed him on the towers and told him he was needed at the site. Martin jumped into his EMS response vehicle and sped toward the Brooklyn Bridge, calling dispatch as he did. "I asked Citywide to do a roll call of EMS officers to determine who was operational and who was not," he said during a debriefing. "No one came over the radio, there was no voice conversation, no one was answering the radio." With no response from Kowalczyk, McCracken, or Gombo, or any other commanding officer, Martin came to the unhappy realization that he might be the only senior EMS chief left. He took a deep breath. "At that point I wasn't sure if people were alive or dead," he said. "It was a very terrifying moment."

Paramedic Kevin Kelleher, Battalion 20 EMS, FDNY, understood the feeling. He faced the same silence as he shuffled through the dust and debris. "It was rather eerie not hearing anything on the radio after the second tower came down," said Kelleher. "We didn't know if we were the only people left down there." Voices, though, slowly came up. Division Chief John Peruggia, EMS FDNY, responded from a point northeast of the towers on Chambers Street; Kowalczyk was with him. Minutes later, McCracken, Gombo, and Chief James Basile, Commander Division 2, EMS FDNY, arrived. Martin hurriedly navigated the roads and parked his car. When he got out, he saw a lifetime of shock and fatigue written across the faces of his fellow chiefs. "(They) were visibly shaken," he said. "They were coping—but you could see that they were really visibly shaken by the incident."[1]

Around the pile, orders were circulating by word-of-mouth or traveling on the radio waves however spotty the coverage—*evacuate to New Jersey; go to the boats*—but no one as yet established a consistent link between Lower Manhattan and the hospitals in New Jersey where patients were being received. So far, the injured had been transported rather well, but inefficiently—there was no central location to triage which meant the EMS crews had been triaging and loading boats from a dozen spots along the seawall. It was a terrible waste of resources at a time when resources were precious. The missing piece was coordination between the EMS crews on the scene and the hospitals in New York and New Jersey. It was a critical problem to be overcome, plus it came with a tricky issue of communication.

As the dust swirled around them, the chiefs put their heads together. "Mind you, we have no communications with the outside world and, in essence, what we were able to see is just what we were able to see on this block," said Chief Gombo speaking of what little information they had versus what the rest of the world was seeing on their televisions. "No phones, no radio communications. We did not know whether there were other buildings in danger of collapsing." What they did know was that the command structure had to be rebuilt, even if it meant creating one in the middle of the devastation and dust. They tossed a spaghetti bowl full of ideas against the wall, and two kept sticking. West Side Highway was blocked; Lower Manhattan was cut off. The division of the site into sectors was still the best way to organize the assets on site, but that had limits. "You couldn't get through West Street, you couldn't get through Liberty Street, you couldn't get through Vesey Street, you couldn't get through Church Street," said Martin. "All the surrounding roadways (were blocked)." But you could get to the ferry terminal, and the ferries could quickly transport patients to the hospitals on Staten Island or over to New Jersey. Why not move the triage sites to places adjacent to the boats, they asked themselves. Everyone knew where these places were and it would speed up the transport of patients and get victims the medical attention they needed, faster. "At that point, the decision was made for the EMS resources to go to two different staging areas on the outskirts of this incident," said Gombo. "The decision was made, on the north, Chelsea Piers because there was a large parking area. On the south, we decided that we would use the ferry terminal, Staten Island Ferry Terminal. So those were the two staging areas that we were going to send (our) EMS resources to. That was the plan."[2]

But another problem loomed. On the average day in the life of EMS, roughly 525 ambulance tours provide 9-1-1 coverage for the city of New York. By late morning, a good portion of those crews were at ground zero—by some estimates 145 ambulances and 31 officers from the 9-1-1 system were there—leaving New York with dangerously thin coverage.[3] Kowalczyk called dispatch to see how the system was faring. Some 4,000 calls had flooded the call center, a nearly two-fold increase over the average day. "When I asked for a call status on the city, the dispatcher indicated that they were holding in excess of 400 assignments [for 9-1-1 help] pending. I had to make a decision. I was looking at the enormity of this situation at the World Trade Center, [but I also] had to be concerned with Mrs. Jones having chest pains in the Bronx or in Brooklyn." Kowalczyk made up his mind. He released 20 ambulance crews back into the 9-1-1 system.[4]

That done, there was one final piece to the puzzle, and it needed to be addressed before they split up. The central EMS dispatch system remained online and was functioning, but there was no centralized EMS command post staffed with senior officers to sort through requests and prioritize orders. Instead, orders were being given on the spot by junior officers without the big picture. Clearly the vacuum had to be filled and a centralized command structure had to be reestablished, and not just for the collapsed towers.[5] "We had to get a citywide command center up because we had a citywide problem," said EMS Chief Goldfarb. "Chief Gombo suggested Police Plaza, so we decided that Gombo and myself would go to Police Plaza to set up the big picture, and Kowalczyk and Pascale would go to Chelsea Piers and work the scene picture and the evacuation piece of it, and we would try and get someone over to the ferry terminal."[6] That "someone" was Chief Basile. A youthful looking veteran,

Basile in fact had more 24 years on the force. "I met with Chief Kowal-czyk, Chief Gombo (and) the other chiefs that were there at the time," said Basile. "I was directed at that point to set up a treatment site over at the ferry terminal."

That decided, they headed out. Basile took a small boat down the Hudson River to the Staten Island Ferry Terminal while Kowalczyk went up to the Chelsea Piers on the Hudson River. Gombo and Goldfarb made their way uptown north to Police Plaza to set up a new EMS command center. "We decided to leave [local decisions] on scene to [the] officers already on scene," remembered Goldfarb, but the big picture would be managed from Police Plaza.[7] Goldfarb was able to get the news out to his first responders in the field. "I was able to break through to citywide dispatcher," he recalled. "We [got] that information to him that we were setting up those two points."[8, 9]

And so the pieces of the puzzle began fitting together. There would be a new command center established and the EMS crews would now have two points from which to stage. "We could [now] coordinate with New Jersey on distributing patients to Jersey hospitals," said Martin.[10] Martin radioed Staten Island and confirmed that their emergency rooms were ready and that they had plenty of ambulances dockside. "[My counterpart on Staten Island] was prepared to transfer numbers of patients from the ferry terminal in St. George to Staten Island hospitals," said Martin. A similar call to the New Jersey EMS services came back with much the same answer: The ambulances were ready, the doctors were ready; all they needed to know was what sort of injuries were headed their way—heart attacks, broken bones, burns, lacerations, and so on—and they'd have the right teams there to meet them.[11]

But there was a hitch. So long as the radios worked, the plan was nearly perfect, but the handheld units were near the end of their battery life and would soon become useless. Thankfully, as Martin got into his car to come downtown he had an afterthought and went back to pick up one more thing. "I brought my little portable radio charger," said Martin. Kowalczyk scarcely hesitated—he made Martin his communications offi-cer and, in turn, said Martin, "we kept just exchanging batteries."[12]

Batteries.

It was a small stroke of genius.

Against the backdrop of two 500,000-ton buildings crumpled to the ground, with the urgent sound of rescue helicopters arcing through the skies and flashing lights on the harbor, and hundreds if not thousands of police, fire, and EMS personal navigating the edges of the pile for survivors, a pocketful of batteries and a small charger did the trick. And in that, there was a comforting familiarity.

CHAPTER 36

"We had to get back in the game."

11:30 a.m.

THE SITUATION NO LONGER LACKED CLARITY—THERE WAS NO MISTAKING what had happened—the shrill alarms of firefighters who were no longer moving was stark witness to that. A brutal attack had leveled much of Lower Manhattan and not even an army of first responders could have done much to change the outcome. "The most frustrating thing was seeing fire trucks collapsed, crushed, firefighters bent over trying to get air, PASS alarms going off," said Chief McCracken. Added EMT Jack Delaney, "We went down there with the expectation of saving a lot of lives. Actuality, for a period of time, we were concentrating on saving our own lives."[1] Said Kowalczyk of his EMS responders, "At this event, the rescuers quickly became victims. We were there to help people, but we became victims."[2]

But hope ran deep. Back in the pile, there were countless "maybes." Maybe there were survivors. Maybe they'd find someone buried in a crevasse that held air. Maybe they'd save one more life. *Check the voids. Check the basements.* It was those thin maybes that were now powering tired muscles and coursing new energy through exhausted bodies.

EMS captain Mark Stone, commanding officer, Battalion 8, was fueled by those "maybes." He survived the collapses with a group of dusty, worn-out firefighters and EMS responders. They escaped to the Hudson River and stopped to collect their thoughts. "That's where we walked, just right to the water, which wasn't far. At that point I said out loud, 'Okay. Let me get my thoughts together. . . . We got to go back to work.' One of the firemen looked at me and he said, 'are you stupid.' I said 'yes, in this case I must be.' I mean, people were jumping on boats at that point, because there were boats lined up on the Hudson, and I thought of doing that [too]."

But if Mark Stone was stupid, they all were. Being tired was one thing; actually getting on a boat was another. It was tempting, but leaving wasn't an option. "I still had a job to do," said Stone. "Being a captain, there are still many people that are under me who are going to look to me for guidance and support. There are also chiefs that really need me to function. So, I took a few seconds. I took a few deep breaths."³

And he went back.

EMT Michael Mejias was as tired and worn out as anyone. He had every right to evacuate. Instead, he loaded a stretcher with as many supplies as he could scavenge. "We had to get back in the game," he said.⁴

"Everybody's running back—firemen, policemen, EMTs, paramedics —because we've got men in there," added Mejias's partner, EMT Jody Bell. "That was everybody's first [priority] not even hesitating, [we] just made a U-turn and started heading back."⁵

"There was just no way of keeping them out," said EMT Lamanna. "A lot of firefighters wanted to be treated [by us so they could] go right back to the scene."⁶ And it worked both ways. "It gave me purpose," said EMT Jennifer Beckham of the time she spent patching people up and watching them go back. "Being able to be an EMT; it kept me sane."⁷

The boat captains went back too, men and women not paid to run *toward* a calamity, not hardened by years of dealing with emergencies. "We knew we had to go back, but we didn't know what was going to happen to us," said Jim Peresi. "We were hearing that there were four planes still in the air. We heard they just hit the Pentagon. You know, you don't know what to expect. We're figuring [the terrorists are] coming back up here so, yeah, going up [to Manhattan to take on passengers], you didn't know if you were coming back. You didn't know. That's probably the hardest part about it."⁸

"We were afraid, but we were not afraid," said EMT Immaculada Gattas, Division 6, FDNY, putting it into her own words. "We never thought about dying, we only thought about helping other people."⁹

New Jersey trooper Joe DeMarino ran back and forth as many as twenty times. The ferries went back and forth. The tugboats went back and forth. And then they all went back again.

Just one life saved made it more than worth it.

━⌣

Robert Wick saved at least one life, maybe more. Wick, an EMT from the medical center in Flushing, New York, found an ESU officer prone on the ground covered in dust and struggling to breathe. "He was gagging and coughing on the debris. I helped him up to walk a block. That was where the water was—New York City Harbor. A harbor patrol started putting everybody into the boat." Wick knew the police officer needed oxygen, so he got on the boat with him and found an oxygen tank and even a mask, but no tools to tighten down the regulator. Police officers have knives and small multipin-purpose pocket tools, so on a gamble he reached into the officer's pockets and found what he needed. "I used the cop's Leatherman [tool] to tighten it down."[10] He attached the mask to the regulator and turned on the gas and heard the wheezing sound of life-saving oxygen pouring into his patient's lungs. Now all he needed was to get to a hospital. Wick watched the captain work the engines and finally breathed a sigh of relief. "There was still a lot of smoke, and you could hardly see anything," said Wick. "[But the boat] took off across the water [toward New Jersey]."[11]

Firefighter Lt. Sean O'Malley could barely see. His eyes were scratched raw by the grit in the air and his lungs were choking on the dust but he too went back in. He ended up down at the marina where he pitched in to help evacuate the injured over to New Jersey. "I had already had my eyes washed out twice by EMS," he said, not that being half blind stopped him. "We were assisting loading injured [firefighters] down into the NYPD and Nassau police boats [in] the North Cove Marina. [They were] dispatching them over to New Jersey." Each departing boatload was a victory of sorts against the violence that surrounded them all."[12]

Firefighter Gerard Casey made it out on his own. He had been in the Marriott when the tower fell. He survived the collapse, but when he got to the streets, all he saw was a cratered moonscape of twisted girders, debris, and bodies. "The street was gone, the restaurant was gone; everything was gone," he said. "One guy from 24 Truck was bleeding really bad. There was a fireman crushed. There was another guy who was screaming, going crazy. I walked another 50 feet and there was another guy that was dead. There were bodies everywhere."

Casey was in considerable pain himself. His knee, his back—he didn't know what sort of injuries he had, but he felt every one of them. He gathered up a survivor and together they limped toward the water. "We just kept walking and we ended up at the water marina," said Casey. "A boat came over and they pretty much threw us on the boat. They said 'You guys are banged up. Get on the boat.' And that was that."[13]

Firefighter Scott Holowach, Engine 3, FDNY, also found himself loading injured firefighters onto the boats. "[There] weren't many civilians at the water," he said. "We were right where Marine 1 ended up being docked. We helped a lot of firemen get on the ferries and shipped them over to New Jersey. Guys from 21 Truck were there with injuries, so we put them on the ferries. A few other guys from other companies, they were injured." One, he thought, was suffering from a heart attack.[14]

The docks were busy over on Ellis Island. "One boat arrived after another, each carrying 50 to 70 passengers," wrote the Ellis Island historian. "The injuries were numerous—burns, broken bones, and respiratory problems, while other victims appeared to be in shock. A few were soaked with jet fuel; almost all were coated in the toxic dust. As each new arrival got off the boat, he or she was wetted down with a hose to remove the dust and soot." A volunteer who watched the boats unloading said the survivors were "grasping for air, coughing, looking like they had been through a snowstorm, a sugar factory, dust and everything covering their bodies." Said another, the evacuees were "shoeless, in torn clothing, with stunned, vacant expressions on their faces."[15] The EMTs and other volunteers needed little more than the vacant expressions and broken bones to understand the devastation that had occurred across the harbor. The lawns were crowded as one boat after boat after the other unloaded survivors. Thousands of evacuees were taken to Ellis Island, at least 275 had injuries requiring attention. Of those, 50 required hospitalization. Hundreds more were simply showered and released. It was a staggering load, and yet everyone expected many more.[16]

⌐ ⌐

EMT Jason Katz was evacuated by boat, not once but twice. During the collapse, building debris hit his hand, tearing the flesh off his fingers, which were bleeding profusely. A fire truck near him was on fire, people around him were screaming. He found Chief Browne. At water's edge they found a group of people trying to board the boats. He ignored his hand. "We started helping civilians onto the fire boat, just helping everybody off the island," said Katz. "From there we started making our way down to Battery City and [heard] something about a report of a gas leak, that they were evacuating the island, and it was kind of a mad rush, and everyone was jumping on police boats that were in the basin, the boat basin down there. We all jumped on the police boats—myself, Bobby Browne, and a couple of other EMTs—and we jumped on the boat. They shot us over to Jersey. After we helped everybody off, we went back [to Manhattan], and at that time we made our way down to Battery Park by the Liberty Ferry Terminal."[17]

From there, Katz walked down to the Staten Island Ferry Terminal and went up to the new triage area where he was examined. His hand was far worse than he had initially self-diagnosed. His fingers hadn't been merely cut. Rather the skin had been peeled off down to the bone. There was no question about it—his next evacuation would be his own. "They cleaned me up a little bit and sent me on the Staten Island ferry to a triage area at the Staten Island Ferry Terminal in Staten Island. I jumped on a bus, and they took me to Staten Island University Hospital. They were degloving injuries, and I fractured the tips on my pointer and middle finger on my left hand."[18] Degloving is skin that has been ripped off the underlying muscle.

⌐ ⌐

No doubt the "other EMTs" on the police boat who evacuated with Browne and Katz were EMTs Beckham and Giebfried. After they rescued the woman on the scooter trapped in the lobby of the South Tower, after the collapses and the suffocating dust, they headed toward the river where they broke into an ambulance and gathered supplies and set up a makeshift triage area next to the railing. As exhausted as they were, if they could treat someone, they did; if not, they put them on a boat. How long they were there, neither remembers, but they were both near exhaustion, triaging people as fast as they could while gradually succumbing to the dust themselves. Said Beckham of her mental state: "I was too busy to think about anything else." But then word came down about the gas leak and Giebfried was already battling the dust for every breath of clean air she could gulp while throwing up whatever fluids she tried to get down, so they had no choice. "They threw us on a New York police boat," said Beckham. "It was named the *Ray Cannon*. I remember the name of the boat because I grew up in the same town as Ray Cannon. He was a police officer, killed in a shooting. Everyone loved Ray. We were the last two or three people to board. I remember the water in the bottom of the boat; I remember kneeling in that water as it took off across the river."[19]

Giebfried doesn't remember any of that. She was beyond the limits of her endurance, lucky perhaps that she had any strength at all, so bad was it for her. Never an asthmatic, her lungs were nonetheless behaving as if she were in the middle of a chronic episode. She was treated with albuterol but her airways were closing. "I passed out on the boat," she said. The next thing she remembers she was being treated in the Bayonne Hospital.[20]

The new EMS command center was up and running and data were coming in and being organized, and a picture was emerging: It wasn't good. "I have a log entry at 1130 and [New Jersey EMS command] tells me they had 4,000 patients between Ellis Island and the Hoboken PATH station and various shore points on New Jersey, that all these people [had come] over by boat," said EMS chief Goldfarb. "[I] told them 'don't send us any mutual aid from Jersey. You guys work your thousands of patients and we'll get the mutual aid elsewhere because obviously you're stretched.'"[21] A tired New Jersey EMS team leader was certainly grateful to hear that. He later reported that his group had triaged more than 1,000 patients in no time at all. How did he know that? "Our supply of 1,000 tags were exhausted in two hours' time," he later said.[22]

Chief Kowalczyk was at the Chelsea Piers. Unlike his New Jersey counterparts, he wasn't stretched; not in the least. His problem was the opposite: Instead of too many people to triage, he had too many EMTs, and they all wanted to go down to the towers. By noon, Chelsea Piers had a line of ambulances parked on the West Side Highway nearly a mile long all waiting for patients to transport. "Ambulances from all over were coming in," he later said. "It was like I was at the gates of Shea Stadium at the end of a game. People were just running toward us. Ambulance crews were approaching me: 'Chief, I'm a Haz-Tac unit, let us go in there.' I said, 'let's get organized,' they know we're here. About ten minutes later that same Haz-Tac crew came to me and got in my face. He wasn't insubordinate, but he was very aggressive." Kowalczyk said the same thing. There were dangers; let's get organized before we run into trouble. "'It's my job to get you home at night, to your family,' I said. 'Let me do that job. A half hour later that same individual came over and thanked me and understood."[23]

That said, nothing had really changed. They all wanted to get in the game.

CHAPTER 37

"Everybody seemed to be migrating down toward the water zone."

11:50 a.m.

THE RAILING ABOVE THE RIVER WAS CROWDED WITH EVACUEES. NEW rescue boats arrived—harbor patrol boats, police boats from Nassau County, boats from the Corps of Engineers, Coast Guard and fishing boats.[1] Wherever a captain saw a cluster of people or a hand waving, they came alongside the seawall and jury-rigged aluminum ladders to help people down. If a 40-foot patrol boat could take on 10 passengers, they took on 20. If a ferry could take on 6,000, they took on 6,001. And if they had no idea what they could carry—the fireboats *McKean* and *Harvey* for example—they took on as many as the captains felt safe. "Everybody seemed to be migrating down toward the water zone," remembered EMT Delaney.[2] No doubt the sea of flashing blue lights on cabin cruisers bobbing on the harbor had the pull of gravity.

At the very onset of the attacks, the National Park Service's tenders began to evacuate its own park workers from Liberty Island and Ellis Island. The first load of passengers was taken off by *Liberty IV*, a 64-foot vessel ordinarily used to transport VIPs and staff to Ellis Island or Liberty Island. Another tender, *Liberty III*, was later used to take doctors, nurses, and extra supplies from Brooklyn to the North Cove Marina.[3]

The marine unit of the National Park's police force was also involved. Their vessels included a 41-foot patrol boat, Marine 4; a 26-foot Whaler, Marine 3; a 25-foot Sea Ark patrol boat, Marine 5; a 30-foot Intrepid patrol boat, Marine 2; and a 27-foot Glacier Bay patrol boat, Marine 1.

Some of their boats were detailed to transport first responders to Ellis Island, others were used to form a security perimeter around Ellis Island and Liberty Island. Interestingly, one boat evacuated the entire New York field office of the Secret Service across the harbor. The building they left behind, 7 World Trade Center, was damaged in the attack and burning out of control. It would collapse before the day was over.[4]

One of the oddest boats that participated was a tour boat that had seats for several dozen passengers, but it was as unlikely a rescue boat as any. With a wide, stable hull and powerful engines in the back, it ran tourists around the harbor at incredibly high speeds. "I was escorting people down toward where the boats were [taking people] over to I guess Liberty Island or to the Jersey side or wherever the boats were taking them," said paramedic Joel Pierce, Battalion 57, EMS FDNY. "I saw this one boat with a camera crew on it. I don't know if you're familiar with it, but the Green Monster is what they call it. It's like a high-speed tour boat that races up and down the water around the island. It gives tours of the island. Well, we saw them and waved them over and I told them go around south to where the bulkheads are and start picking up people and get them out of here. They listened to me. They actually did that. It was pretty good."[5]

Powerboats from the Merchant Marine Academy at Kings Point, New York, entered the logbooks sometime around noon. "They told us we've been requested to help transfer the injured," said midshipman David Monk, the skipper of one of the academy boats.[6] Kimberly Dutchberg, an instructor at the academy, took a hard-bottom inflatable down the East River past Throgs Neck and under the several bridges and through the Coast Guard blockade. On her first run she was told to pick up physicians waiting for a ride at Manhattan's South Street Seaport. She was told to take them around to North Cove. But there was a problem. "[South Street Seaport] was basically engulfed in black smoke from the flames," said Dutchberg. Feeling her way forward, though, Dutchberg navigated through the smoke without radar, docked safely, and loaded the physicians. "We carried doctors from the South Street Seaport, what I called a triage barge, and transported them over to North Cove, which was close to where the disaster was so they could go and work in another triage spot where they may have been more needed."[7]

As she came back, and again rounded the tip of Manhattan, Dutchberg went past the tugboats lining the seawall shoulder-to-shoulder. "Most of the tugboats [in the harbor] had stopped working and had gone to help out with the relief effort," she said. "You could basically walk across all the bows to get around the bottom of the island." Dutchberg's next pickup was a load for firefighters on Long Island. "We took them from the Brooklyn shipyard over to North Cove, which was the closest place, and we dropped them off there. Then they went into the disaster area."[8]

Behind Kimberly Dutchberg, up at Kings Point, the entire academy wanted to be where she was. "Within an hour we probably had 150 midshipmen and another 50 members of the faculty and staff who were down at the waterfront saying, 'Put us on boats, get us to the city to help,'" she said.

As rough-and-tumble as any vessel on the harbor was a rugged working boat that took commercial divers out to do underwater repairs on bridge stanchions and piers. Even before the towers were hit, Kurt Erlandson of the company Randive had a crew diving near the Verrazano-Narrows Bridge. Erlandson saw the smoke and debris from the collapse and worried that semi-submerged debris or a length of discarded rope or some other troubling material would eventually foul the propellers or otherwise jam up the rescue boats. His divers were seasoned professionals and knew how to fix such problems even in the swiftest currents and darkest waters. They often cleared fouled rudders and propellers on the sterns of the tankers and container ships and other ocean-going vessels that used New York Harbor. He felt compelled to act. He took his divers off the job and sent them downtown. "I pulled them out of there and dispatched them to assist the evacuation. Then the rest of the crew and I arrived in New York . . . with a complete diving spread about 11:30, after we got clearance to go to the Battery." Erlandson's intuition wasn't for naught. Quite the contrary. Fouled propellers were a near constant. "[T]he divers averaged six jobs a day clearing cables and hawsers from the response boats and tugboats," said Erlandson.[9]

For all the gear and his compliment of seasoned divers, one of his jobs had nothing to do with fouled propellers or jammed rudders. His dive boat was very likely the one that evacuated Lee Grusin to safety, a resident of Battery Park City on the Hudson River. "We went onto a boat that turned out to be a private boat owned by a Marine dive company," remembered Grusin. "I just remember going aboard and big arms helping us aboard and everything was blue. I've since learned it was their tarp over their dive equipment and they had blue bumpers. But I just remember this bright blue and holding on and thinking, 'thank God the river's here, thank God the river's here.' And 'thank God the air is fresh.'"[10]

Chief Basile's boat had a jammed propeller. He almost didn't make it down to the Staten Island Ferry Terminal to take over the triage area there. He was with paramedic Louis Cook, Division 2, EMS FDNY. They both knew that the walk from North End Avenue down to the Staten Island Ferry Terminal would take too long even on a good day, much less with the two towers blocking the way. "Louis," said Basile, "there's no way we're going to make it to the south ferry from here walking."

"Well," said Cook, "we'll have to find us some alternate transportation."

Cook saw boats in the marina and yelled down to a deckhand. "'Your boat and motor work now?' He looked at me and he said, 'Yeah.' I said, 'Let's go.' We told him, 'we have to go to the south ferry, and we have to get there now.' So, the guy just fires up the boat, and we go. We make it out into the Hudson, and we're going down the Hudson River. We're looking back, and all we see is this big cloud of smoke and dust. We're just like in shock, how could this happen? Actually, it was a good respite because we were able to get away from the scene for a little bit and clear our heads," said Basile. "The air was clear, and we were able to see the magnitude of what had just happened with us."

But problems cropped up. Cook sat at the bow of the boat and Basile sat at the console with the pilot. "One of the pontoons in the back of the boat was flat," said Cook. "Something must have hit it and flattened it. I looked at it and I laughed. I said 'Oh, great. We survived all this and now we're going to drown.' So, we make it to the south ferry, and the boat dies. They get me up to the ladder to climb up onto the dock, and I tell [Basile], 'Just stay. I'll get [you the] dock line. Don't worry about it.'" But Cook discovered that a spare line was hard to find, and while he looked, the current pulled the boat away from the docks and out into the harbor. "Something jammed in the propeller, so we're stranded out there," said Basile. "I saw some Coast Guard, or some New York City cops in another Zodiac. I tried to wave them down, [but] they zipped by. Five minutes later Louie is trying to throw me a life preserver on a rope, which got about two feet off the pier. It was comical, to say the least."[11]

Basile ultimately waved down a Coast Guard boat and was brought ashore. "The prop was fouled," explained Cook. "[The Coast Guard boat] cleared it to get the boat started [and they helped bring] it back up to the dock, and Basile climbs up the ladder."[12]

- ◆ -

The plan to relocate the triage centers was well received. Inside the Staten Island Ferry Terminal, a wholesale transformation of the cavernous second floor was underway. Said EMT Dominick Maggiore, Battalion 50, EMS FDNY: "We probably had 30, 40 beds set up." There was an area for critical care patients and one for the noncritical patients. They were ready for burns, broken bones, lacerations, and other critical injuries.[13] EMT Vincent Marquez, Battalion 20, EMS FDNY, liked the new arrangement. "That's why we secured the Staten Island Ferry Terminal," he said. "If we had patients, the only way we figured we were getting them out of there was by ferry. [To do that], we wanted a secure area where we could treat them and get them out."[14]

Best of all was the return to the ordinary cadence of EMS operations, a welcome rhythm for EMT John Rothmund. "We got to the terminal, and it was like a godsend, because everybody's in there. All the triage stuff was set up. Anybody [who] was walking and [we could] treat was treated and sent off that island."[15]

CHAPTER 38

"Every vessel in the harbor was moving."

11:59 a.m.

BY AND LARGE THE INJURED HAD BEEN EVACUATED, THE FIRST RESPOND-ers were being treated, and the first of the survivors from around the base of the towers were safely offsite. But the job was far from done. Essentially the entire population of Lower Manhattan from Chambers Street down to the tip of the island had no way off. Pat Moore lived in a tower directly across from the World Trade Center. "Everything that was in the World Trade Center came into our apartment," he said. "There were huge boulders and a computer from one of the towers. There was stuff everywhere."[1] A survivor named Janice went to help a neighbor whose apartment faced the towers. The rooms looked a war zone. "There was dust and glass everywhere, all the windows on one side of his apartment had blown in, and his belongings on that side were scattered all over the place," she wrote in her digital archive.[2]

Incredibly long lines formed at the ferry stop the likes of which had never been seen before in Manhattan. Some of them stretched across Lower Manhattan for four or five blocks, then doubled back on them-selves once, sometimes twice. Those in line moved forward in a steady but slow shuffle. "We finally got to the ferry pier. It was amazing," wrote Sommer Everson, a law student that evacuated that day. "Thousands of people waiting in line, no ropes, just people taking their place in a line that stretched four city blocks and wound around." While in line, the evacuees saw first responders as they rocketed from one problem to the next. They also saw cameras. "CNN was set up there," continued Sommer. "We watched tour busses carrying police officers speeding toward Lower

Manhattan. All kinds of boats were waiting to get us across the river. Tug-boats, tourist boats. As we waited to board a boat, any boat, a man came around carrying bottled water and cups for anyone thirsty."[3] Said EMT Alex Loutsky: "They had ferries going to Brooklyn, they had ferries going to Staten Island, ferries going to New Jersey and so forth."[4]

At the New York Waterway World Financial Center Terminal the land-side staff was calm and that helped keep the people in line calm. "I found huge lines [there]," wrote an evacuee in his digital archive. "It was difficult to determine where the lines began, where they ended, and/or even how wide they were. There was little supervision with the exception of a few New York Waterway employees trying to maintain some order. Considering the size of the crowds, which looked like it was in the tens of thousands, it was amazing the calmness that existed. There was an African American uniformed employee who had a beaming smile on her face. I could not remember the exact reassuring words she chose but it did not matter. Whatever those specific words were, it made everyone within the sound of her voice feel a whole lot better."[5]

Comparisons about the size of the crowds abounded. Variously, people compared the long lines to a war novel, or a scene from a movie, perhaps a postapocalyptic scene of a city in collapse. "I finally got to Chelsea Piers, from which boats were traveling to Weehawken, [New Jersey]," wrote an evacuee named Luke. "I waited in line for a couple hours. It was like being herded in some sensationalistic movie like 'Red Dawn,' although the herders were much more friendly."[6]

The deckhands were key to the operation. They ushered people on board, filled every seat until they were full, then they squeezed people between bulwarks and coils of rope and on rubber fenders or, depending on what type of boat you were on, tug or ferry or patrol boat, even on tool-boxes and storage chests. Life vests were pulled out and dispersed. Incredibly, otherwise jaded New Yorkers promptly complied and put them on. As the captains shoved off, they immediately called for another boat to come in behind them. "At some point we were loading three and four boats at a time," remembered Paul Amico, the builder of piers who was on-scene with New York Waterway.

Downstream by the Battery, the stubby, blue-and-white ferries were using their blunt bows to evacuate survivors off the seawall. This made loading convenient for the evacuees but tricky for the pilots. To hold their bows in place against the tide, the captains had to keep their engines turning. "The ferries powered in fairly hard," said Paul Amico. "There's a very strong current along that wall." [7]

New York Waterway later tallied their service. On an ordinary day, they carried roughly 34,000 passengers. On September 11, operating from their terminals and the seawall in a hurried "load and go" mode, they evacuated 158,506 people of whom as many as 1,500 to 2,000 were injured. [8]

As New York Waterway president Arthur E. Imperatore Jr. said, "We just went ahead and did it." [9]

—◦—

The boats were narrowing the gap between fear and freedom. What started as a trickle of emergency vessels was now a flood of boats of every size and shape. "Every vessel in the harbor was moving," said Staten Island ferry captain Jim Parese. "Us and some of the small boats, the smaller ferries, the police boats [who] were there, the Corp of Engineer boats. I couldn't believe the number of tugboats. As we were going down on our first trip, there was like a sea of tugboats coming from Staten Island heading for Manhattan." [10]

Imperatore had his entire fleet of 20-plus ferries in evacuation mode. [11] "[We] picked up people at our terminals and also nosed the boats into the seawalls, letting people jump over the railings onto the boats." [12]

On the waterfront the crowds were thick, but orderly and quiet. The captains, on the other hand, were as loud as a ringmaster at a carnival. "The ferries, they are yelling out, 'I can take 75. I can take 200,'" said EMT Frank Pastor, Battalion 31. "That's when we started putting the people on the boats." [13] "We got on the island and we just started telling tugboats where you're going to go," added Peterson. "We put 100 to 150 people on each boat. Any place people wanted to go—that there were enough people —we would send them there. The boats would go and come back." [14]

Liz Finn, the assistant vessel master for the Army Corps of Engineers, the one who had seen the attacks from across the harbor at Caven Point, New Jersey, was in the wheelhouse of the 85-foot vessel *Gelberman*. She went to the wall. Finn was impressed by the general calm of the evacuees. Despite the collapse of two towers, despite the terrible sight of bodies and body parts, they showed no panic. "Everyone was great," Finn said. "No one got hysterical, there wasn't any pushing or shoving, and every small boat in the harbor was helping."[15]

The 124-foot MV *Hayward*, a drift collector, cast off, as did the survey vessel *Hatton*. Down the docks, the 53-foot research vessel *Hudson* headed across the harbor as did the DCV *Driftmaster*, with its two 20-ton drift nets stowed, and New York Survey Boat #1. "We were all in just disbelief," said Captain Joe Meyers. "Everybody went to their boats and got underway to help however we could." Meyers was captain of the 65-foot patrol vessel *Hocking*. "When we arrived, the people on the pier had a deep stare and were covered in dust," said Tony Hans of the Corps' New York District. "They were afraid to leave and afraid to stay."[16]

The staff at Caven Point used their docks to create space for the injured arriving from Manhattan and to stock the boats with supplies for the return trips. "The first marina was for the uninjured, the second marina was for the injured," wrote the official historian. "The third marina was for the critically injured." The plan was for the Corps' vessels to evacuate a load of passengers one way and return to Manhattan with emergency personnel or supplies the other way. "The boats ferried more than 200 firefighters and other emergency personnel from New Jersey to Lower Manhattan," said Joe Myers also from the New York District of the Corps. According to their records, the United States Army Corps of Engineers evacuated 2,333 people from New York City. Finn, whose job description made no mention of emergency rescues, evacuated 525 people on the *Gelberman* alone.[17]

On the East River, Fox Navigation was filling its ferries as fast as it could. It put two high-speed boats to work, the 148-foot catamarans *Sassacus* and *Tatobam*. Fox's bread-and-butter route was from

Manhattan to Glen Cove, New York, on Long Island, just up the East River. Their ferries were sleek ships with tucked-in cockpits and rakish profiles, and their interiors were accented in traditional nautical finishes of teak and brass. The seats were comfortably suited for the 45-minute commute and they boasted a well-stocked cocktail bar to take the edge off a day's combat. Each ship could carry 300 passengers and their jet-like turbine engines could easily power them up the East River, no matter the tides.[18] On 9/11, they altered their route. Instead of going up and down the East River, they were hurrying evacuees over to New Jersey, then racing back for more.[19] Fox would evacuate 1,300 survivors before the day was over.[20, 21]

Captain Richard Naruszewicz was taking evacuees on his ship, the 350-passenger ferry the *Finest*. The *Finest* ran between Pier 11 in Manhattan and the marina at Atlantic Highlands, a pickup spot for the bedroom communities of New Jersey near the entrance to New York Harbor.[22] Naruszewicz did nine runs that day. His company had a second ship, the *Bravest*. Both used the slips at Atlantic Highlands, quickly refueling and heading back for more.[23, 24] NY Fast Ferry evacuated four thousand people from Manhattan.[25]

The word to evacuate was generally accompanied by instructions to head to the Staten Island Ferry Terminal. That made some sense. The Staten Island ferry system was a public system with large capacity boats each ideally suited to move thousands of people off the island in one trip. The trick was getting there; September 11 would be a day of long walks. "The police closed off all the streets and made announcements on the megaphone," remembered a survivor who was directed that way. "The first announcement was that the Staten Island ferry was open, and it was the only way out of New York. I remember asking the policewoman, 'How do I get there?' 'Walk,' she said. I walked a total of over 200 blocks that day. I had relatives in Staten Island, so I figured I'd be safe with them, at least."[26]

Staten Island ferry's port captain John Maudlin somehow managed to put seven of his vessels into service, two more than on an ordinary day.

Inside the terminals, deckhands were tying off the boats as fast as they came in, coiling rope and turning the ferries around with the dexterity and efficiency of an Indy 500 pit crew. Said Port Captain Maudlin: "The men on the docks [at Whitehall and St. George terminals] really took the brunt of all this. They somehow kept everyone and everything moving, allowing the boat crews to do what they had to do. It would never have happened without them."[27]

But big boats, like a Staten Island ferry, created problems of their own, particularly when the waterways were as crowded as they were. In general, big boats don't maneuver well in tight spots or with sudden moves, but these ferries had a few tricks up their sleeves. Ferries were in fact surprisingly agile. In addition to the main engines, a ferry had bow thrusters underneath the hull that could move a ferry laterally. "[The *Newhouse*] can spin in its own wake," said Parese. "It can walk sideways. It has all kinds of maneuverability. During that day, most of the propulsion system was used in order to get out of tight situations. We had to be able to swing the boat around, not hit any targets, and get the thousands of people that just experienced that [collapse] back home to safety."[28] Jim Parese asked his engineers for as much speed as they could get him. "I contacted the chief engineer. I wanted to know how fast I could make that boat run, because I didn't want to be in open water for any extended amount of time. So, he told me I could push it up over 800 RPMs." That gave him 16 knots, the nautical equivalent of a Ferrari. Gil Rosshead, the head engineer, pushed the 7,000-hp engines on the ferry to their very limits. "We just wanted to get over there as fast as we could without blowing up the engines and disabling the boat."[29]

On September 11, the Staten Island ferries would transport 50,000 people to safety.[30]

The numbers of evacuees climbed as a boat lift began to operate from every conceivable nook and cranny of the harbor. From one corner, the Seastreak Ferry Company put four of its catamaran-style vessels into service, each with room for some 500 passengers.[31] Within minutes of the first collapse, they took on passengers despite the thick smoke that blanketed their slips. "You could only see about five feet ahead," remembered Captain Gordon Young of the Seastreak ferry *Liberty*, as he came into Pier 11 on the East River. "We had to come into the dock using the radar. It was really bad." But as Young readily admitted, their arrival couldn't have been better timed. The air was filled with fear and the pier was crowded with dust-covered and shoeless evacuees. "If I would have pulled in with a rubber raft, these people would have jumped on it without hesitation. They just wanted to get the hell out of there," said Young.[32]

Seastreak evacuated 3,000 people that day.[33]

World-famous Circle Line Sightseeing Cruises operated from another corner of the harbor. They had three of their boats shuttling to and from Weehawken, New Jersey, free of charge, and had the 160-foot Circle Line XI, the *Calypso*, evacuating people, which could take on 575 passengers per trip.[34] Peter Cavrell, vice president of Circle Line, had been able to pull two vessels from their docks on the East River, which added to the lift capacity and expedited things considerably. "By 10:15 [in the morning] people started coming to the pier," said Cavrell.[35] "We also sent a few staffers into midtown to tell any people walking north that we were offering free service to New Jersey," he added. "We moved about 30,000 people on our boats. It wasn't a kind of coordinated effort. We just started doing it. We wanted to do our part."[36]

Spirit Cruises evacuated 8,000 people.[37] Their handsome yacht-like dinner boats took evacuees from Chelsea Piers to their terminal at Lincoln Harbor in Weehawken.[38] The 600-passenger *Spirit of New York*, the 400-passenger *Spirit of New Jersey*, and the 350-passenger *Spirit of the Hudson* each transported evacuees off Manhattan. Those who boarded these ships were struck by the contrast between the destruction at ground zero and the comfort of these vessels that catered to well-heeled customers clinking wine glasses on a New York Harbor dinner cruise. The main deck had intimate table settings for groups of four clustered around a dance floor, with a second deck above with even more tables. It was "a fancy dinner cruise ship," said an evacuee. "We joked about this luxury treatment. How else do you deal with witnessing, firsthand, an act of war against your country?"[39]

—✦—

VIP Yacht cruises had their boat the *Horizon* coming down to New York City for a 2 p.m. jazz cruise that sailed from Pier 63, a multiuse facility inside Hudson River Park. John Kervey, the operator of Pier 63, radioed the boat to say that the city was essentially locked down and the harbor was closed to all but emergency vessels. There would be no jazz cruise today. "They decided to come anyway," said Kervey. "I talked to them about possibly being involved in a relief effort to get some of the people out, because I saw all these thousands of people and there just didn't seem to be any other way off the island."[40]

Horizon docked and started loading evacuees, while to the south, in the North Cove Marina, Bob Hayward Sr., the owner of VIP Yacht Cruises, was trying to put together a crew so he could get his other cruise vessel the *Royal Princess* underway. In a stroke of good fortune Patrick Harris appeared. Harris had taken his sailing yacht *Ventura* over to New Jersey and docked it and then came back over in a small dinghy. Harris immediately joined Hayward and sailed the *Royal Princess* up to Pier 63 to help people out.

Instead of a profitable afternoon with music and cocktails and paying customers, the *Horizon*, the *Royal Princess*, and two sister ships, the *Excalibur* and the *Romantica*, were able to evacuate 1,800 dust-coated survivors off the island.

CHAPTER 39

"We know evil."

12:00 p.m.

CHARLIE WELLS HAD IT RIGHT—*GET THE HELL OUT OF THE CITY.* "THE subways were down; they closed the bridges down. We were basically the only way out," said Jim Parese.[1] As one survivor put it, "No buses, no trains, no tunnels," she wrote. "The boats provide freedom."[2]

But freedom came with a dose of reality that was hard to swallow. From the distant repose of the river the evacuees were now seeing the smoke, the dust, the devastation that once was the World Trade Center. "We rode the ferry past the Statue of Liberty and stared at the mess we had left behind," wrote Michele, the evacuee who left with her new friend Shira. "It was like a bad movie. The smoke just kept pouring into the sky and the towers were gone. It made no sense."[3]

"It was such a depressing sight to behold," wrote another evacuee. "There was a solemn silence among the passengers as we passed Lower Manhattan and saw the smoke billowing into the sky."[4]

A survivor named Luke saw things he hoped to never see again. He saw emergency vehicles as they raced down dust-coated roads. He saw fighter jets flying combat air patrol sweeps above him. He saw death around him. "[I] finally got to Chelsea Piers, from which boats were traveling to Weehawken, [New Jersey]," he later wrote. "We got on the boat—which held 600 at a time—and pulled away from the pier. As we did, the entire southern tip of Manhattan came into view . . . the most unbelievable sight of the day. People were talkative until this point; and then a silence fell over the crowd, and everyone looked in horror at what used to be there."[5]

In Lower Manhattan, Yolanda Pickering shouldered her way through the crowds to the Staten Island Ferry Terminal, which was packed, but the people waiting there were calm, or so she remembered. In fact, unlike a normal crowded day, people didn't surge onto the ferries when their doors opened. "When the boat started to pull out of the pier, I looked out of the windows of the ferry only to see the tower totally engulfed in smoke," she wrote in her digital archive. "I kept looking and said to someone 'where are the towers?' and they said, crying, 'they are gone.' I couldn't see clearly anymore because the tears blurred my vision."[6]

James Matulevich was well south of the towers after their collapse. He likened the streets of Lower Manhattan to an apocalyptic movie. "Somewhere about Liberty Street there was a curtain of black smoke that stretched across Broadway toward Brooklyn cutting us off from the rest of Manhattan," he later wrote. "It seemed like a scene from *On the Beach*." Matulevich headed west toward the Fort Clinton historical site in the Battery hoping the breeze would blow the smoke away. It did. "Once we got around to the harbor side of the fort, it was like finding an oasis," he wrote. "But best of all, there were boats there taking people to Jersey." Because it was low tide and a ten-foot drop, a policeman helped him down to the deck of a tugboat. Once he was safely on board, he walked around until he saw a vantage point that afforded him a good view of the city. "I climbed up the front of the boat to the highest place I could until I reached a spot in front of the wheelhouse," he said. "The tug backed away from the bulkhead, turned and headed away from the city. As we plowed our way across the harbor, everybody had their eyes glued to the smoke that was coming up from where the WTC once stood, some still shaking their heads in disbelief." They docked in New Jersey and disembarked, about 100 of them in all. "When I finally got onto the dock, I did the same thing that everybody who went before me did. I stopped to look back across the river almost hoping that when I looked this time the towers would be there, but they weren't."[7]

Back in Manhattan, yet another survivor joined the flow of people headed to the ferries, this time to the terminal on the East River. "Finally making it to the seaport at Pier 17, we were directed to a police launch that would evacuate us to safety," he later wrote in the digital archives.

"Once on this boat, we were outfitted with life rafts and given water to drink. A police officer on board was talking to us about what we would see, or not see, as we rounded the southern tip of Manhattan. What the officer told us did not prepare me for what I saw—but nothing could. As we came to the Hudson River, we finally got a view of the devastation from the backside. I just could not believe that these symbols were destroyed and no longer existed. Adding to this was the unimaginable amount of humanity lost and the extended pain and suffering we all are—and will be—going through. Looking back toward New York was just so unreal. The smoke and altered skyline brought tears and disbelief. How and why could this happen?"[8]

"I just wanted to get home," wrote another survivor who was also evacuated by boat. "I was beginning to feel like a war refugee as I waited the hours in line. Lower Manhattan continued to billow huge amounts of smoke. F-16s continually streaked the skies overhead as FBI agents dressed in fatigues and armed with machine guns stood watch. I was finally able to get on a ferry to Weehawken and stood on the upper deck and viewed Lower Manhattan as we crossed the river. It felt strange to be one of the fortunate ones as I thought of the less fortunate that perished this day."[9]

"I was not concerned about the particular destination of the ferry as long as it crossed the Hudson River and put me a step closer to home," said a survivor named James. "The ferry pushed across the calm Hudson; I welcomed the noise of the ferry's engines." Out on the river he got his first view of ground zero. "I looked at Lower Manhattan and saw the smoke drifting upward. Perhaps the smoke would carry the unfortunate souls of those lost that day to a better world."[10]

"The boat trip over was quiet," said Jonathan Segal. "Everyone stood and stared southward as the sun set. Some people were crying but most just stood with their mouths open, hands on their head."[11]

Strangers connected with strangers and comforted each other. Commuters who had scarcely glanced at each other for years sat together, some hugging, some holding hands, some silent in their shared grief. "I remember being on that ferry, coming around the tip of Manhattan and seeing the first tower collapse," wrote one of the evacuees. "A wonderful woman—I wish I even had gotten her name—sat with me, held my hand,

and gave me her water to drink. She tried to calm me and comfort me. On that 15-minute ferry ride back, which seemed like hours, she showed me such kindness that I will never forget her, and I wish I could thank her. She hugged me as I got on the ferry bus, said God-bless and I managed to get home."[12]

Kenneth Austin Walsh was on a ferry bound for the Atlantic Highlands. His boat took him into the middle of the harbor and across the upper bay. His ferry was one of those plush commuter ferries outfitted for the daily Wall Street crowd. On this day, though, the bar was closed, the police searched bags, and the fare, ordinarily $18, was free. "They gave us water, and there were two clergymen on the boat, a Catholic priest and a minister, both associated with the Highlands Fire Department," Walsh later wrote in his digital archive. Walsh wasn't a devote Christian, but he probably knew the old saying that there are no atheists in a foxhole—and ground zero had been his foxhole. "A call comes over the loudspeaker asking for 50 volunteers to take the next boat. People get up and leave, willingly with no problems. I see the priest and yell out, 'Father, are you riding this boat?' He says 'yes.' I decide to stay." The priest sat beside Walsh and they spoke to each other. He was a war veteran, said the priest. He had done two tours in Vietnam. He had seen carnage over there, so they let it out quietly, two men touched to the core by unspeakable things no one should have to see. They decided to pray. "It's my first time praying in public since I was 14," wrote Walsh. "We arrived in New Jersey, the minister walks me off the boat and asks if he can do anything else, and I tell him he did more for me than anyone in a very long time."[13]

Cory Baker, a law student at the time, felt the sting of death when he saw the empty driveways in his neighborhood. "All those people I had just been on the bus with. Dead. And my neighbors. We take the ferry into the city together every morning. That's where they work. Some of the driveways in my neighborhood are frighteningly empty of cars. They are all still parked in the ferry parking lot waiting for their owners to come home. Some of them never will."[14]

Survivors were profoundly changed by the experience. "As we [rode] the boat toward New Jersey, we [turned] back and [saw] the black towers of smoke where the two towers of prosperity once stood," wrote an evacuee in the digital archives. "One year later, the hurt remains. We say I love you more, we leave work earlier to get home to our family, we know fear—we know strength, we know God, and we know evil."[15]

"I felt like I was on a landing craft going into the beach at Normandy."

12:05 p.m.

Replacement firefighters streamed into Manhattan, many of them to the applause of the evacuees impatient to get off the island. Charles Blaich and his brother experienced it. Their ferry docked to a crowd of anxious people, but when they saw who was arriving, they broke into cheers. "They all stopped and applauded us," said Blaich, which was a welcome shot in the arm.[1]

Frank Chaney, a New York City employee, was on the New Jersey side of the river when the towers came down. Anxious to get back, he somehow managed to talk his way onto a returning ferry only to discover that it was filled with firemen, police officers, and other officials, all headed to ground zero. As they approached Manhattan he watched as the firefighters prepared to debark. "The firemen began to don their gear," he later wrote. "I felt like I was on a landing craft going into the beach at Normandy."[2]

Jay Swithers, the EMS captain, was already on the New York side when a boatload of replacements arrived. They were part of the general recall of firefighters that saw a nearly 100 percent response. "Looking down where the ferry allows the cars to come out, it looked like thousands of firefighters," said Swithers. "They walked up in their bunker gear and there was a crowd of people that applauded the firefighters as they were coming off the ferry. They marched off, uptown, like in twos and fours, almost as if they were [an] army carrying equipment."[3]

Michelle Reuter, the one who joined up with her new friend named Shira, saw it at the Staten Island Ferry Terminal. "When the boat finally docked and they opened the doors, we saw that it was completely full with firefighters, EMTs, and their trucks," she wrote. "As they walked off the boat, everyone began to cheer and applaud. It was amazing and kind of eerie. These people were heading into the war zone and we were all scrambling to get out."[4]

On Staten Island, Battalion Chief Jack Calderone, Battalion 22, FDNY, arrived at the ferry terminal expecting to join the flow of replacements headed into Manhattan. Instead, he was tasked with preparing the terminal for the arrival of patients from ground zero. A job less appealing to a firefighter could scarcely be imagined, but orders were orders. "We were told we would be on the next ferry [over to Manhattan], but before it came in, somebody from the ferry [operations office] came out and told us we had a phone call. We went in and took the call and were given instructions to set up a triage and staging area, that they were going to start bringing victims and bodies over." Calderon accepted his assignment and started to organize rescue assets. He coordinated with the Staten Island–based EMS crews and had 20 or so ambulances staged on the street outside. He asked the operations people in the terminal to stretch a phone line out to a command post on the lower level. He called the National Guard to bring in refrigerated trucks to house the deceased and the Transit Authority to line up buses at the doors to move people onward after they got off the boats. "After about an hour and a half, we had everything set up to handle whatever was going to be thrown at us," he said. "Our EMS personnel arranged a full operating room staff, doctors, nurses. We were ready for anything that was going to come our way." But little did. The ferries came and went delivering a few walking wounded, but not much more. "We sat there for approximately six hours and I think we had a total of 16 injuries," he said. "The most serious was a broken bone."[5]

The story was much the same inside New York's Whitehall terminal. It was crowded with thousands of people anxious to evacuate the island, but they were healthy, part of the endless stream of evacuees simply wanting to get as far away as they could. The array of cots so perfectly set up on the second floor were empty, or nearly so. "Essentially, I spent the best part of the day there thinking that there was going to be a mass exodus to the ferry terminal, patients looking for treatment," said Chief Basile. But it never happened. "In essence we didn't treat that many patients. We did about five transports."[6]

Nurse Michele Okamoto made it down to the Staten Island Ferry Terminal and saw the empty cots. She was hesitant to say anything, and it had nothing to do with her being the new person from Hawaii. "As the hours went by, the reality of there being so few survivors was dawning on us. We had no television and were inundated by rumors regarding planes being shot down, a thousand survivors in the parking garage, etc. We saw no dramatic pictures like all of you did. But we knew instinctively that [receiving only a few] patients was the worst sort of sign." She huddled with the physicians as they spoke about what it meant. Around them, weary firefighters and police officers were arriving drenched in sweat, covered with dust, and needing a break. They were tossing off their coats and slumping against a wall, taking a breather to gather themselves, getting some water, gulping down some reasonably clean air, and washing their eyes. "The police [including the hard-hit Port Authority officers], firemen, EMTs, and paramedics began to use this as a rest and recovery station," wrote Okamoto. "Their stories were astounding, such as diving under a truck as a fireball 'rolled over our heads.' They would come into the room shouting out for colleagues. . . . 'Did John make it? . . .' One female FD paramedic lost her rig when eight ambulances were crushed. She looked noble and calm to me. A medic told me she was there as the bodies plunged down. She and others saw things that will haunt their nights for the rest of their lives. I was treated so kindly by all the rescue personnel, introduced around as the nurse from Hawaii that just moved here. A few half-hearted jokes about welcome to New York. Anything was a welcome distraction from a disaster that altered lives too fast, too profoundly, too soon to take in."[7]

The realization that there were too few survivors was keenly felt by those who were evacuated from the pile. EMS Captain Janice Olszewski, the one who had one of the sectors north of the towers under her command, was caught in the collapses and was having trouble breathing. She was evacuated by ambulance to the NYU hospital. "They opened up the back door [of the ambulance] and an entire team of doctors and nurses surrounded me," she later told interviewers. "I was attacked with patient care. They were doing everything. They started a line, gave me oxygen. I looked around. I wanted to say, 'Where are your patients? How many have you treated from the incident?' And [then I] remembered, this was about two to two and a half hours later. I finally asked, 'How many did you treat?' They said, 'Twelve.' *Twelve*? I couldn't believe it. It hit me like a ton of bricks. Then I said, 'I hate to say this, but they're all dead. You're not going to get a lot of patients. You're going to get maybe rescuers later on.'"[8]

Chief McCracken's experience was no different. He made his way down to the Staten Island Ferry Terminal and was shocked by the empty cots. "Numerous boats [had taken the injured] to Jersey," he said, but the empty cots puzzled him. "When I got there, I met [FDNY EMS] Dr. [Allen] Cherson and Chief [James] Basile who had set that up [the treatment area]. I said to the guys, 'How many patients made it to you?'"

"This is it."

"You gotta be kidding me—that's it?"[9]

Dr. Kelly, the one who interrupted her rounds to race down to the scene, put a blunt point to it. "We weren't getting any injuries because people were essentially dead," she said.[10]

CHAPTER 41

"No one was talking."

Afternoon

ON THE NEW JERSEY SIDE OF THE RIVER, EVACUEES ARRIVED AND WERE treated or immediately released. The docks and piers were crowded but people were moving from one station to the next. What started as a choppy affair soon found its rhythm. The evacuees were tired, shell-shocked, confused, looking for a loved one—it was a mix of nearly every emotion possible, but foremost among them it was a feeling of relief. They were out of the toxic cloud, out of the dust, away from the bodies, away from the blood, away from the cries for help. Survivors would later remember the smallest acts of kindness. "The launch docked at the Liberty State Park Marina and we were sent to a reception center where we were offered food, drink, and medical attention if necessary," wrote one survivor. "We were treated with care and understanding, [and] this was comforting and helpful."[1]

Precautions were taken, though, including some unpleasant ones. After passing through the medical tents or the initial triage areas, evacuees were sent to an area set up as a decontamination station. The new arrivals were divided into two groups—one for immediate release and the other for those who would require a shower. "When we reached the banks of Hoboken, New Jersey, we were forced to stay on board the ferry," wrote one evacuee. "No one understood why we couldn't leave the boat, until we saw people dressed in white protective suits setting up a decontamination station. As we exited the ferry, we were required to stand under a shower while someone in a white suit sprayed us with water, at least I think it was water. I asked one of the workers why we were being decontaminated. She responded that no one was sure what exactly was in the cloud of smoke and dust, possibly asbestos. At first, I was concerned, but then I reflected on the fact that I was at least alive. I was lucky enough to see the people I loved once again."[2]

At another location evacuees were simply hosed off. "A hazmat team greeted [our] ferry," wrote an evacuee. "All those who had been within 10 blocks of the Trade Center [including me] were separated from the crowd and brought to a decontamination area. We were given a plastic bag to place our electronic equipment into, and then made to walk into a series of tents, where a fireman hosed us off with a fire hose. The water was cold, and everything I had on was soaked."[3]

Across the bay out in Sandy Hook, the system was better organized. "I remember there were two trailers set up, one for men, one for women," said ferry captain Jim Naureswitz. "People would go in to take a shower and get clean clothes and blankets."[4]

For the thousands of people who were evacuated from Manhattan by boat, the boats were just a stepping-stone on an uncertain road back to home and family. Buses were brought in to take them nearby train stations where trains would take them to other transportation centers that looped back into Manhattan. Crowds were a constant. A survivor who worked at Merrill Lynch in the World Financial Center just across the West Side Highway self-evacuated as the South Tower came down. Her home was in Brooklyn, but her first stop was on the other side of the Hudson River. "New Jersey never looked so good," she later wrote in her digital archive. "The boat took us to Liberty State Park, and I wandered around there among hundreds of people waiting for announcements. There was a large triage center there with dozens of emergency workers and dozens of ambulances. Most of us just wandered and waited." She was able to contact her husband and reassured him that she was alright, then she boarded a bus that took her to the Army Reserve Center at Caven Point. Like the rest of New Jersey's waterfront, the Army Reserve Center was overflowing with evacuees. "There were several hundred people at the center, and when some food arrived near 3:00 p.m., it was all gone before most of us could get to it." To relieve the crowding, she and others were sent on yet another bus, this one to a gymnasium in Bayonne near the Marine Ocean Terminal. Once there, nearly any need they had was met, and then some. "The mayor of Bayonne, the local police, firemen, and EMTs and other citizens did their best to help us through that stay. We had two priests among us offering grief counseling. We had a full-course dinner donated by a local Italian eatery, cookies and milk at 10:00 p.m., and nonstop coffee, tea, sodas, and water." There were radios for those who wanted news; there were telephones, mattresses, and sheets brought in by the Boy Scouts, plus toothpaste, brushes, soap, towels, and even T-shirts to sleep in, those donated by a local company. But sleep was hard to come by. "At 4:00 a.m., I couldn't sleep," she wrote. "Every time I closed my eyes, I saw the burning towers. We would go outside and look across the water and see the fires burning under a clear night sky . . . there were many of us wandering around at 4:00 a.m. The policemen stood by the doors and asked if they could help us in any way. Did we want to talk? Shortly before dawn, newspapers were delivered to the gymnasium. We all gathered around to see the papers, and suddenly I realized what I had escaped."[5]

James Matulevich, the evacuee who thought Lower Manhattan looked like a scene from *On the Beach*, arrived in Jersey City. When he got off the boat, he turned around hoping the towers would magically reappear, but they didn't. Instead, the police hurried him off the pier and he began his journey home. His first stop was personal. "I was hoping to stop at Flamingo's or the Iron Monkey to get a bite to eat or more importantly a drink, but all the businesses in Exchange Place were closed." Instead, he was directed to a bus station five blocks away that would connect him to Penn Station in Newark. Matulevich headed that way and joined a cluster of other survivors all waiting for the same transportation. They talked. "One guy had an office at the American Stock Exchange that had the windows blown in. The other told me he was outside watching the fire in the North Tower when the South Tower was hit. He saw what he believed to be one of the plane's engine crash through a walkway above a group of firemen. He didn't think they could have survived."[6]

Before he got on his bus, Matulevich was asked if he wanted to be hosed down, but it was optional, so he declined. The bus weaved its way through the crowded streets and got to the train station. "The train was jammed with people and there were barely a few places left to stand," he wrote. "Being packed-in on the train wasn't unusual but nobody was complaining and that was unusual, in fact it was strangely silent. A few EMTs managed to squeeze onto the train asking if anyone was hurt or needed medical help. I guess they were looking for people who might be in shock." Matulevich looked at his fellow passengers. "Just before the train started to move, I asked a woman standing next to me how she was. In a quivering voice she said she saw people jumping out of the towers. Her eyes began to tear, and she choked back some sobs. She didn't speak again during the trip and neither did I."[7]

Lines and more lines marked the waypoints on the journey home. A survivor in Lower Manhattan started his evacuation in a long line of people waiting to board a ferry to Weehawken. While waiting, the people around him wanted to know what had happened but the story he told only amplified their fears of the unknown. He shuffled forward. Weehawken was by no means his home. He lived in the bedroom community of Belmar, New Jersey, thirty miles in the other direction, but getting out of Manhattan was a step in the right direction. He boarded his ferry. As they approached the docks of New Jersey, his boat had to wait in line offshore. "It took a long time to get across [the river] since there were more boats than docks," he later recorded in his digital diary. "The ferry finally docked, and we headed for busses to go to Hoboken." On the sidewalks and in the parking lots, the route was dotted with people who were manning tables on which were arrayed snacks and bottled water. The streets were jammed with cars, which altogether made for a longer than normal bus ride to the nearby Hoboken train station. When he finally got to the station, it, too, was crowded, although there were plenty of volunteers lending assistance. "A man with a NJ Transit jacket came over to us and asked if he could help," he said. "I told him I wanted to go to Belmar. He said the next train was leaving in 4 minutes on track 14, the other end of the station. For the first time since the first plane hit 1 WTC, I looked at my watch. It was 4:45 p.m. I couldn't believe a whole day had passed. I had no conception of time."[8]

For many that night, home would be a refugee shelter. An evacuee who had an apartment in the closed off areas of Battery Park City was wheeling a suitcase across the parking lot of an enormous shopping mall in Jersey City. Steve Featherstone, the reporter, saw him and offered to let him spend the night in his spare bedroom. "He politely declined and said he'd take his chances with the shelters, wherever they were. I directed him toward a giant glowing red JC Penney's sign at the Newport Centre mall."[9]

On the docks, at train platforms, and at the bus terminals, countless people stood on their tiptoes and waved as crowds watched the arrivals for a familiar face. The stress, emotions, the pent-up worries were all easy to read. "The anxious faces of family members searching for loved ones confronted everyone as they left the boat," wrote one survivor.[10]

That night the restaurants in Hoboken were crowded. People were out and about, evacuees and locals alike, but everyone seemed to be cocooned in their own thoughts. "Hoboken was full of people," wrote one resident. "But it was eerily silent. The restaurants and bars were busy, but no one was talking."[11]

And so it went on the New Jersey side as the evacuation continued. One boat arrived, then another. People were helped off and escorted away. That's not to say there weren't hitches. At peak of the evacuation there were often more boats that spaces to dock so the boats idled offshore waiting their turn. An analysis of data would later determine that some 2,000 survivors were triaged through Exchange Place in Jersey City while another 2,000 were triaged in Hoboken. More came through Weehawken, although the number is unclear. However, on top of those needing medical triage, tens of thousands more were arriving simply to get off of the island, to get away from it all, to find a way home, whatever or wherever that was.

"By 12:30 p.m., we had established a water supply."

Afternoon

By noon, the fireboats were finally fighting fires, and they were busy indeed. On Vesey Street the 47-story tower called 7 World Trade Center was burning top to bottom. On Liberty Street, the top four floors of the nine-story 5 World Trade Center were in flames. At Albany and West Side, the stone-glad 23-story high-rise called 90 West was on fire. "Fires were burning everywhere," wrote a newly arrived firefighter from Engine Company 166, Staten Island. "It looked like hell."[1]

On Vesey Street the 47-story granite tower called 7 World Trade Center was burning. On Liberty Street the top four floors of the nine-story 5 World Trade Center were in flames. At Albany and West Side, the stone-clad 23-story high-rise called 90 West was on fire.[2]

Captain Fuentes's plan to place fireboats around the tip of Manhattan quickly proved to be prescient. The collapse of the towers released spears of 12-ton I-beams that pierced the streets and severed underground water lines, which cut off the flow of water to the fire hydrants around the towers. The only way to fight the fires was to draft water from the Hudson River and feed it into hoses that would be stretched to pumpers closer to the flames. Engine Company 166 pitched in to help make this happen. "The chief told us to dig out the satellite unit [which has a high-volume hose] and to start stretching the line up Vesey Street [out] to the water," wrote one of the firefighters. "A fireboat was moored there and we had to hook up the line to it so it could start pumping water into the site."[3] In actuality, there were several fireboats moored there. Pilot Campanelli had the *John McKean* tied up along the seawall at the foot of Albany Street in the southern sector from which lines were stretched to the fire at 90 West. Upriver, fireboats *Firefighter* and *Kevin C. Kane* were drafting water and pumping it inland to the firefighters battling the flames at 7 WTC.

But Captain Paul Mallery, Ladder 10, FDNY, wanted even more water. "I figured water; Hudson River, so, I start making my way to the Hudson," he said. "We already had the tender *Smoke Two*—it was inside the marina hooked up to pump—and he was pumping. I could see up and down the river; Marine 9 [*Firefighter*] was in; Marine 1 [*John McKean*] was down by Albany."[4] But out on the Hudson, he saw yet another red boat, the fireboat *John J. Harvey*. Mallery asked nearby firefighters to radio the boat, but they couldn't get through, so instead the crew of the *John McKean* reached them.[5] Said Huntley Gill, a volunteer on the *Harvey*, "As we passed the two big working city fire boats, they called us on the radio and said, 'this is the *McKean, John J. Harvey*, get rid of your passengers as fast as you can. We don't have any hydrants; we need your water.'"[6]

The *Harvey*, however, was in the process of taking a load of survivors upriver when they got the call, so first they had to deliver their evacuees then return to the seawall. When they arrived, Captain Mallery went over to talk to them. "It's a museum buff boat, so I [say to one of them civilians on her], 'can you get water out of that thing?' The guy goes 'I got no hose; I got no fuel.' I said what the hell kind of fire boat is that, no hose no fuel? I said, 'all right I will get you the hose we will see about the fuel.' I bump into Lieutenant Sean O'Malley. 'Sean we need hose to the boat.' [Sean] musters up some guys—they start stretching from some pumper somewhere, west back to the boat. I see a Port Authority guy. I said, 'could you get fuel into that boat?' He said, 'all right let me see'; he gets on his radio."[7] The Corps of Engineers boat *Hayward* took care of the fuel.[8]

Lieutenant O'Malley, Engine 10, had no doubt the *Harvey* could help. "I recall having seen the *Harvey* doing water displays for cruise ships," he said. "So, I left [Mallery] on the promenade at the North Cove marina area to coordinate the area [with Chief Basile]. He said, 'take as many guys as you need . . . you're on your own.'"[9]

Still, a larger and more fundamental problem seemed ready to derail their plans. The 70-year-old *Harvey* was a retired New York City fireboat operated by volunteers as a working museum boat. Using its powerful deck guns, it was often called upon to throw a ceremonial arc of water under which a newly arriving ship would enter New York Harbor, but deck guns were not what the firefighters needed on September 11. They needed the water to be pumped into hoses and that was a capability that the *Harvey* had long ago given up. "We had no interest in pumping into hoses, why would we? It's not something we ever thought we'd have to do," said Gill.[10] "None of the valves that were on the big manifolds, which are like massive bronze fire hydrants, worked. So, we had to quickly improvise. [We] ended up shoving coke bottles and soft balls into the guns that we weren't using, and we ended up putting the fire hoses directly onto the deck pipes [that we could use]."[11] That done, the *Harvey* began pumping water into four hoses, delivering roughly the equivalent of two home swimming pools a minute.[12] Taken as a whole, the many fire boats were together pumping some 60,000 gallons of water a minute, or roughly the equivalent of 30 to 40 land-based engines.[13]

After retreating for the better part of the morning, first responders were now making headway. Optimism began fueling tired muscles. Said a relieved Chief Hayden, "By 12:30 p.m. we had established a water supply."[14]

And with that, firefighters began doing what they do best.

CHAPTER 43

The Last Ship

Night

NO BOOK ON SEAMANSHIP SPELLS OUT HOW TO EVACUATE AN ISLAND the size of Manhattan—or, for that matter, how to evacuate *anyone* from Manhattan—but the captains of the boats executed an evacuation of more than a quarter of a million people as if they had been training for it since the day Neptune rose from the deep. "The response was incredible," said Coast Guard Rear Admiral Richard Bennis, who at the time was USCG Captain of the Port. "Every single vessel in the Port of New York responded to Lower Manhattan. All you could see was vessels streaming into the harbor ... every fast ferry, every tugboat, the pilot boats, the Army Corps of Engineers boats, Coast Guard boats—every able boat in the harbor responded to Lower Manhattan."[1]

During World War II a total of 338,226 soldiers were evacuated by boat from Dunkirk, France. In New York, 272,539 were evacuated by boat from Manhattan.[2] Dunkirk took nine days, May 26 through June 4, 1940. The boat lift of Manhattan took less than 12 hours. The boat lift of Manhattan was thus the largest single-day boat lift in recorded history.[3] The tugs, emergency patrol boats, dinner cruise boats, Randive, the Corps of Engineers, Circle Line, and New York Waterways Spirit—all of them came to the assistance of a paralyzed city.

"I was amazed at the calm and orderly evacuation," said the senior operations manager for New York Waterway. "New Yorkers really stepped up to the plate that day."[4]

While a hard and fast number is difficult to come by, most sources agree that there were 46 ferries and as many as 100 other boats that participated in the evacuation of Lower Manhattan. The largest vessels were the 6,000-passenger Staten Island ferries; the smallest was the Zodiak that carried Cook and Baisle. Irrespective of size or how many people they took, around the harbor there was a feeling of quiet satisfaction. "I felt good [about] what I did," said tugboat captain Ken Peterson. "I got calls from every tugboat and every boat that was there saying, 'Thank you, Kenny, and I'll work with you anytime.'"[5]

However, the boat lift carried a price that was both physical and emotional. Later, most of the boat captains would say that of the two, the boat lift was the hardest on their hearts. "I stayed there for four days," said John Ackerman, the harbor pilot. "It was definitely more emotional than it was physical."[6]

The North Tower of the World Trade Center was attacked at 8:46 a.m. The South Tower was attacked at 9:03 a.m. The South Tower collapsed at 9:59 a.m. The North Tower came down at 10:28 a.m. Thousands were dead. Thousands more were looking for help.[7]

The ferries began the boat lift within minutes of the attacks and continued for the better part of the day. Around 3:00 p.m. the volume of people began to taper. Owing to the enormous lift capacity of the many boats that pitched in to help, the crowds thinned out, the lines largely gone. "After the initial surge of evacuation, we went down to about five boats on scene," said Peter Keyes, VP in charge of the New York operations for the Moran tugboats.[8] Ferry captain Naruszewicz brought in his boat, the *Finest*, for one more load. He came up the East River well past sunset. "By 10 p.m., Manhattan was completely dark," he said. "We went in, lowered the ramp, and no one came. I looked into the beam of the spotlight, and it looked like it was snowing dust—a complete whiteout. We almost couldn't see the ramp. We sat there quietly for about five minutes and people started to trickle on. Some of them looked like they were sleepwalking."[9]

Many of the boats stayed at ground zero well into the night. Some began delivering supplies, others moved people around from one location to another. Some boats delivered hot meals. "Someone mentioned to us that they didn't have hot food for the firemen and rescue workers," said Ken Peterson. "There was a gentleman over in Jersey City named Jim Riley who worked for Marple Tech, a trading company. We heard him on the radio saying he will be there to help us. Twenty minutes later he calls and says he had 5,000 hamburgers. He got a verbal agreement from Outback Steak House to set up a tent at the Jersey City [docks] where the boats were going back and forth. They continually cooked for three days."[10]

At least one new vessel arrived that night, and it was a welcome addition indeed. The 210-foot oil spill recovery ship the *Responder*, based in Edison, New Jersey, arrived on scene and docked in the North Cove Marina. It had a bank of floodlights on board. They were promptly used to illuminate a landing spot for emergency helicopters.

Within minutes of the attacks, and despite the overwhelming obstacles, including the blockage of the West Side Highway, the injured began arriving at emergency rooms. By noon, the tragedy peaked at 90 patients arriving an hour, and from there it began a steady decline. However, the number of injured rescue workers climbed from one or two an hour at the onset to eighteen an hour and continued at that rate well into the early afternoon.[11]

On September 11, the New York Fire Department had 11,336 firefighters and 2,908 EMS workers on the payroll.[12] A total of 145 ambulances responded to the attacks, and more than 400 total EMTs were on scene, including 31 supervisors from the FDNY system.[13] By noon, a total of 121 engine companies, 62 ladder companies, and 27 fire chief officers had been assigned to the incident or self-assigned. By the end of the day half of all of FDNY units in the city had been involved with the World Trade Center.[14] A total of 343 first responders perished including two paramedics from the EMS division of FDNY. Six others EMTs died, those from other EMS services.[15]

Some 240 rescue workers (158 firefighters and 82 EMS workers) were taken to area emergency departments.[16] A total of 6,202 patients were treated in New York area hospitals of which 1,061 were treated in

New Jersey.[17, 18] Five patients died during their emergency care at St. Vincent's, perhaps others elsewhere, but thousands more had been saved.[19]

In the aftermath of the attacks, much thought was given to the day. Against the backdrop of death and destruction, lives had been saved, as impossible as that seemed. "We were able to help people who were coming out of the buildings," said Jack Delaney, director of EMS at New York Presbyterian. "We were able to direct them and get them into ambulances. There were actually thousands and thousands of people who got out of the buildings successfully."[20]

Al Fuentes put in years of decorated service as a land-based firefighter. He knew what it was like to fight fires, he knew what it was like to risk everything.

Fuentes saw firsthand what it took to survive, which led to his own perspective of that day, a perspective that very well summed it up for countless other survivors. It was not just an historic boat lift. It was not just a monumental evacuation that went into the record books.

Said Captain Fuentes, nearly 20 years afterward—of the grit, determination, and selflessness of the medics, mariners, and firefighters who persevered around the base of the towers, "It was the greatest rescue in the history of the civilized world."[21]

And that said it all.

Epilogue

A Peanut Butter Sandwich

"IT WAS JUST ONE CRAZY DAY," SAID EMT LONNIE PENN. "I MEAN I KIND of say it's all in a day's work, but that [day] you will never forget. This is a timeline in history."

Karen DeShore's journey was far from over. After shepherding her band of survivors down to the marina—and staying with them as they crossed over to New Jersey—she herself needed help. Call it exhaustion, call it what you will, DeShore's legs were shot. "When we got over to Jersey, they told me to get the hell out of the area and I said, 'I can't get up right now.' I just couldn't get up. I didn't have the strength to get up." Rescue workers helped her to her feet and got her out of the boat. There were some bed sheets on the pier, a makeshift setup at best, and that's where they put her. "We were just lying there, and they gave us water and they irrigated our eyes [but] that just made it worse. By then we were vomiting. Some of us were vomiting blood. Maybe 45 minutes to an hour later [they] got some vans to take us to Jersey City Medical Center." At the medical center she was taken into an auditorium and received basic treatment including medicines to clear her airways. "I got albuterol treatments and got an injection. They got an ophthalmologist and they cleaned out my eyes and my ears." DeShore felt better but hadn't dropped her guard. There was one accommodation she insisted on. "I refused to give up my helmet. I would not surrender my helmet because I didn't know when the next thing was going to come."[1]

DeShore never saw the face of the man who reached out to hold her hand but she knew he was sent from heaven, that his presence was nothing less than a divine miracle. "His hand left my hand, and that was it," she later recalled. "I never heard his voice again. I never saw him again. I never knew who he was."[2]

Captain Ed Metcalf didn't make it back to the fireboat *John McKean*, at least not the way he planned it. As soon as the boat reached the seawall near the base of the North Tower, Metcalf left to tell the fire chiefs he could pump water. He was caught in the parking garage on the West Side Highway during the first collapse only to claw his way out and reconnect with Chief Downey before the second tower came down. "I saw Downey and started to go south with him," said Metcalf. "I was in the middle of West Side Highway. We helped an injured EMT and got her moving when I heard the rumble again." In seconds he was again plummeted into darkness and overwhelmed by the avalanche of debris. "I realized that God had called me home," remembered the father of seven. "I prayed that God would take care of my family."[3]

But not quite yet. Although the steel beams had crushed cars and killed people around him, incredibly, he survived relatively unscathed. "As numb as I was," he said. "the only thing I had in my head was 'I've got to get back to the river and I've got to supply water.' That was my job that day. After the second collapse, I knew I had to get back to the boat."[4]

Make it back he did only to discover that his crew had used the fireboats to evacuate more than 100 survivors and had helped a great many more of the injured. "By the time I got back they had returned from their voyage across the river. Now they were stretching lines."[5] But the crew promptly sent him away. He was covered in dust and had a sore back. At the very least he needed a doctor or a medic to look him over, they said. "I was put on Marine 6," said Metcalf. "We sailed around the tip of Manhattan. We stopped at the first hospital we could get to, but they weren't able to take me. They loaded me on a police boat and took me to Brooklyn."[6] Metcalf saw doctors there and was treated, but he insisted on being released and managed to get back to the fireboat by early evening—but even that was short-lived. He had a family too.

It was nearly midnight on September 11, 2001, when Metcalf finally arrived home and stood at his front door. "I went inside. I hugged and kissed my wife."

After looking in at his children—after even more hugs and kisses—Metcalf turned around and went back to ground zero.[7]

Countless others did exactly the same thing.

—◆—

The world had forever changed. People had forever changed.

Across the ocean, two naval war ships were passing at sea. One was American, the other German. "Today, during my watch, they [the German ship *Lutjens*] signaled that they would like to come close aboard to say goodbye, as they are moving on from our present operation area," remembered ENS Jeff McCaffrey, USN, of the encounter. "When they came alongside, they were flying their flag at half-mast, and had an American flag at half-mast on their starboard halyard. The crew manned the starboard rail in dress uniforms, and as they completed their approach, they unfurled a banner that read, 'We stand by you.' It was very moving, and I think finally made the whole World Trade Center event 'real' for the crew. It also brought home, in a very real way, this event has affected the entire international community, not just the US."[8]

"[I] learnt a lot in the aftermath of the attacks," said a survivor from Australia. "I learnt what it was to be American. I learnt [that] Americans are fiercely patriotic. I learnt that I am not Australian. You are not Americans. We are citizens of the world."[9]

A photojournalist was walking uptown and saw that very message written on the street corners of his city. "As I approached the Javits Center there were people gathered around cars listening to the latest news updates from the radio. I'm not sure why that was so surprising, but the image of various types of people [black, Hispanic, and white] huddled around the car with the doors and windows open and the radio turned up for all to hear made me think of my escape from N. Moore Street that morning. Each of us from different walks of life, ethnic backgrounds, and religious beliefs. Each of us standing side-by-side. Each of us running for our lives. Now, each of trying to figure out how to move on."[10]

Two days after the attacks, a firefighter was working the pile. Exhausted, he took a break for lunch. "They brought a couple of crates of sandwiches up and some sodas and stuff," he later recalled. "One of the bosses said, 'these baloney sandwiches in this box over here, don't eat those, they'll make you cry.' So, I think, 'they'll make me cry? What are they spicy or something?' He just shook his head and walked away." Puzzled by that, the firefighter reached in and pulled out a brown paper bag and looked inside. "[I] opened the flap and there's a little crayon picture of a rainbow and flower and 'we love you' written in crayon. So, I open the bag up and there's two peanut butter and jelly sandwiches in there and another little note from a girl named Megan and a girl named Melissa. [It says] 'We love you firemen. Keep up the good work.' [There was] like a little drawing of a stick figure and the Trade Center and a flower. On the back of the note it said, 'Made with love from the Coman Hill Elementary School Kindergarten Class.' We're sitting there, grown firemen, rough, tough guys getting chocked up and teary eyed over a frickin' peanut butter and jelly sandwich."[11]

The Numbers

How many people were evacuated by boat on 9/11? In the immediate aftermath of the crisis, estimates ranged from 500,000 to 1 million. Eventually, the press and some authors seemed to settle on 500,000 and that number was repeated so often that it became the quasi-official number. A more accurate estimate might be found in data then released by the boat operators. Based on those data, the following table is a zero-based estimate of the number of people evacuated from New York by boat on 9/11.

TOTAL EVACUATIONS BY BOAT ON SEPTEMBER 11, 2001

NY Waterway	158,506[1]
Staten Island ferry system	50,000[2]
Circle Line	30,000[3]
Spirit Cruises	8,000[4]
Tugboats	5,000[5] (author estimate based on photos, and cited reports)
NY Fast Ferry	4,000[6]
Other dinner boats and cruise boats	3,000 (author estimate based on photos, reports, and interviews)
Seastreak	3,000[7]
Harbor patrol boats	3,000 (DeMarino extracted as many as 300 people—he ran at least 20 trips. The scuba unit had at least six boats and ran multiple trips. Author estimate based on photos, reports, and interviews)
US Army Corps	2,333[8]
Others	2,000 (Randive, *Little Lady*, *Chelsea Screamer*, *Green Machine*, *Lexington*, combined with author estimate based on photos, reports, and interviews)[9]
VIP Yacht Cruises	1,800[10]
Fox Navigation	1,300[11]
Fireboats *Harvey*, *McKean*, *Kevin Kane*, *Smoke*, etc.	600[12]
TOTAL	**272,539**

1. https://www.marinelog.com/news/remembering-maritime-heroes-on-9-11/
2. Milton, Joel, *Marine Lift,* Workboat, November 2001, p. 58
3. https://www.marinelog.com/news/remembering-maritime-heroes-on-9-11/
4. https://www.marinelog.com/news/remembering-maritime-heroes-on-9-11/
5. https://www.morantug.com/site/news/29. Operators spoke of 100 people per tug per trip. Nearly 50 tugs evacuated people. The lowest estimate was 3,300 people evacuated by tug that day, per: https://alisonbate.ca/2019/06/18/armada-rescues-trapped-new-yorkers-9-11/; see also http://www.harborheroes.com/boats.html

6. https://www.kitsapdailynews.com/news/we-stopped-counting-former-captain-of-kings tons-newest-ferry-recalls-evacuating-thousands-on-9-11/ see also Milton, Joel, Marine Lift, Workboat, November 2001, p. 58

7. Milton, Joel, *Marine Lift,* Workboat, November 2001, p. 58

8. https://www.nan.usace.army.mil/About/History/9-11-Remembrance-10-Years-Later/; see also Milton, Joel, *Marine Lift,* Workboat, November 2001, p. 58

9. See also, https://www.theepochtimes.com/captain-of-the-ship_3033598.html

10. *Horizon, Excalibur, Romantica, and Royal Princess; Dust to Deliverance, p. 154*

11. https://www.workboat.com/news/passenger-vessels/calling-all-boats-9-11/

12. Marine 1, FDNY and The Marine Fire Fighting Institute Newsletter #9. www.marine fighting.com/pages/newsletters/newsletter9.htm

Notes

Epigraph
1. Peter Josyph, *Liberty Street: Encounters at Ground Zero* (Albany, NY, Excelsior Editions 2006), p. 272.

Foreword
1. www.wtc.com/about/history

Chapter 1: September 12, 2001
1. Fire Department of the City of New York, *World Trade Center Task Force Interview*, Prezant interview.

Chapter 2: September 10, 2001
1. http://www.spokesman.com/picture-stories/readers-remember-twin-towers-photos/
2. Matt Liddy, 9/11 Remembered—Ten Years On, ABC News, Monika Bravo interview, https://abc.net.au/news/specials/september-11-remembered/2011-09-09/eye witness-accounts-of-september-11/2866958

Chapter 3: "There should be a law against working on such a beautiful day."
1. US Army Corps of Engineers, Ground Zero, *New York District Times*, Fall 2001.
2. Ken Belson, "If It Floats Near the City, They Want It," *New York Times*, April 26, 2008.
3. Harbor data, https://en.wikipedia.org/wiki/Port_of_New_York_and_New_Jersey, last accessed 9/2020.
4. Chief Petty Officer P.J. Capelotti, Rogue Wave: *The U.S. Coast Guard on and after 9/11* (Washington, DC, U.S. Coast Guard Historians Office), p. 5.
5. David Tarnow, interviewer, "All Available Boats: Harbor Voices from 9/11," South Street Seaport Museum, https://transom.org/2002/all-available-boats/
6. Author interview, Joseph DeMarino, July 2020.
7. Author interview, Edward Metcalf, September 2020.

8. Mitchell Fink and Lois Mathias, *Never Forget: An Oral History of September 11, 2001* (New York, HarperCollins, 2002), p. 181.

9. Marine 1 FDNY, September 11, 2001, http://marine1fdny.com/911_new.php

10. Tug characteristics: http://www.reinauer.com/RTCWeb/DesktopHtml/nyTugList.aspx

11. Ground Zero, *The New York District Times*.

12. Description of his morning from Jessica DeLong, *Dust to Deliverance: Untold Stories from the Maritime Evacuation on September 11*, [New York, McGraw Hill, 2017], p. 10; see also; All Available Boats; American Dunkirk.

13. https://tidesandcurrents.noaa.gov/waterlevels.html?id=8518750&units=standard&bdate=20010910&edate=20010911&timezone=GMT&datum=MLLW&interval=h&action=data

Chapter 4: *"Lower Manhattan is really MCI (Mass Casualty Incident) City."*

1. "story2936.xml" (untitled), *September 11 Digital Archive*, accessed April 25, 2019, http://911digitalarchive.org/items/show/4133

2. Statistics per *The Guardian*. https://www.theguardian.com/world/2002/aug/18/usa.terrorism

3. A.J. Heightman, "Out of the Darkness," *Journal of Emergency Medical Services*, vol. 9, no. 1, 2011.

4. http://exhibitions.nysm.nysed.gov/wtc/about/facts.html

5. "story nmah5427.xml" (untitled), *September 11 Digital Archive*, accessed April 25, 2019, http://911digitalarchive.org/items/show/19423

6. "Out of the Darkness."

7. Fire Department of the City of New York, *World Trade Center Task Force Interview*, Monroe interview.

8. "Out of the Darkness."

9. Data per the 9/11 Commission Report, _____, The National Commission on Terrorist Attacks Upon the United States, *The 9/11 Commission Report* (New York: W. W. Norton), p. 4.

Chapter 5: *"We had a view of the World Trade Center."*

1. Author interview with Beckham, August 2020.

2. "I get cranky," A.J. Heightman, "Live To Tell," *Journal of Emergency Medical Services*, vol. 9, no. 30, 2001.

3. Fire Department of the City of New York, *World Trade Center Task Force Interview*, Loutsky interview; see also "Live to Tell."

4. Fire Department of the City of New York, *World Trade Center Task Force Interview*, Hansen interview.

5. Fire Department of the City of New York, *World Trade Center Task Force Interview*, Cuniffe interview.

Chapter 6: "Eric, look at that! Look how low that plane is."

1. Fire Department of the City of New York, *World Trade Center Task Force Interview*, Lorocco interview.

2. Loutsky interview.

3. Fire Department of the City of New York, *World Trade Center Task Force Interview*, Pastor interview.

4. Live to Tell.

5. Out of the Darkness.

6. Live to Tell.

7. Fire Department of the City of New York, *World Trade Center Task Force Interview*, Ramos Interview.

8. Live to Tell.

9. Fire Department of the City of New York, *World Trade Center Task Force Interview*, Puma interview.

10. Fire Department of the City of New York, *World Trade Center Task Force Interview*, Martinez interview, p. 3.

11. Jim Dwyer and Kevin Flynn, *102 Minutes: The Untold Story of the Fight to Survive Inside the Twin Towers* (New York: Henry Holt, 2005), p. 20; see also 9/11 Commission Report.

12. Body strapped to her seat, Dean Murphy, *September 11: An Oral History* (New York: Doubleday, 2002), p. 195.

13. 102 Minutes, p. 37.

14. Fire Department of the City of New York, *World Trade Center Task Force Interview*, Abed interview.

15. Live to Tell; Fire Department of the City of New York, *World Trade Center Task Force Interview*, Davila interview.

16. Fire Department of the City of New York, *World Trade Center Task Force Interview*, Mallery interview.

17. The 9/11 Commission Report estimate was ten thousand gallons; the 767 could carry twenty-four thousand gallons.

18. "story2936.xml" (untitled), *September 11 Digital Archive*, accessed April 25, 2019, http://911digitalarchive.org/items/show/4133

19. Some accounts say a 10-60 was transmitted.

20. 10-40 per EMS response, Fire Engineering.

21. https://forums.firehouse.com/forum/firefighting/firefighters-forum/2716-wtc-box

22. Fire Department of the City of New York, *World Trade Center Task Force Interview*, Merced interview,

23. Out of the Darkness.

24. Fire Department of the City of New York, *World Trade Center Task Force Interview*, Z. Goldfarb interview.

Chapter 7: "No one would be allowed off the boat."
1. David Tarnow, interviewer, "All Available Boats: Harbor Voices from 9/11," South Street Seaport Museum, https://transom.org/2002/all-available-boats/
2. A.J. Heightman, "Exodus Across the Hudson," *Journal of Emergency Medical Services*, vol. 9, no. 1, 2011, p. 8.
3. "All Available Boats," p. 45.
4. "All Available Boats," p. 46.
5. Jessica DeLong, *Dust to Deliverance: Untold Stories from the Maritime Evacuation on September 11*, (New York, McGraw Hill, 2017), p. 10.
6. Michael Sirak, interviewer, Airmen on 9/11: SMSgt Edward Metcalf, *Air Force Magazine*, September 11, 2011, https://www.airforcemag.com/PDF/MagazineArchive /Magazine%20Documents/2011/September%202011/0911airmen.pdf
7. *Air Force Magazine*, SMSgt. Edward Metcalf; see also Marine 1 FDNY.
8. Author interview with Metcalf, September 2020.
9. Author interview with DeMarino, July 2020.
10. Rogue Wave, p. 6.
11. Rogue Wave, p. 6.

Chapter 8: "A major, major MCI."
1. "story4992.xml" (untitled), *September 11 Digital Archive*, accessed April 25, 2019, http://911digitalarchive.org/items/show/12450.
2. Fire Department of the City of New York, *World Trade Center Task Force Interview*, Moritz interview
3. "story1859.xml" (untitled), *September 11 Digital Archive*, accessed April 25, 2019, http://911digitalarchive.org/items/show/17905.
4. Fire Department of the City of New York, *World Trade Center Task Force Interview*, Giaconelli interview.
5. Fire Department of the City of New York, *World Trade Center Task Force Interview*, Smith interview, p. 11.
6. Out of the Darkness.
7. _____, "Courage Under Fire: 9/11 Responders Show Their True Valor," *Journal of Emergency Medical Services*, September 9, 2002.
8. Fire Department of the City of New York, *World Trade Center Task Force Interview*, Mallery interview.

Chapter 9: "Our fireboats can get in close to the Manhattan shoreline."
1. https://en.wikipedia.org/wiki/Port_of_New_York_and_New_Jersey
2. "email301.xml" (untitled), *September 11 Digital Archive*, accessed April 25, 2019, http://911digitalarchive.org/items/show/36894.
3. USDOT, Effects of Catastrophic Events on Transportation System Management and Operations, New York City, September 11, 2001, p. 4.
4. *Rogue Wave.*
5. *Never Forget*, p. 98.

6. *Never Forget*, p. 68.

7. https://www.timesofisrael.com/the-jews-of-the-us-coast-guard-always-ready -during-hurricane-season/

8. Alfredo Fuentes, *American by Choice*, (Long Beach, NY, Fire Dreams Publishing Co., 2004) p. 5.

9. www.marinefirefighting.com/pages/newsletters/newsletter9.htm

10. http://www.capecodfd.com/PAGES%20Special/Fireboats_FDNY_H8_Hist-1958 -1992.htm

11. Fuentes, *American By Choice*.

Chapter 10: *"We had more patients than we had ambulances."*

1. Fire Department of the City of New York, *World Trade Center Task Force Interview*, William Green interview.

2. Fire Department of the City of New York, *World Trade Center Task Force Interview*, Moncherry interview.

3. Fire Department of the City of New York, *World Trade Center Task Force Interview*, J. Bell interview.

4. Fire Department of the City of New York, *World Trade Center Task Force Interview*, K. Davis interview.

5. Martinez says they parked at Vesey; Puma remembers Fulton.

6. Out of the Darkness.

7. Fire Department of the City of New York, *World Trade Center Task Force Interview*, Sloutsky interview.

8. Fire Department of the City of New York, Sloutsky interview.

9. Fire Department of the City of New York, *World Trade Center Task Force Interview*, M. Delgado interview.

10. Live to Tell.

11. Live to Tell.

12. Bellevue data, The World Trade Center Attack: Observations from New York's Bellevue Hospital.

13. Live to Tell.

Chapter 11: *"The hand was charred black."*

1. "nmah5018.xml" (untitled), *September 11 Digital Archive*, accessed April 25, 2019, http://911digitalarchive.org/items/show/40592.

2. Live to Tell.

3. Live to Tell; https://www.jems.com/articles/supplements/special-topics/courage -under-fire/live-tell.html

4. "All Available Boats," p. 122.

5. "All Available Boats," p. 114.

6. https://nypost.com/2001/03/05/heroes-of-keriks-police-posse/

7. *Never Forget*, p. 90.

8. "nmah5410.xml" (untitled), *September 11 Digital Archive*, accessed April 25, 2019, http://911digitalarchive.org/items/show/41016.

9. Fire Department of the City of New York, *World Trade Center Task Force Interview*, P. Ashby interview, p. 9.

10. "story670.xml" (untitled), *September 11 Digital Archive*, accessed April 25, 2019, http://911digitalarchive.org/items/show/12609.

11. "story2936.xml" (untitled), *September 11 Digital Archive*, accessed April 25, 2019, http://911digitalarchive.org/items/show/4133

Chapter 12: "We couldn't put the fire out."

1. Data: http://nymag.com/news/9-11/10th-anniversary/first-responses/

2. Hospital data, The World Trade Center Attack: Lessons for Disaster Management.

3. Bellevue data, The World Trade Center Attack: Observations from New York's Bellevue Hospital.

4. The World Trade Center Attack: Is critical care prepared for terrorism?; other data, The World Trade Center Attack: Lessons for Disaster Management.

5. Ground Zero, Paterson Fire History, www.patersonfirehistory.com/ground-zero.html

6. The Jersey Journal Remembers, Liberty State Park Triage Center, September 11, 2001.

7. US Army Corps of Engineers, Responding on the Water, Corps Vessels Answered Call on NT Harbor, *The New York District Times*.

8. "story9290.xml" (untitled), *September 11 Digital Archive*, accessed April 25, 2019, http://911digitalarchive.org/items/show/15972.

9. Goldfarb interview.

10. Fire Department of the City of New York, *World Trade Center Task Force Interview*, Kennedy interview.

11. Fire Department of the City of New York, *World Trade Center Task Force Interview*, L. Garcia interview.

12. Daniel Nigro, Report from the Chief of the Department, *Fire Engineering*, 2002, https://www.fireengineering.com/2002/09/01/234254/report-from-the-chief-of -department/#gref

13. Fire Department of the City of New York, *World Trade Center Task Force Interview*, Callan interview.

14. Peter Hayden, North Tower Command, *Fire Engineering*, 2002, https://www.fire engineering.com/2002/09/01/233141/north-tower-command/#gref

15. "story1001.xml" (untitled), *September 11 Digital Archive*, accessed April 25, 2019, http://911digitalarchive.org/items/show/12087

Chapter 13: "With the second plane in, I knew this was no accident."

1. Harbor Voices.

2. *Rogue Wave*, p. 7.

3. Harbor Voices.

4. *Never Forget*, p. 98.

5. "nmah5018.xml" (untitled), *September 11 Digital Archive*, accessed April 25, 2019 http://911digitalarchive.org/items/show/40592

6. Fire Department of the City of New York, *World Trade Center Task Force Interview*, Hyland.

7. "story2936.xml" (untitled), *September 11 Digital Archive*, accessed April 25, 2019, http://911digitalarchive.org/items/show/4133

8. "story6328.xml" (untitled), *September 11 Digital Archive*, accessed April 25, 2019, http://911digitalarchive.org/items/show/8805

9. Live to Tell.

10. Live to Tell.

11. Fire Department of the City of New York, *World Trade Center Task Force Interview*, Donovan interview.

12. *Never Forget*, p. 57.

13. http://www.nyppa.org/todd-911

14. Fire Department of the City of New York, *World Trade Center Task Force Interview*, Swithers interview.

15. Fire Department of the City of New York, *World Trade Center Task Force Interview*, Sean O'Malley interview.

16. Fire Department of the City of New York, *World Trade Center Task Force Interview*, Smith interview.

Chapter 14: "We needed the maneuvering room."

1. Report from Ground Zero, p. 94.

2. Fire Department of the City of New York, *World Trade Center Task Force Interview*, Gombo interview.

3. *Never Forget,* p. 98.

4. Dust to Deliverance, p. 29.

5. "All Available Boats," p. 44; see also Edward Marek, *Talking Proud, Invisible Waterfront Hands: Evacuation of Manhattan 9/11*, p. 10; www.talkingproud.us/culture/man hattanevacuation/911evauationnyc/html, p. 28.

6. "story911.xml" (untitled), *September 11 Digital Archive*, accessed April 25, 2019, http://911digitalarchive.org/items/show/17062.

7. "story911.xml" (untitled), *September 11 Digital Archive*, accessed April 25, 2019, http://911digitalarchive.org/items/show/17062.

8. Fire Department of the City of New York, *World Trade Center Task Force Interview*, Norris interview.

9. *American Dunkirk*, p. 96.

10. Richard O. Aichele, A Shining Light in Our Darkest Hour, *Professional Mariner*, March 2, 2007, https://www.professionalmariner.com/a-shining-light-in-our-darkest -hour/

11. *American Dunkirk*, p. 101.

12. Harbor Voices.

13. "Six boats" per John Snyder, Remembering maritime heroes on 9/11, MarineLog, https://www.marinelog.com/news/remembering-maritime-heroes-on-9-11/

14. U.S. Department of Transportation, Rescue at Water's Edge: The U.S. Merchant Marine Response to 9/11, https://www.youtube.com/watch?v=yc66PsnXPoA
15. *American Dunkirk*, p. 116.
16. Harbor Voices.
17. Mmah6682.xmlseptember11thremembrance
18. "nmah6382.xml" (untitled), *September 11 Digital Archive*, accessed April 25, 2019; see also Trade Center Burn Victim's Long Road, NYT,2019, http://911digitalarchive.org/items/show/43202; see also Marine 1, September 11, 2001.
19. Author interview with Metcalf, September 2020.
20. Ibid.
21. Harbor Voices.
22. 9/11 Burn Victim Recounts Story of His Rescue by Stranger, CBS New York.
23. 9/11 Burn Victim Recounts Story.

Chapter 15: "It was just hell."

1 "All Available Boats."
2. Author interview with Fuentes, September 2020.
3. Author interview with Metcalf, September 2020.
4. Nancy Rigg, After The Fall, *Journal of Emergency Medical Services*, 9.30.2001,https://www.jems.com/2001/09/30/after-fall/
5. Rigg, After The Fall.
6. Harbor Voices.
7. Harbor Voices; see also Untold Story of 9/11 Resilience.
8. Harbor Voices.
9. Exodus Across the Hudson, p. 8.
10. Exodus Across the Hudson, p. 9.
11. "story2160.xml," September 11 Digital Archive, accessed April 15, 2019, http://911digitalarchive.org/items/show/14721.
12. "story1402.xml," September 11 Digital Archive, accessed April 16, 2019,
13. Fire Department of the City of New York, *World Trade Center Task Force Interview*, Prezant interview.
14. Jennifer Tripucka, A First Responder's Story of Hoboken on September, 11th, Hoboken Girl, September 10, 2018; see also "nmah5410.xml" (untitled), *September 11 Digital Archive*, accessed April 25, 2019, http://911digitalarchive.org/items/show/41016.

Chapter 16: "They looked like zombies."

1. Dust to Deliverance, p. 43.
2. Untold Story of 911 Resilience, transcribed.
3. https://seastreak.com/what-to-know/faq/njnyc-commute/; scholastic magazine. http://teacher.scholastic.com/scholasticnews/indepth/911/teachers/resources_mccabe.htm
4. Harbor Voices.
5. "All Available Boats."

6. "All Available Boats.".
7. James McGranachan, "'My God, We Are Under Attack:' U.S. Coast Guard Activities New York: Eyewitness to War." *Sea Power* 45, No. 9 (September 2002), pp. 36-40.
8. "All Available Boats."

Chapter 17: "Improvise."
1. Zachary Goldfarb, FDNY EMS Response, *Fire Engineering*, 9/1/2002, https://www.fireengineering.com/2002/09/01/233392/fdny-ems-response/#gref
2. 58 BLS ambulances, 29 ALS, JEMS Courage Under Fire.
3. Charlie Wells, Live to Tell states ambulances' "1,000 first responders" per 9/11 Commission Report,
4. Out of the Darkness.
5. https://www.rcshf.org/pages.php?PageID=2&col=detail&id=36
6. Live to Tell.
7. Goldfarb interview.
8. Out of the Darkness.
9. Fire Department of the City of New York, *World Trade Center Task Force Interview*, R. Browne interview.
10. Mechel Handler, "Through the Valley of Death," *Jewish Action*.
11. JEMS Courage Under Fire.
12. Fire Department of the City of New York, *World Trade Center Task Force Interview*, Olszewski interview.
13. Live to Tell.
14. Live to Tell.

Chapter 18: "That shuts down New York Harbor."
1. https://en.wikipedia.org/wiki/Closings_and_cancellations_following_the_September _11_attacks
2. https://www.newsday.com/911-anniversary/9-11-01-when-the-subways-went -still-1.790103
3. http://content.time.com/time/nation/article/0,8599,174912,00.html
4. Staff Statement No. 13, The National Commission on Terrorist Attacks Upon the United States, p. 13.
5. Fire Department of the City of New York, *World Trade Center Task Force Interview*, Medjuck interview, p. 4.
6. Staff Statement No. 13, The National Commission on Terrorist Attacks Upon the United States, p. 13.
7. USCG Historian's Office, Attack on America: September 11, 2002 and the U.S Coast Guard, Interviewee: Rear Admiral Richard E. Bennis.
8. USCG Historian's Office, Attack on America: September 11, 2002, and the U. S Coast Guard, Interviewee: Rear Admiral Roy Casto.
9. USCG Historian's Office, Attack on America: September 11, 2002, and the U. S Coast Guard, Interviewee: Rear Admiral Richard E. Bennis.

10. Pentagon.www.workboat.com/news/passenger-vessels/calling-all-boats-9-11/
11. Dust to Deliverance, p. 36.
12. 150 targets, *Rogue Wave*, p. 27.
13. https://www.timesofisrael.com/the-jews-of-the-us-coast-guard-always-ready
-during-hurricane-season/
14. Because Air Force jets were already in the sky, the helicopter was forced to land
before they could attempt rooftop rescues. The crews were bitterly disappointed. *Rogue Wave.*
15. *Rogue Wave*, p. 16.
16. USCG Historian's Office, Attack on America: September 11, 2001, and the US
Coast Guard.
17. Pentagon.www.workboat.com/news/passenger-vessels/calling-all-boats-9-11/
18. *Rogue Wave*, p.15.
19. *Rogue Wave*, p. 29.

Chapter 19: "It just looked like too much, high-rise towers, free burning like that."
1. Live to Tell.
2. Fire Department of the City of New York, *World Trade Center Task Force Interview*,
Wells interview.
3. Author interview, August 2020.
4. Fire Department of the City of New York, *World Trade Center Task Force Interview*,
DeShore Interview.
5. Fire Department of the City of New York, *World Trade Center Task Force Interview*,
R. Moore interview.
6. Fire Department of the City of New York, *World Trade Center Task Force Interview*,
K. Kelly interview.

Chapter 20: "The tower might come down in the harbor"
1. Janey A. McDonnell, Responding to the September 11 Terrorist Attacks, *National
Park Service* (Washington, DC).
2. "My God We Are Under Attack."

Chapter 21: "That's your evacuation plan—everybody goes south."
1. 102 minutes, p. 193; see also p. 251.
2. https://www.washingtonpost.com/archive/lifestyle/2001/09/20/for-an-extraordinary
-week-nielsen-puts-the-ratings-aside/52bf74fc-af28-4c43-bbd8-d86509843b9c/
3. https://www.mediapost.com/publications/article/306848/a-day-of-television-like-no
-other-a-911-memory.html
4. Fire Department of the City of New York, *World Trade Center Task Force Interview*,
Gregory interview.
5. DeShore interview.
6. Beckham interview with author, August 2020.
7. Giebfried interview with author, August 2020.

8. 102 Minutes, p. 193.

9. Live to Tell; see also DeShore interview.

10. Author interview Giebfried, August 2020.

11. Live to Tell; see also DeShore interview.

12. Courage Under Fire, see also Fire Department of the City of New York, *World Trade Center Task Force Interview*, Fran Pascale interview.

13. Live to Tell.

14. Live to Tell.

15. Live to Tell.

16. Live to Tell.

17. Breier, *Even in the Darkest Moments*, p. 29.

18. Breier, *Even in the Darkest Moments*, p. 29.

19. Live to Tell.

20. Live to Tell.

Chapter 22: *"The debris went well into the Hudson."*

1. Building stats: https://hypertextbook.com/facts/2004/EricChen.shtml

2. Digital Archives, File #80454: 144.mp3.

3. Annette Wright, "We stopped counting": Former captain of Kingston's newest ferry recalls evacuating thousands on 9/11, *Kitsap Daily News*. https://www.kitsapdailynews.com/news/we-stopped-counting-former-captain-of-kingstons-newest-ferry-recalls-evacuating-thousands-on-9-11/

4. Fire Department of the City of New York, *World Trade Center Task Force Interview*, Bell interview.

5. Out of the Darkness.

6. Never Forget, p. 90.

7. https://www.popphoto.com/american-photo/91101-photographers-stories-pt-3-youre-too-close#page-2

8. Harvey Eisner, This Is Their Story.

9. Joseph Pfifer, First Chief on the Scene, *Fire Engineering*, 9.01.02. https://www.fireengineering.com/2002/09/01/233840/first-chief-on-the-scene/#grefhttps://www.fireengineering.com/2002/09/01/233840/first-chief-on-the-scene/#gref

10. Steve Featherstone, Across the River, Jersey City Online, http://www.jerseycityonline.com/wtc/911_story.htm

11. Meg Cabot, Meg's blog, https://www.megcabot.com/2012/09/9112001/

12. Mary Marshall Clark, Peter Bearman, Catherine Ellis, and Stephen Drury Smith, eds., *After the Fall: New Yorkers Remember September 2001 and the Years That Followed* (New York: The New Press, 2011).

13. Fire Department of the City of New York, *World Trade Center Task Force Interview*, Steffens interview.

14. Fire Department of the City of New York, *World Trade Center Task Force Interview*, Gregory interview.

15. Fire Department of the City of New York, *World Trade Center Task Force Interview*, N. Sweeting interview.

16. Out of the Darkness.

17. Raven Walker, After the Towers Fell (iUniverse), p. 95.

18. Out of Darkness.

19. Live to Tell; see also Out of Darkness.

20. Mechell Handler, "Through the Valley of Death," Jewish Action.

21. Clark et al., After the Fall, p. 54.

22. Fire Department of the City of New York, *World Trade Center Task Force Interview*, Pilla interview.

23. Clark et al., After the Fall, p. 76.

24. Fire Department of the City of New York, *World Trade Center Task Force Interview*, Wood interview.

25. Joseph Pfifer, First Chief on the Scene.

26. Liberty Street. Encounters at Ground Zero, p. 263.

Chapter 23: "It was blacker than midnight."

1. Fire Department of the City of New York, *World Trade Center Task Force Interview*, Fitzpatrick, p. 13.

2. https://www.tms.org/pubs/journals/jom/0112/eagar/eagar-0112.html

3. Fire Department of the City of New York, *World Trade Center Task Force Interview*, Lamanna interview.

4. Fire Department of the City of New York, *World Trade Center Task Force Interview*, H. Sickles interview.

5. Fire Department of the City of New York, *World Trade Center Task Force Interview*, D. Prezant interview.

6. Fire Department of the City of New York, *World Trade Center Task Force Interview*, Bendick interview.

7. DeShore interview.

8. Fire Department of the City of New York, *World Trade Center Task Force Interview*, M. Stone interview.

9. 9/11 in "Firefighters' Words: Surreal Chaos and Hazy Heroics," Kevin Flynn and Jim Dwyer, *New York Times*, January 31, 2002.

10. Author interview, August 2020.

11. N. Sweeting interview.

12. Live to Tell.

13. John A. (Jay) Jonas, Ladder 6: Rescue of the Rescuers, https://www.fireengineering .com/2002/09/01/234457/ladder-6-rescue-of-the-rescuers/#gref

Chapter 24: "People kept coming down to the seawall just looking to get away."

1. Maritime Administration, Merchant Marine Heroes of 9/11, video, https://www .youtube.com/watch?v=Xo07tAFzWgw1. Both the *Finest* and the *Bravest* were using the pier, however, contemporary reporting places both captains on the *Finest*.

2. Aichele, A Shining Light.

3. "story3359.xml" (untitled), *September 11 Digital Archive*, accessed April 25, 2019, http://911digitalarchive.org/items/show/13203.

4. Boatlift—Tom Hanks Narrates "An Untold Tale of 9/11 Resilience." https://www.americanwaterways.com/media/videos/boatlift-tom-hanks-narrates-untold-tale-911-resilience

5. *Never Forget*, p. 98.

6. John Snyder, Remembering maritime heroes on 9/11, MarineLog, https://www.marinelog.com/news/remembering-maritime-heroes-on-9-11/; see also *Rogue Wave*, p. 7.

7. Harbor Voices.

8. "story48.xml" (untitled), *September 11 Digital Archive*, accessed April 25, 2019, http://911digitalarchive.org/items/show/3914

9. . . . *monsoon . . . Rogue Wave*, p. 7.

10. Dust to Deliverance, p. 51.

11. Harbor Voices.

12. Merchant Marine Heroes of 9/11.

13. https://workboatdc-static.s3.amazonaws.com/uploads/2015/09/WorkBoat_November_2001_CoverStory.pdf

14. Author interview with Brian Gestring, August 2020.

15. New Jersey State Police, Marine Services, Search and Rescue Stories, September 11, 2002, Rescue—Newark Bay Station.

16. Author interview with DeMarino, August 2020.

Chapter 25: "Is anyone there?"

1. Author interview, August 2020.

2. Fire Department of the City of New York, *World Trade Center Task Force Interview*, Penn interview, NYFD.

3. DeShore interview, p. 13.

4. Fire Department of the City of New York, *World Trade Center Task Force Interview*, J. Jefferson interview, p. 12.

5. Wells interview, p. 16.

6. DeShore interview.

7. DeShore interview.

8. Author interview with DeShore, August 2020.

Chapter 26: "The group started jumping over the wall into the boat."

1. https://web.archive.org/web/20140718195213/http://www.nabe-web.com/am2001/mckee.htm

2. "story3745.xml" (untitled), *September 11 Digital Archive*, accessed April 25, 2019, http://911digitalarchive.org/items/show/14423.http://911digitalarchive.org/items/show/14423

3. Fire Department of the City of New York, *World Trade Center Task Force Interview*, F. Burgos interview, p. 7.

4. *Never Forget*, p. 98.

5. Fire Department of the City of New York, *World Trade Center Task Force Interview*, Fitzpatrick interview.

6. Marine 1 FDNY, September 11, 2001; see also "All Available Boats: Harbor Voices from 9/11."

Chapter 27: "[It was] a lot of chaos, a lot of people running around, a lot of screaming, a lot of people asking for help."

1. Joyce Ng, *Hotel 9/11: An Oral History from the Survivors of 3 World Trade Center* (Fayville, MA, JSW Books, 2016), p. 70.

2. Fire Department of the City of New York, *World Trade Center Task Force Interview*, M. Ruppert interview, p. 4.

3. Joyce, *There were a lot* p. 104.

4. Author interview, August 2020.

5. https://www.firehouse.com/home/news/10545160/wtc-this-is-their-story-part-i

6. NJ State Police, Search and Rescue Stories.

7. NJ State Police, Search and Rescue Stories.

8. DeShore interview, p. 12; see also Penn interview.

9. DeShore interview.

10. Author interview with Fuentes, September 2020.

11. American By Choice, p. 9.

12. Author interview with Fuentes, September 2020, *American by Choice*, p. 9.

Chapter 28: "The building was a quarter-mile high, and we were way too close."

1. Fire Department of the City of New York, *World Trade Center Task Force Interview*, C. Fenyo interview.

2. Fire Department of the City of New York, *World Trade Center Task Force Interview*, Stone interview, p. 17.

3. Joseph Pfifer, First Chief on the Scene.

4. N. Sweeting interview, p. 10.

5. "story9207.xml" (untitled), *September 11 Digital Archive*, accessed April 25, 2019, http://911digitalarchive.org/items/show/4793.

6. "story9438.xml" (untitled), *September 11 Digital Archive*, accessed April 25, 2019, http://911digitalarchive.org/items/show/3973

7. http://livingmemorial.voicesofseptember11.org/911-stories/journal-entry-submitted-victor-colantonio

8. Hotel 9/11, p. 151.

9. American By Choice, p.17.

10. Ibid.

11. Harvey Eisner, This Is Their Story.

12. Fire Department of the City of New York, *World Trade Center Task Force Interview*, Ruppert interview, p. 4.

13. American by Choice, p. 216.

14. Hotel 9/11, Death count in Introduction.

15. American by Choice, pp. 19, 22.

16. Author interview with DeMarino, July 2020.

17. DeShore interview; see also Penn interview.

18. Fire Department of the City of New York, *World Trade Center Task Force Interview,* M. Cain interview, p. 5.

19. Cain interview, p. 5.

20. Author interview with DeMarino, July 2020.

21. Author interview with DeMarino, August 2020.

22. Penn interview, p. 13.

23. DeShore interview.

24. "He Found Fuentes," *Firehouse Magazine,* WTC: This Is Their Story Part I, p. 2; others tell this story but do not mention Flatley one way or the other. See Lt. Haughney, American by Choice, p. 224.

25. American by Choice, p. 217.

26. American by Choice,, p. 216.

27. American by Choice,, p. 217.

28. American by Choice,, p. 233.

29. American by Choice,, p. 227.

30. American by Choice, p. 84.

31. Author interview with Captain Fuentes, September 2020.

32. Gregory Fried, Life on the Thin Blue Line: Tales of a NYPD Executive Chief Surgeon (Bloomington, IN, Archway Publishing, 2017), p. ix.

33. *Never Forget,* p. 97.

34. http://www.liherald.com/stories/Former-NYPD-chief-surgeon-shares-911 -story,83937

35. *Never Forget,* p.97

36. *Never Forget,* p. 97.

37. http://www.liherald.com/stories/Former-NYPD-chief-surgeon-shares-911 -story,83937

38. Author interview with DeMarino, July 2020.

39. *Never Forget,* p. 123.

40. American by Choice, p. 234.

41. American by Choice, p. 217,

Chapter 29: *"They give us water and comfort."*

1. "email503.xml" (untitled), *September 11 Digital Archive,* accessed April 25, 2019, http://911digitalarchive.org/items/show/38911

2. Brendon Brewer. Being in Lower Manhattan on 9/11, *The Crisis Communicator,* https://thecrisiscommunicator.com/2014/09/11/being-in-lower-manhattan-on-911/

3. https://www.megcabot.com/2012/09/9112001/

4. "story2060.xml" (untitled), *September 11 Digital Archive,* accessed April 25, 2019, http://911digitalarchive.org/items/show/6443

5. Being in Lower Manhattan on 9/11, The Crisis Communicator

6. "story10855.xml" (untitled), *September 11 Digital Archive*, accessed April 25, 2019, http://911digitalarchive.org/items/show/12482

Chapter 30: "The only way out [for the injured] was by boat."
1. https://en.wikipedia.org/wiki/Winter_Garden_Atrium
2. https://placesnomore.wordpress.com/2010/09/07/3wtc/
3. https://www.silive.com/northshore/2013/09/12_years_ago_3_generations_on.html
4. https://www.nycop.com/Jan_02/Terrorism_and_Emergency_Manage/body_terrorism_and_emergency_manage.html
5. Post Collapse: Liberty Street Sector Operations.
6. Blaich interview.
7. Ibid.
8. Cohen interview.
9. Blaich interview.
10. Live to Tell.
11. Harvey Eisner, WTC: This Is Their Story.
12. https://www.firehouse.com/home/article/10567885/deputy-chief-peter-hayden

Chapter 31: "We started putting the women and children on boats to get them over to New Jersey."
1. "story10860.xml" (untitled), *September 11 Digital Archive*, accessed April 25, 2019, http://911digitalarchive.org/items/show/18314.
2. Rescue at Water's Edge.
3. Penn interview.
4. *Rogue Wave*, p. 20.
5. Boatlift—Tom Hanks Narrates "An Untold Tale of 9/11 Resilience." https://www.americanwaterways.com/media/videos/boatlift-tom-hanks-narrates-untold-tale-911-resilience
6. Untold Story of 9/11 Resilience.
7. "All Available Boats: Harbor Voices from 9/11" transcript.
8. Untold Story of 9/11 Resilience.
9. https://njmonthly.com/articles/jersey-living/leading-giants-by-the-helm/
10. Aichele, A Shining Light.
11. "All Available Boats: Harbor Voices from 9/11" transcript.
12. "All Available Boats: Harbor Voices from 9/11," South Street Seaport Museum, https://transom.org/2002/all-available-boats/
13. *Rogue Wave*, p. 21.
14. Recorded in both Untold Tale of 9/11 Resilience and Dust to Deliverance, p. 114.

Chapter 32: "There are twenty-seven to thirty tugboats sitting there."
1. Fire Department of the City of New York, *World Trade Center Task Force Interview*, DeRubbio interview, p. 9.
2. Live to Tell.
3. All Available Boats, Peterson transcript.

4. "Standing offshore," in *American Dunkirk*, p. 48; twelve tugs per Bate, Alision, Armada; Rescues Trapped New Yorkers, *Cargo Business News*, September 2001.

5. "All Available Boats," Peterson transcript.

6. WTC: MARITIME 9/11—Carolina Salguero, https://portsidenewyork.org/911 -maritime-response

7. WTC Maritime 9/11 – Carolina Salguero interviews, https://portsidenewyork.org /911-maritime-response

8. "email368.xml" (untitled), *September 11 Digital Archive*, accessed April 25, 2019, http://911digitalarchive.org/items/show/39589

9. "All Available Boats," Peterson transcript.

10. George Matteson, *Tugboats of New York* (New York University Press, New York), p. 213.

11. Aichele, A Shining Light.

12. Joel Milton, Marine Lift, *WorkBoat*, November 2001, https://workboatdc-static.s3 .amazonaws.com/uploads/2015/09/WorkBoat_November_2001_CoverStory.pdf

13. Milton, Marine Lift.

14. They cheered, *Rogue Wave*, p. 21.

15. Alision Bates, Armada Rescues Trapped New Yorkers (9/11), *Cargo Business News*, September 2001.

Chapter 33: "Get the hell out of the city"

1. Live to Tell.

2. Live to Tell.

3. Fire Department of the City of New York, *World Trade Center Task Force Interview*, D'Amato interview, p. 11.

4. Fire Department, D'Amato interview, p. 11.

5. American Photo, 9.11.01: The Photographers Stories.

6. Author interview with Wells, September 2020.

7. Author interview with Wells, September 2020.

8. Author interview with Wells, September 2020.

9. Live to Tell.

Chapter 34: "Just like the Titanic."

1. Browne interview, p. 17.

2. Lamanna interview, p. 25.

3. Browne interview, p. 17.

4. Fire Department of the City of New York, *World Trade Center Task Force Interview*, Scott interview.

5. Fire Department of the City of New York, *World Trade Center Task Force Interview*, Blacksberg interview, p. 7.

6. Michelle Reuter (untitled), *September 11 Digital Archive*, accessed April 25, 2019, http://911digitalarchive.org/items/show/96817

7. "story616.xml" (untitled), *September 11 Digital Archive*, accessed April 25, 2019, http://911digitalarchive.org/items/show/13418.

8. "story273.xml" (untitled), *September 11 Digital Archive*, accessed April 25, 2019, http://911digitalarchive.org/items/show/5133.

9. "story273.xml" (untitled), *September 11 Digital Archive*, accessed April 25, 2019 http://911digitalarchive.org/items/show/5133.

10. Julia Frey interview, Al l Available Boats.

11. Hotel 9/11, p. 107.

12. Never Forget, p. 76.

13. Brenda Flanagan, At 9/11 ceremony, Jersey City remembered as "last refuge," *NJTV News*, September 11, 2018.

14. "Burned out ambulance," Testaments: Reflections on September 11, https://www.jems.com/2011/09/30/testaments-reflections-sept-11/

15. Out of Darkness.

16. Fire Department of the City of New York, *World Trade Center Task Force Interview*, E. Kennedy interview, p. 9. They were in the general area.

17. Fire Department of the City of New York, *World Trade Center Task Force Interview*, Boeri interview.

18. Fire Department, Boeri interview.

19. *Never Forget*, p. 98.

Chapter 35: "We have no communication with the outside world."

1. Martin interview.

2. Gombo interview.

3. Lisa Dionne, EMS Untold, *Journal of Emergency Medical Services*, 9.30.2001.

4. Fire Department of the City of New York, *World Trade Center Task Force Interview*, W. Kowalczyk.

5. Data on EMS system per https://www.nydailynews.com/new-york/new-york-ems-long-1870s-article-1.2196826

6. Goldfarb interview.

7. Live to Tell.

8. Goldfarb interview.

9. FDNY EMS Response, *Fire Engineering*.

10. Martin interview.

11. Ibid.

12. Ibid.

Chapter 36: "We had to get back in the game."

1. Live to Tell.

2. Live to Tell.

3. Fire Department of the City of New York, *World Trade Center Task Force Interview*, Mark Stone interview.

4. Fire Department of the City of New York, *World Trade Center Task Force Interview*, M. Mejias interview, p. 6.

5. Fire Department of the City of New York, *World Trade Center Task Force Interview*, J. Bell interview, p. 11.

6. Fire Department of the City of New York, *World Trade Center Task Force Interview*, Karen Lamanna interview, p. 25.

7. Author interview with Beckham, August 2020.

8. Merchant Marine Heroes of 9/11.

9. Fire Department of the City of New York, *World Trade Center Task Force Interview*, Gattas interview, p. 14.

10. Live to Tell.

11. Live to Tell.

12. Fire Department of the City of New York, *World Trade Center Task Force Interview*, S. O'Malley interview, p. 22.

13. Fire Department of the City of New York, *World Trade Center Task Force Interview*, Casey interview.

14. Fire Department of the City of New York, *World Trade Center Task Force Interview*, S. Holowach interview, p. 8.

15. McDonnell, Responding to the September 11 Terrorist Attacks.

16. McDonnell, Responding to the September 11 Terrorist Attacks.

17. Fire Department of the City of New York, *World Trade Center Task Force Interview*, J. Katz interview.

18. Fire Department, Katz interview.

19. Author interview with Beckham, August 2020.

20. Author interview with Giebfried, August 2020.

21. Goldfarb interview.

22. Exodus Across the Hudson, p. 5.

23. Kowalczyk interview.

Chapter 37: *"Everybody seemed to be migrating down toward the water zone."*

1. *Never Forget*, p. 98.

2. Live to Tell.

3. McDonnell, Responding to the September 11 Terrorist Attacks.

4. McDonnell, Responding to the September 11 Terrorist Attacks.

5. Pierce interview, p. 13.

6. Merchant Marine Heroes of 9/11.

7. "All Available Boats: Harbor Voices from 9/11" transcript.

8. "All Available Boats."

9. Aichele, A Shining Light.

10. "All Available Boats: Harbor Voices from 9/11" transcript.

11. Fire Department of the City of New York, *World Trade Center Task Force Interview*, Bastile interview, p. 10.

12. Cook interview, p. 25.

13. Fire Department of the City of New York, *World Trade Center Task Force Interview*, Maggiore interview, p. 3.

14. Fire Department of the City of New York, *World Trade Center Task Force Interview*, Marquez interview.

15. Rothmund interview.

Chapter 38: "Every vessel on the harbor seemed to be moving."

1. Edward Marek, Talking Proud, p. 10.

2. "story11271.xml" (untitled), *September 11 Digital Archive*, accessed April 25, 2019, http://911digitalarchive.org/items/show/10110

3. New York Law School, "Eight Blocks Away, Memoirs of September 11, 2001" (2011) (*Tribeca Square Press*. Book 3) http://digitalcommons.nyls.edu/tribeca_square _press/3, p. 12.

4. Loutsky interview.

5. "nmah6262.xml" (untitled), *September 11 Digital Archive*, accessed April 25, 2019, http://911digitalarchive.org/items/show/43026.

6. "email193.xml" (untitled), *September 11 Digital Archive*, accessed April 25, 2019, http://911digitalarchive.org/items/show/38471.

7. "All Available Boats: Harbor Voices from 9/11."

8. John Snyder, Remembering maritime heroes on 9/11, MarineLog., https://www .marinelog.com/news/remembering-maritime-heroes-on-9-11/; 1,500 victims per Pat Smith and quoted in Peter Bowles, 9/11/01: Treating the Victims, *Newsday*.

9. Aichele, A Shining Light.

10. "All Available Boats," Peresi interview transcript.

11. Remembering maritime heroes on 9/11, MarineLog.

12. Aichele, A Shining Light.

13. Fire Department of the City of New York, *World Trade Center Task Force Interview*, Pastor interview.

14. "All Available Boats," Peterson interview transcript.

15. Remembering September 11, 2001, US Army Corps of Engineers, Engineer Update, Modern Dunkirk, USACE boat operations on 9/11, p. 11.

16. Remembering September 11, 2001, US Army Corps of Engineers, Engineer Update, Modern Dunkirk, USACE boat operations on 9/11, p. 11.

17. Joel Milton, "Marine Lift, WorkBoat," *Work Boat*, November 2001, p. 58.

18. https://loripotter.wordpress.com/2012/05/11/a-boat-named-sassacus/; and also https://www.courant.com/news/connecticut/hc-xpm-1997-06-12-9706120320-story .html

19. https://loripotter.wordpress.com/2012/05/11/a-boat-named-sassacus/

20. https://www.workboat.com/news/passenger-vessels/calling-all-boats-9-11/

21. Fox ridership per http://www.schallerconsult.com/pub/lowermn.pdf

22. Annette Wright, "We stopped counting."

23. Aichele, A Shining Light.

24. Details about the *Finest* per Annette Wright, "We stopped counting." https://www
.kitsapdailynews.com/news/we-stopped-counting-former-captain-of-kingstons-newest
-ferry-recalls-evacuating-thousands-on-9-11/
25. Estimate per Annette Wright, "We stopped counting." https://www.kitsapdailynews
.com/news/we-stopped-counting-former-captain-of-kingstons-newest-ferry-recalls
-evacuating-thousands-on-9-11/
26. "story820.xml" (untitled), *September 11 Digital Archive*, accessed April 25, 2019,
http://911digitalarchive.org/items/show/13383
27. Joel Milton, "Marine Lift, WorkBoat," *Work Boat*, November 2001, p. 58.
28. "All Available Boats," Peresi interview transcript.
29. https://workboatdc-static.s3.amazonaws.com/uploads/2015/09/WorkBoat_Novem
ber_2001_CoverStory.pdf; see also South Street Seaport Oral Histories
30. https://www.workboat.com/news/passenger-vessels/calling-all-boats-9-11/
31. https://seastreak.com/about-seastreak/strong-capable-fleet/
32. https://seastreak.com/about-seastreak/strong-capable-fleet/; https://workboat
dc-static.s3.amazonaws.com/uploads/2015/09/WorkBoat_November_2001_Cover
Story.pdf
33. Joel Milton, Marine Lift, p. 58.
34. https://goingcoastalmagazine.wordpress.com/2008/09/15/circle-lines-wwii-cutter
-may-take-its-final-manhattan-cruise/
35. http://www.professionalmariner.com/March-2007/A-shining-light-in-our
-darkest-hour/
36. Remembering maritime heroes on 9/11, MarineLog.
37. Evacuation numbers, Remembering maritime heroes on 9/11, MarineLog.
38. Boat capacity, https://www.spiritcruises.com/new-york-metro/about/faq
39. New York Law School, "Eight Blocks Away: Memoirs of September 11, 2001."
40. "All Available Boats: Harbor Voices from 9/11"

Chapter 39: We know evil.

1. "All Available Boats: Harbor Voices from 9/11."
2. "story2681.xml" (untitled), *September 11 Digital Archive*, accessed April 25, 2019,
http://911digitalarchive.org/items/show/5837
3. Michelle Reuter, (untitled), *September 11 Digital Archive*, accessed April 25, 2019,
http://911digitalarchive.org/items/show/96817
4. "story10241.xml" (untitled), *September 11 Digital Archive*, accessed April 25, 2019,
http://911digitalarchive.org/items/show/6329.
5. "email193.xml" (untitled), *September 11 Digital Archive*, accessed April 25, 2019,
http://911digitalarchive.org/items/show/38471
6. "story4297.xml" (untitled), *September 11 Digital Archive*, accessed April 25, 2019,
http://911digitalarchive.org/items/show/11368
7. James F. Matulevich "story10886.xml," (untitled), *September 11 Digital Archive*,
accessed April 25, 2019, http://911digitalarchive.org/items/show/19423, Copyright 2003.

8. "story9701.xml" (untitled), *September 11 Digital Archive*, accessed April 25, 2019, *September 11 Digital Archive*, accessed May 19, 2019, http://911digitalarchive.org/items /show/11339

9. "story10324.xml" (untitled), *September 11 Digital Archive*, accessed April 25, 2019, http://911digitalarchive.org/items/show/15134

10. "nmah6262.xm," (untitled), *September 11 Digital Archive*, accessed April 25, 2019, http://911digitalarchive.org/items/show/43026

11. "story2936.xml" (untitled]), *September 11 Digital Archive*, accessed April 25, 2019, http://911digitalarchive.org/items/show/4133

12. "story1657.xml" (untitled), *September 11 Digital Archive*, accessed April 25, 2019, http://911digitalarchive.org/items/show/6402

13. "story10855.xml" (untitled), *September 11 Digital Archive*, accessed April 25, 2019, http://911digitalarchive.org/items/show/12482

14. Eight Blocks Away, Memoirs of September 11, 2001, NY Law School.

15. "story2681.xml" (untitled), *September 11 Digital Archive*, accessed April 25, 2019, http://911digitalarchive.org/items/show/5837

Chapter 40: *"I felt like I was on a landing craft going into the beach at Normandy."*

1. Charles Blaich, Post Collapse: Liberty Street Sector Operations, *Fire Engineering*, https://www.fireengineering.com/2002/09/01/232635/postcollapse-liberty-street -sector-operations/

2. New York Law School, "Eight Blocks Away: Memoirs of September 11, 2001."

3. Clark et al., *After the Fall*, p. 177.

4. Michelle Reuter (untitled), *September 11 Digital Archive*, accessed April 25, 2019, http://911digitalarchive.org/items/show/96817

5. https://www.firehouse.com/home/news/10545160/wtc-this-is-their-story-part-i

6. Basile interview.

7. "nmah5427.xml" (untitled), *September 11 Digital Archive*, accessed April 25, 2019, http://911digitalarchive.org/items/show/45076

8. Live to Tell.

9. Live to Tell.

10. Fire Department of the City of New York, *World Trade Center Task Force Interview*, K. Kelly interview.

Chapter 41: *"No one was talking."*

1. "story9701.xml" (untitled), *September 11 Digital Archive*, accessed April 25, 2019, http://911digitalarchive.org/items/show/11339

2. "story10241.xml" (untitled), *September 11 Digital Archive*, accessed April 25, 2019, http://911digitalarchive.org/items/show/6329

3. "email600.xml" (untitled), *September 11 Digital Archive*, accessed April 25, 2019, http://911digitalarchive.org/items/show/37436

4. Annette Wright, "We stopped counting."

5. "story670.xml" (untitled), *September 11 Digital Archive*, accessed April 25, 2019, http://911digitalarchive.org/items/show/12609.

6. Copyright 2003 James F. Matulevich "story10886.xml" (untitled), *September 11 Digital Archive*, accessed April 25, 2019, http://911digitalarchive.org/items/show/19423.

7. Matulevich, "story10886.xml."

8. "story938.xml" (untitled), *September 11 Digital Archive*, accessed April 25, 2019, http://911digitalarchive.org/items/show/13614.

9. Featherstone, http://www.jerseycityonline.com/wtc/911_story.htm

10. "story3359.xml" (untitled), *September 11 Digital Archive*, accessed April 25, 2019, http://911digitalarchive.org/items/show/13203.

11. "story1853.xml" (untitled), *September 11 Digital Archive*, accessed April 25, 2019, http://911digitalarchive.org/items/show/10695.

Chapter 42: "By 12:30 p.m., we had established a water supply."

1. "story991.xml"(untitled), *September 11 Digital Archive*, accessed April 25, 2019, http://911digitalarchive.org/items/show/9063.

2. https://en.wikipedia.org/wiki/5_World_Trade_Center

3. "story991.xml" (untitled), *September 11 Digital Archive*, accessed April 25, 2019, http://911digitalarchive.org/items/show/9063.

4. Fire Department of the City of New York, *World Trade Center Task Force Interview* Mallery interview.

5. Mallery interview.

6. Harbor Voices.

7. Mallery interview.

8. Which fireboats responded per US Fire Administration, Case Study #3 New York City—World Trade Center Collapse, Five Fireboats Conduct Rescue, Transport and Suppression, https://www.usfa.fema.gov/downloads/pdf/publications/tr-146.pdf, p. 19; also, Tom Gulner, Marine Firefighting Institute, What Else Can Fireboats Do? https://www.marinefirefighting.com/Pages/Newsletters/Newsletter9.htm#:~:text=What%20Else%20Can%20Fireboats%20Do%3F&text=We%20all%20know%20that%20large, extinguish%20even%20the%20largest%20fires.&text=This%20approach%20must%20be%20taken,an%20attack%20onboard%20the%20vessel.

9. O'Malley interview, p. 19.

10. "All Available Boats, Harbor Voices from 9/11."

11. "All Available Boats, Harbor Voices from 9/11."

12. http://www.capecodfd.com/PAGES%20Special/Fireboats_FDNY_01.htm

13. http://www.capecodfd.com/PAGES%20Special/Fireboats_FDNY_01.htm

14. North Tower Command, *Fire Engineering*.

Chapter 43: The Last Ship

1. Rogue wave, p. 24.

2. See "The Numbers" section of this book.

3. https://www.historic-uk.com/HistoryUK/HistoryofBritain/Evacuation-of-Dunkirk/

4. "story911.xml" (untitled), *September 11 Digital Archive*, accessed April 25, 2019, http://911digitalarchive.org/items/show/17062.

5. "All Available Boats: Harbor Voices from 9/11" transcript.

6. "All Available Boats: Harbor Voices from 9/11" transcript.

7. FDNY EMS Response, *Fire Engineering*.

8. _____, US Department of Transportation, The News, Moran Crews Cited for 9/11 Evacuation Endeavors.

9. Annette Wright, "We stopped counting."

10. "All Available Boats: Harbor Voices from 9/11" transcript.

11. Centers for Disease Control, Rapid Assessment of Injuries Among Survivors of the Terrorist Attack on the World Trade Center—New York City, September 2001, January 11, 2002, https://www.cdc.gov/mmwr/preview/mmwrhtml/mm5101a1.htm

12. https://nypost.com/2003/12/12/fdny-at-pre-911-numbers/; see also Glenn Asaeda, World Trade Center Attack, FDNY, The Second National Emergency Management Summit, 2/8/2008, http://www.ehcca.com/presentations/emsummit2/1_08.pdf

13. Glenn Asaeda, World Trade Center Attack, FDNY, The Second National Emergency Management Summit, 2/8/2008, http://www.ehcca.com/presentations/emsummit2/1_08.pdf; see also EMS Untold, JEMS, 9.30.2001.

14. http://www.nyc.gov/html/fdny/pdf/mck_report/fire_operations_response.pdf

15. EMS Response, *Fire Engineering*.

16. CDC, Injuries and Illness Among New York City Fire Department Rescue Workers After Responding to the World Trade Center Attacks, September 11, 2002, Issue 51; https://www.cdc.gov/mmwr/preview/mmwrhtml/mm51SPa1.htm

17. Jim Dwyer and Ford Fessenden. "One Hotel's Fight to the Finish," *New York Times*, September 11, 2002.

18. Injuries and Illness Among New York City Fire Department Rescue Workers After Responding to the World Trade Center Attacks.

19. Rapid Assessment of Injuries Among Survivors of the Terrorist Attack on the World Trade Center.

20. https://www.salisburypost.com/2011/09/08/students-chat-with-911-paramedic-via-skype/

21. Author interview with Fuentes, September 2020.

Epilogue: A Peanut Butter Sandwich

1. Penn Interview.

2. DeShore interview, p. 17.

3. Author interview with DeShore, August 2020.

4. Author interview with Metcalf, September 2020.

5. Author interview with Metcalf, September 2020.

6. Author interview with Metcalf, September 2020.

7. Author interview with Metcalf, September 2020.

8. SMSgt. Edward Metcalf, *Air Force Magazine*.

9. "story9438.xml" (untitled), *September 11 Digital Archive*, accessed April 25, 2019, http://911digitalarchive.org/items/show/3973

10. 9/11 Remembered—Ten Years On, Matt Liddy, ABC News, https://abc.net.au /news/specials/september-11-remembered/2011-09-09/eyewitness-accounts-of -september-11/2866958

11. "story9438.xml" (untitled), *September 11 Digital Archive*, accessed April 25, 2019, http://911digitalarchive.org/items/show/3973

12. "All Available Boats: Harbor Voices from 9/11," by WNPR.

Index

Note the photo spread images are indicated by *p1, p2*, etc.

About the Author

L. Douglas Keeney earned his bachelor's and master's degrees from the University of Southern California. A pilot and scuba diver, he lives in Louisville, Kentucky, with his wife, the journalist Jill Johnson Keeney.